THE DIOCESAN QUINQUENNIAL FACULTIES
FORMULA IV

THE CATHOLIC UNIVERSITY OF AMERICA
CANON LAW STUDIES
No. 248

THE DIOCESAN QUINQUENNIAL FACULTIES FORMULA IV

A HISTORICAL SYNOPSIS AND COMMENTARY

BY THE
REVEREND GEORGE EAGLETON, S.T.B., J.C.L.
OF THE
DIOCESE OF RENO

A DISSERTATION

SUBMITTED TO THE FACULTY OF THE SCHOOL OF CANON LAW
OF THE CATHOLIC UNIVERSITY OF AMERICA
IN PARTIAL FULFILLMENT OF THE REQUIREMENTS
FOR THE DEGREE OF
DOCTOR OF CANON LAW

THE CATHOLIC UNIVERSITY OF AMERICA
WASHINGTON, D. C.
1948

Nihil Obstat:
JOHN ROGG SCHMIDT, A.B., J.C.D.
Washingtonii, die 21 iulii, 1948

Imprimatur:
+ THOMAS K. GORMAN, D.D.
Episcopus Renensis

Reno, Nev., die 23 iulli, 1948

A. CARLISLE & COMPANY, RENO, NEVADA.
PRINTED IN THE UNITED STATES OF AMERICA
2

TO

THE MOST REVEREND THOMAS K. GORMAN, D.D.

D. Sc. Hist et Moral.,

TABLE OF CONTENTS

Part II

CANONICAL COMMENTARY

FOREWORD

The historical development of the Canonical Institute of Quinquennial Faculties, as discussed in the first part of this dissertation, may be described as a corollary of the development of the legal system of the Church. It is an Institute which grew out of the exceptions to the law, and which resulted from the necessity of mitigating and adjusting the universal law of the Church to widely divergent needs. From the time of their inception the Faculties were granted for the sake of facilitating the treatment of problems which arose out of the extraordinary needs of indivdual Bishops in particular places, especially those far removed from the Holy See.

The Institute has its origin in the time of Pope Gelasius I (492-496), and was kept alive through the subsequent acts of Popes John VIII (872-882), Paschal II (1099-1118), and others. The use of the Faculties received a new impetus and growth as a result of the Reformation, which placed new demands on the legál system of the Church. The discovery and colonization of the New World gave added impulse to the use of the Faculties. The rapid expansion of the Church, as a consequence of this discovery and colonization, gave rise to difficulties in communication between the Holy See and the distant missions. Such difficulties could be obviated only by an Institute such as Quinquennial Faculties.

The limitation of the Faculties to a definite number of cases or for a set period of time was required by their very nature. Unlimited, they would have become the law rather than the exception. Then, too, the conditions which called for the granting of the Faculties were constantly changing, a fact which required constant vigilance on the part of the Sacred Congregation to whose care and control the Faculties were committed.

The logical consequence of the ultimate pre-Code crystallized doctrine and practice, deriving from the constant vigilance exercised by the Sacred Congregations in the past, is now revealed in the Code of Canon Law, which, in canon 66, gives to the Faculties a true canonical status, and which in various other canons furnishes guiding rules for their interpretation.

The second part of this dissertation deals with the Faculties and their use according to the Code of Canon Law. It strives to demonstrate in what manner the Faculties are to be employed in the ministration of the benefits of the Church, and the administration of the affairs of the Church, and in what manner the employment of the Faculties is affected by the common law of the Church.

The author wishes to avail himself of this occasion to express his gratitude to His Excellency, The Most Reverend Thomas K. Gorman, D.D., D. Sc. Hist., Bishop of Reno, for providing for him the opportunity of graduate study in the School of Canon Law, and who by his generosity made possible this publication. The writer likewise wishes to express his gratitude to the members of the Faculty of The School of Canon Law, The Catholic University of America, Washington, D. C., for their learned guidance and valuable assistance in the preparation of this dissertation.

CHAPTER I

PRELIMINARY NOTIONS

The faculties granted to the bishops of the United States under Formula IV have undergone some slight changes since the practice of issuing them each five years was instituted. They are now issued under one formula, designated Formula IV, by the Sacred Consistorial Congregation, even though the grants are made by a number of the Roman Congregations. Since the promulgation of the present Code of Canon Law, American bishops request and receive the faculties at the same time that their regular diocesan report is made according to the provision of canon 340, § 2. When making this report the bishops are requested to petition a renewal of the faculties. The years referred to by the words of the canon, *"in quarto"*, now fall on those years which end in the numerals four (4) and nine (9); thus the latest faculties are those which were granted in 1944 and will remain in force until the designated date of 1949.

As a canonical institute Quinquennial Faculties, as we know them, are of comparatively recent origin, and legal writers of the earlier countries of Church Law did not make mention of them as such.[1]

Habitually delegated jurisdiction was known, however, and this is the fundamental concept of the institute of Quinquennial Faculties.[2]

---

[1] Wernz, *Ius Decretalium* (2. ed., 6 vols., Romae et Prati, 1906-1913), I, n. 163, p. 206; Verneersch, "Commentaria de Formulis Facultatum Quas S. Cong. de Prop. Fide Concedere Solet,"—*Periodica de Re Canonica et Morali utili praesertim Religiosis et Missionariis* (Burgis, 1905—), XI (1922), (33)—(143) (Hereafter cited Vermeersch, "Commentaria," *Periodica*, XI.

[2] Wernz, (*Ius Decretalium*, I, 206): "Facultas hoc loco generatim definitur potestas, per quam Superior ecclesiasticus jurisdictione in foro externo praeditus subdito concedit aliquid sive in foro poenitentiali vel conscientiae tantum, sive etiam pro foro externo valide aut licite aut saltem in tuto agendi"; Coronata, *Institutiones Iuris Canonici* (5 Vols., Taurini: Marietti, 1928-1936), I, 82; Motry, *Diocesan Faculties According to the Code of Canon Law*, The Catholic University of America Canon Law Studies, n. 16 (Washington, D. C.: The Catholic University of America, 1922), p. 17. (Hereafter cited *Diocesan Faculties.*)

In the early centuries of the Church's existence bishops had the power of instituting new feasts, and also of making laws and of dispensing from them. But since the constitution of the Church demanded unity as one of its attributes, the gradual bringing of this power of the bishops under the head of the Church, the Roman Pontiff, was only a matter of time and development. The supremacy of the Pope always existed; it was the practical use and recognition of this power that developed during the course of history.[3]

The possibility of dispensing in particular cases from an ecclesiastical law was considered and recognized as necessary by the early leaders of the Church. During the first few centuries there were few laws, and those laws which did exist were of such a nature that little reason for dispensing from them could be found. Reilly quotes St. Augustine (354-430) and St. Cyril of Alexandria (376-444) as the earliest authors in defense of the opinion that, despite the paucity of universal ecclesiastical laws and the practice of rigorous observance, the relaxation of a law in a particular case was observed and recognized as necessary.[4]

That the Bishop of Rome was supreme among the bishops of the world was recognized from the beginning by most of the bishops of the Western Church. The clarification of the doctrine and the extent of the Pope's jurisdiction was more distinctly determined later. It was only after the persecution of the Church had temporarily ceased, and the possibility of easier communication was established, that the unification process could begin. Those active in ecclesiastical administrative law saw both the need for the principle of dispensation and at the same time the absolute necessity of keeping the oneness of the Church by acknowledging the Pope in his rightful supremacy. This doctrine was firmly established much later, but its existence was recognized from the beginning.[5]

---

[3] Brys, *De Dispensatione in Iure Canonico, praesertim apud Decretistas et Decretalistas usque ad Medium Saeculum Decimum Quartum* (Burgis: Beyaert, 1925) p. 11 (hereafter cited *De Dispensatione in Iure Canonico*).

[4] Reilly, *The General Norms of Dispensation*, The Catholic University of America Canon Law Studies, n. 119 (Washington, D. C.: The Catholic University of America Press, 1939). pp. 5-7.

[5] Pius IV, Const. "*Auctorem Fidei*", 28 aug. 1794, *Prop. Synodi Pistorien.* damn.—*Codicis Iuris Canonici Fontes*, cura Emi Petri Card. Gasparri editi (9 vols., Romae Postea Civitate Vaticana: Typis Polyglottis

Vaticanis, 1923-1939, [Vols. VII, VIII, et IX,] ed. cura et studio Emi Justinium Card. Seredi.) n. 475 (hereafter cited *Fontes*); Ryan, *Principles of Episcopal Jurisdiction*, The Catholic University of America Canon Law Studies, n. 120 (Washington, D. C.: The Catholic University of America Press, 1939) p. 65.

CHAPTER II

APOSTOLIC FACULTIES FROM THE FOURTH TO THE TWELFTH CENTURY

ARTICLE I

PRACTICE OF THE COUNCILS IN THE EARLY FOURTH CENTURY

It was in the early councils of the Church that there was the initial manifestation of the notion of delegating to bishops powers which they lacked, either by reason of reservation or in view of their lack of jurisdiction. The Council of Ancyra (314) acknowledged the faculty of dispensing to bishops in canon 2. The words, *in eorum potestate,* were used with reference to what was shared with the bishops in their habitual faculty of dispensing and reinstating deacons who had lapsed in their faith. Otherwise this faculty seemed reserved to the Council itself, since the members held the conciliar legislation superior to the bishops' dispensatory powers. If such had not been the view then held, the explicit statement of the bishops' powers in any particular case would not have been necessary.[1] However, the statement of the principle was repeated in the canons of the Council of Nicaea (325). Canon 8 of this Council gave to bishops the permission to exercise their own judgment in permitting the *cathari,* if they had been bishops before their lapse, to retain the episcopal dignity. In Canon 12, concerning the *lapsi* among the laity, certain penalties were prescribed, but the canon also stated that it was within the power of the bishop to treat them with greater leniency. In both canons there seems to be implied a delegation of power by the Council to the bishops, a

[1] H. Th. Bruns, *Canones Apostolorum et Conciliorum Saeculorum* IV-VII, 2 vols., 2. ed., (Berolini, 1839) I, p. 66 (hereafter cited as Bruns); Mansi, *Sacrorum Conciliorum Nova et Amplissima Collectio* (53 vols. in 60, Paris-Arnhem-Leipzig, 1901-1927), II, 514 (hereafter cited as Mansi); C. Hefele-H. Leclercq, *Histoire des Conciles* (10 vols. in 19, Paris, 1907-1938) I, nn. 223-225 (hereafter cited as Hefele-Leclercq).

delegation which the bishops needed to mitigate or dispense from the legislation of the Council which otherwise was above their jurisdiction.[2]

The Pope was represented at this Council by two Roman priests, Victor and Vincent. Accordingly, it may be said that the faculties habitually granted to bishops in canons 8 and 12 were granted, if not directly, then at least indirectly, by the Holy See. Though the legislation was more that of a limitation than that of a concession, the Council of Antioch (341) approved many laws designed to determine the extent of the bishops' jurisdiction, and to care for those cases which perchance would be brought to their attention, but which fell outside the limits established.[3]

ARTICLE 2

PRACTICE OF THE POPES FROM THE FOURTH TO THE TWELFTH CENTURY

Strictly considered the grants of the councils were not habitual faculties in the same sense that this term implies today, that is, as it is used in canon 66 in reference to quinquennial faculties. Pope Siricius (385-399) was the first to indicate that other forms for the delegation of jurisdiction were in use. In a letter to Himerius, Bishop of Tarragona, he exhorted all priests and bishops to follow strictly all papal and conciliar legislation, unless they had first applied to Rome for either the faculties to dispense or for the grant of a dispensation. Although he did not grant any faculties on that occasion, he did indicate that the practice was neither unknown nor condemned.[4]

More closely approximating the modern concept was the letter of Pope Gelasius I (492-496) to all the bishops in the provinces of Lucania, Brutium and Sicily. The Pope did not invent nor did he employ a new principle when he granted to those bishops the faculties of dispensing from the interstices required for the con-

---

[2] Mansi, II, 671 and 674; Bruns, I, 16 and 17; Hefele-Leclercq, I, nn. 408-412 and nn. 415-416.

[3] Mansi, II, 1307-1319; Bruns, I, 80-87.

[4] Jaffe, *Regesta Pontificum Romanorum ab condita Ecclesia ad annum post Christum natum MCMXCVIII*, (2. ed., correctam et auctum auspiciis Gulielmi Wattenbach, curaverunt S. Lowenfied, F. Kaltenbrunner, P. Ewald, 2 vols., Lipsiae, 1885-1888), n. 255 (hereafter cited as Jaffe); Mansi, III, 655-661.

ferring of sacred orders through an acknowledged rule established by custom. He merely used a device already demonstrated by the councils as acceptable. In his letter the Pope recounted the reasons in consideration of which he was making the concession. In order to delegate to the bishops the necessary power he used the words, "*Sic spatia dispensanda concedimus*". The phrase, as used, seemed to indicate the grant of habitual faculties.[5]

Records of particular grants are lacking through the next three centuries but in the ninth century Pope John VIII (872-882) made use of the device to orders on the part of certain clerics who had been guilty of grave sin, the Pope commanded the bishop not to deny them promotion. Thus the Pope not only conceded the faculty of dispensing, but even commanded that it be put to use.[6]

Even though grants of jurisdiction to bishops increased during the centuries that followed, the use of the institution was by no means common. Pope John X (914-928), in a letter to Hermann, the Archbishop of Cologne, granted the faculty of dispensing from the censure and irregularity certain priests who had been found guilty of directly perpetrating homicide.[7] Pope Urban II (1088-1099), in a letter to Bishop Pibo of Toul which dealt with the matter of priests who had been ordained without canonical title, wrote that he committed the matter to the discretion of the bishop.[8] To Altman, Bishop of Passau (1065-1091), the Pope wrote using the words, "*Hanc potestatem concedimus*", when he dealt with the question of absolving and readmitting to the ministry some priests who had been convicted of the guilt of fornication.[9]

At the turn of the century Pope Paschal II (1099-1118) made wide use of the granting of habitually delegated jurisdiction. Brys indicates that this Pope was noted for the many and varied faculties which he conceded to bishops during his reign.[10] No

[5] Gelasius I, Epistola XIV, Thiel, *Epistolae Romanorum Pontificum Geniunal a S. Hilario usque ad Pelagium*, I, *Epistolae Romanorum Pontificum a S. Hilario usque ad S. Hormisdam* (Brunsbergae, 1868), 362 (hereafter cited as Thiel); n. 636.

[6] Mansi, VII, 105; Migne, *Patrologiae Cursus Completus, Series Latina*, (221 vols., Parisiis, 1844-1864), CXXVI, 817 (hereafter cited as *MPL*).

[7] Jaffe, n. 3568.

[8] Jaffe, n. 5409; Mansi, XX, 676.

[9] Jaffe, n. 5275.

[10] Brys, *De Dispensatione in Iure Canonico*, p. 63: "Celeber est ob multiplices facultates dispensandi quas episcopis concessit."

special nor any fixed formula was used in the concession of these grants, but it is evident that the granted faculties implied a delegated jurisdiction for particular bishops, and not the bestowal of special privileges, such as were granted to monasteries during the same period. The faculties given were very broad and general; they practically constituted the bishop as the sole authority over the questions involved.[11]

In a letter to Anselm, Archbishop of Canterbury (1093-1109), the Pope made reference to grants conceded by Pope Urban II (1088-1099) and then extended the faculties to cover practically any contingency.[12] It is to be noted, however, that the expressions used were in no way similar to the words employed in extending privileges to the religious orders and monasteries. As an example, the words, *"privilegium dat"*, were used by Pope Urban II in his letter to Rudolph, Abbot of the monastery of St. Vitianus (1074-1089).[13]

It is apparent that the delegation of jurisdiction to individual bishops grew into a not uncommon practice by the beginning of the twelfth century. Of more importance is the fact that from the use made of the institution it may be concluded that bishops recognized and admitted the supremacy of the Roman Pontiff in many cases which were excluded from their jurisdiction.[14]

Aside for the fundamental question of the Pope's supremacy in power as legislator of the Church, the use and development of the institute of faculties had little place for the consideration of the jurists and the collectors of Church Law. Their interest was almost necessarily directed towards the universal law of the Church; particular law, as represented by faculties, was not in their immediate field. It is not strange, then, to note in the collections both the scarcity of letters containing grants of faculties and he lack of comment upon them on the part of Gratian and his predecessors.

[11] Mansi, XX, 1063: " - - - et cetera - - - ": "nos dispensationem hanc solicitudini tuae comittimus, caetera etiam quae in regno illo pro necessitate temporis dispensanda sunt, juxta gentis barbariem, juxta ecclesiae opportunitatem, sapientiae ac religionis tuae sollicitudo dispenset"; Jaffe, n. 5909.

[12] Jaffé, n. 5871.

[13] Jaffé, n. 5307.

[14] Brys, *De Dispensatione in Iure Canonico*, pp. 66-67.

CHAPTER III

APOSTOLIC FACULTIES FROM THE TWELFTH TO THE SIXTEENTH CENTURY

ARTICLE I

IN THE DECREE OF GRATIAN AND IN DECRETAL LAW

The collections of law which preceded Gratian's *Decree* (c. 1140) supported the Pope as the supreme legislator of ecclesiastical law, though in many cases the terms used in them were not unmistakably clear. This was especially true during the reform started by Gregory VII (1073-1085). There was some confusion over the question of a bishop's power and the Pope's delegation of power, in all probability because of the lack of clear-cut notions regarding the dispensing and absolving from penances and the failure to distinguish clearly between jurisdiction in the external and the internal forums. In practice, however, a majority of the bishops referred the more serious cases to the Holy See.[1] The forms to be used and the procedure to be followed by the Pope in the granting either of the dispensation or of the faculty to dispense were not commented upon.

Gratian, in coordinating and synthesizing the earlier legislation and collections of law, considered that the dispensatory power was a correlative of the legislative power, and that consequently the power of dispensing from the universal law of the Church belonged exclusively to the Pope.[2] His extensive use of papal letters and decrees exemplifies the growth and development of the concept of universal pontifical law, and of the Pope as supreme legislator who

---

[1] Thomassinus, *Vetus et Nova Ecclesiae Disciplina Circa Beneficia et Beneficiarios* (3 vols., Venetiis, 1730), Pars II, lib. III, c. 26.

[2] C. 16, C. XXV, q. 1: "Licet itaque sibi contra generalia decreta specialia privilegia indulgere, et speciali beneficio concedere quod generali prohibetur decreto." and " . . . nisi auctoritis Romanae Ecclesiae aliter fieri mandaverit vel permiserit . . . ": Gratian's comment was based on a letter of Pope Leo IV (847-855) to Geolnoth, Archbishop of Canterbury (833-870). Cf. Jaffé, n. 2609.

was himself not subject to the canons inasmuch as he was above the law.[3] Gratian did not speak of habitual faculties other than those granted as such by the law itself. By interpreting the principles evidenced by Gratian and the comments furnished by the glossators it may be concluded that, although he did not commit himself absolutely on the point, he at least favored the opinion that bishops should not dispense from universal Church law without delegation from the Holy See.

The delegation of judicial power was in wide use; it existed as a recognized institution, with much legislation governing the exercise of the power when of necessity it had been bestowed. The granting of privileges also received extensive treatment. The delegation of administrative jurisdiction as exercised today through the quinquennial faculties was not included in either of the two mentioned ways for the conferring of special powers. Probably the lack of a clear distinction in the terms and the private nature of the faculties kept an extensive treatment of them out of the collections.

The increasing study of the science of Canon Law in the schools devoted to that purpose produced more exact terms and distinctions. Important in the question of faculties were the distinctions between dispensation and absolution, and the teaching of the two schools of thought on the power of bishops to dispense. Some held that bishops could dispense in all matters unless the granting of a dispensation by them was expressly forbidden by the law. This conclusion seems to be drawn from the words of Pope Innocent III (1198-1216) who, in speaking of the right to absolve a penalty, stated that the bishops may dispense (absolve) unless the founder of the law reserved that right to himself.[4]

In the Decretals of Pope Gregory IX (1227-1241) the same idea was repeated as reflecting the doctrine set forth by Pope Alexander III (1159-1181) in a letter to the Archbishop of Salerno. An unsigned gloss on the canon cited, among others, Laurentius (+ after 1212), Tancredus (+ 1235), and Vincentius (+ 1240) as supporters of the opinion that a bishop could dispense unless by the law itself

[3] C. 16, C. XXV, q. 1: "Oportet ergo primam sedem, ut diximus, observare ea, quae mandavit decernendo, non necessitate obsequendi, sed auctoritate impertiendi."

[4] Brys, *De Dispensatione in Iure Canonico*, p. 244.

he was prohibited from doing so. A clear distinction between dispensing and absolving was not evident.[5] In many cases power was directly delegated to bishops and metropolitans by the law itself. This is exemplified in a canon attributed to Innocent III.[6]

Two cases were thus provided for. Either the law did not admit the existence of any right on the part of the prelates to grant a dispensation, or, when it did, the existence of that right was traceable to an express concession within the law itself or to a previous recourse to Rome. Pope Honorius III (1216-1227) declared invalid all dispensations granted without proper authority.[7]

The manner in which Rome either granted or denied the petition, that is, for the dispensation, or for the faculty to dispense in some given number of cases or for a fixed period of time, was not clearly indicated. As has been demonstrated, the Popes were accustomed to grant such concessions through personal, private letters. The form of each letter indicated the type of the grant. How the Popes reasoned that they could delegate the powers inherent in their office had its full expression in a *Regula Juris* of Boniface VIII (1294-1303): *"Potest quis per alium, quod potest facere per se ipsum."*[8]

Article 2

Practice of the Popes in the Sixteenth Century

Under decretal law the practice of issuing faculties became quite common. In the centuries that preceded the Council of Trent (1545-1563) many and varied letters containing concessions of jurisdiction were written.[9] For example, Pope Urban VI (1378-1389) granted to Conrad, the Archbishop of Trier, faculties for the

[5] C. 4, X, *de iudiciis*, II, 1, Glossa: " . . . Alia est magis communis opinio quod episcopus ubicumque potest dispensare ubi non invenitur prohibitum . . . "

[6] C. 13, X, *de officio iudicis ordinarii*, I, 31.

[7] C. 15, X, *de temporibus ordinationum et qualitate ordinandorum*, I, 11.

[8] Reg. 68, R. J. in VI°; the gloss on this *Regula* as offered by Ioannes Andreae (+1348) indicated the Roman Law source for this rule: *de vi et de vi armata*, D. (43. 16) 1, § 12, "Deiecisse autem etiam is videtur, qui mandavit vel iussit, ut aliquis deiiceretur: parvi enim referre visum est, suis manibus quis deiciat an vero per alium."

[9] L. Mergentheim, *Die Quinquennalfakultäten pro foro externo. Ihre Entstehung und Eintilung in Deutschen Bistümern* (2 vols., Stuttgart, 1908), II, 171, (hereafter cited *Die Quinquennalfakultäten pro foro externo*). Seventeen concessions, all given to John, Bishop of Meissen, are listed as having been granted during the month of November, 1540.—Ibid., 180-209.

delegating of priests to perform the act of reconsecration in regard to violated churches and cemeteries.[10] The effects of legislation and of the curial practice may be seen in a comparison of these faculties with the ones granted by Pope Paschal II (1099-1118) to Archbishop Anselm (1093-1109).[11] While the faculties granted to Archbishop Anselm were not limited any more definitely than with the words, *"pro necessitate temporis"* and *"et utilitate ecclesiae"*, those granted to Archbishop Conrad were limited expressly to three years for their use, *"post triennium minime valituri."* Thus there was introduced the note expressed currently with the word "Quinquennial" in the faculties of the present day.

In addition to the new element of limitation as to time, there was also a considerable difference in the cases for which the jurisdiction was granted. The faculties granted to Archbishop Anselm were of such an extent that they covered practically all cases wherein the need for faculties would arise, *"caetera etiam quae in regno illo . . . "*, while the ones granted to Archbishop Conrad were limited to the explicit case of delegating priests for the task described, and the conditions were clearly and completely indicated under which the faculties could be used. Taken in its entirety the letter of Pope Urban reveals a considerable advance in the science of Canon Law and in the practice of the Roman Curia by its preciseness and completeness, when contrasted with the broad use of terms and the lack of details evidenced in the letter of Pope Paschal II.

During the reign of Pope Clement VII (1523-1534) faculties were granted to John III, Archbishop of Treves, on July 1, 1553. This concession was made to cover the matrimonial impediments of consanguinity and affinity, as also the irregularities of clerics, which factors were treated in detail in the indult. Similarily the grant was made for a term of three years, with even a clear statement as to how the time was to be computed, over the signature of H. E. Card. Blosius: *"Presentibus ad triennium ab earum dato computandum dumtaxat duraturis. Datum Romae apud Sanctum Petrum, sub annulo piscatoris, die prima Julii 1553, pontificatus nostri anno decimo."*[12]

---

[10] Mergentheim, *op. cit.* II, 171.
[11] Mansi, XX, 1063.
[12] Mergentheim, op. cit., II, 174.

Mergentheim cited as examples numerous grants made to John Bishop of Meissen, during 1540. Although the fixed limitation of time did not appear in all the grants, the complete description of the cases covered, the reasons for which the faculties were being given, and the explanation why they were or were not needed, are all to be found in each of the letters.[13] The need for standardized formularies which could be used in granting faculties can easily be seen.

Extensive concessions of faculties were made to the Religious Orders both prior to and during the years of the celebration of the Council of Trent. While the issued faculties were most frequently contained in papal bulls, which at the same time either confirmed or extended previously granted privileges, a clear distinction was made through the use of the words, *"facultas, facultates"* and *"privilegium, privilegia"*, to point to the two varying types of concession. Usually there was no indication as to the time limit within which or the number of cases for which the faculties were to be used. Examples of such grants may be found in the Bulls issued by Pope Clement VII (1523-1534), Pope Paul III (1534-1549), and Pope JJulius III (1550-1555).[14]

Article 3

Legislation of the Council of Trent (1545-1563)

The Ecumenical Council of Trent which opened during the reign of Pope Paul III (1534-1549) concerned itself with legislation and regulations to direct the universal Church . Exceptions to the law, as also privileges contrary to the law could not, by reason of their very nature, receive any direct treatment. In some cases, however, faculties were extended to bishops in the law itself, that is, faculties were conceded, *"de iure."*[15] In other cases bishops were referred to as delegates of the Holy See.[16] Many decrees of the Council dealt

[13] Mergentheim, *Die Quinquennalfakultäten pro foro externo*. II, 180-209.

[14] *Bullarum Diplomatum et Privilegiorum Sanctorum Pontificum Taurinensis editio* (24 vols., et Appendix, Augustae Taurinorum, Neapoli 1857-1872), VI, (1860), 65, 173, 427.

[15] E. g., Conc. Trident., sess, XXIV, *de ref. matrim.*, c. 1; c. 6; sess, XXIII, *de ref.*, c. 11; c. 13; c. 14.

[16] E. g., Conc. Trident., sess. V, *de ref.*, c. 1, " . . . episcopi locorum in hoc ut Sedis Apostolicae delegati . . . "; c. 2, " . . . quo casu episcopus auctoritate apostolica et tamquam Sedis Apostolicae delegatus procedat."

with the obligations of bishops towards their dioceses,[17] and with their duties and their rights of jurisdiction.[18] But nothing was pronounced on the question of exceptions to the law. These exceptions were to receive their due consideration only as temporal, local and personal circumstances demanded.

---

[17] E. g., Conc. Trident., sess. VI, *de ref.*, c. 1 sqq.; sess. XIII, *de ref.*, c. 1 sqq.

[18] E. g., Conc. Trident., sess. XXIV, *de ref.*, c. 2; c. 3; c. 10.

CHAPTER IV

APOSTOLIC FACULTIES FROM 1637 TO THE PROMULGATION OF THE CODE OF CANON LAW

During the years following the promulgation of the decrees of the Council of Trent, both faculties and dispensations emanating from Rome were granted by means of letters, issued by the Apostolic Chancery on the orders of the Holy Father. This procedure rapidly became too awkward and time-consuming.[1] In addition, the extension of the boundaries of civilization by the discoveries of the Americas and the opening up of new routes to the Orient quickly placed distance between the missionaries and Rome that defied the ordinary means of communication. At the same time the reception of large numbers of pagan converts, the accommodation of Christianity to their cultures, and the combating of the Protestant heresies combined together as reasons which demanded a greater faculty for handling exceptions to the general Church law.[2] Pope Urban VII (1623-1644) in recognizing that need appointed a Commission, made up of Cardinals from the Holy Office of the Inquisition and from the Sacred Congregation for the Propagation of the Faith, for the purpose of composing formulas and regulations to be used in the issuing of faculties to the Ordinaries.[3]

Article I

Composition of the Faculties

The two Congregations mentioned were institutions of Church government organized to meet specific needs. The Sacred Office of the Inquisition, the older of the two, was instituted in the thirteenth century, and given new life by each succeeding Pontiff.

[1] Praefatio R. D. Francisci Gaudé, S. C. de Propaganda Fide Secretarii, in Formulas Facultatum—*Collectanea S. Congregationis de Propaganda Fide* (Romae: Typographia Polyglotta S. C. de Propaganda Fide, 1893), n. 89; (hereafter cited as *Collect.* (1893).

[2] *Collect.* (1893), nn. 88, 89.

[3] *Collect.* (1893), n. 88.

The official name of "Holy Office" was given the Congregation by Piux X (1903-1914) in the Constitution *"Sapienti Consilio."* Its jurisdiction has always been very extensive and complete.[4]

The Congregation for the Propagation of the Faith was erected by Gregory XV (1621-1623) in the Bull *"Inscrutabili"* of January 14, 1622.[5] All mission lands were placed under the jurisdiction of this Congregation, that is, the lands where the hierarchy had not yet been securely established; religious superiors in the missions were also subject to the acts of this Congregation, which acts were given the force of Apostolic Constitutions.[6]

The Commission for the composition of the Faculties, organized in 1633 by Pope Urban VIII, was composed of five Cardinals, two from the Sacred Office of the Inquisition and three from the Sacred Congregation for the Propagation of the Faith. In addition an Assessor and a Secretary were appointed to the Commission. The Secretary was R. D. Franciscus Ingoli of the Propagation of the Faith Congregation.[7] After three years of considerable effort five general *formulae* and seven *regulae* were composed. There were chiefly the work of R. D. Franciscus Ingoli, and were derived from previous letters granting faculties to bishops. Both the rules and formulas were submitted to and approved by the Commission on February 10, 1637.[8]

The seven rules written for the use of the Commission were in the form of general regulations governing both the drafting and the issuing of the faculties. Rule 1 concerned regions in which the practice of the Catholic religion was unimpeded and public.

> 1. In locis in quibus exercitium catholicae religionis est liberum et publicum, non est concedenda missionariis facultas administrandi infra scripta sacramenta parochialia, videlicet, baptismum, matrimonium, communionen in Paschate, et extremam unctionem, nisi cum clausula, "Si in

[4] For a short history of this Congregation, cf. Monin, *De Curia Romana* (Louvain, 1912), pp. 12-77.

[5] *Collect.* (1893), n. 3.

[6] *Collect.* (1893), n. 101; as to the force of the acts of the Congregation, cf. n. 119; for a short history of the Congregation, cf. Monin, *De Curia Romana*, pp. 64-70.

[7] Vermeersch, "Commentaria"—*Periodica*, XI, (1922), (39).

[8] Vermeersch, "Commentaria"—*Periodica*, XI, (1922), (41).

illis non sint Ordinarii vel parochi, vel si adsint, de eorum licentia."

Rule 2 had respect to localities where the Faith was practiced freely but not publicly.

2. In locis in quibus exercitium catholicae religionis est liberum sed non publicum, id est secretum, praedicta prima regula servanda est in tribus sacramentis parochialibus, videlicet baptismo, matrimonio, extrema unctione, nisi in casu necessitatis, et respectu matrimonii, ubi non est publicatum sacrum Concilium Tridentinum. In aliis vero sacramentis, Missionariis concedi potest facultas illa administrandi sine praedicta clausula, de licentia Ordinariorum et Parochorum.

Rule 3 concerned localities where the practice of the faith either public or private was prohibited.

3. In locis in quibus exercitium catholicae religionis tam publicum quam secretum prohibitum est, facultas administrandi sacramenta parochialia concedenda est missionariis cum clausula, "nisi de facile et sine periculo Ordinario vel parocho adiri possint," vel sine huiusmodi clausula, si ita expedire videbitur.

Rule 4 applied to localities where recourse to the Holy See for any reason, principally that of distance, was difficult.

4. In locis in quibus ob distantiam vel alias causas est difficilis recursus ad Sedem Apostolicam, facultas absolvendi a casibus Sedi Apostolicae reservatis, concedi potest Missionariis ad tempus pro ratione distantiae et locorum limitatum, sine clausula de praeterito.

Rule 5 was written for those places in Italy, France, Germany, and Belgium which had missions, and was designed to facilitate conversions and to guard against apostasy.

5. In locis Italiae ubi habentur missiones, et in locis Galliae, Germaniae et Belgii facultas absolvendi a praedictis casibus concedi potest pro haereticis primo conversis ad fidem catholicam; pro aliis vero ibi commorantibus, Nuntiis Apostolicis cum potestate illam subdelegandi in casibus et

locis particularibus. Ratio huius regulae est, quia expedit ut facilis sit recursus pro huiusmodi facultate, ne catholici veteres inter haereticos versantes a ministrisi haereticis pervertantur dum in angustiis sunt propter difficultatem obtinendi absolutionem, et ne de novo conversi ob eandem difficultatem in haeresim relabantur.

Rule 6 referred to matrimonial dispensations to be granted in missionary territories, that is, in territories attended by missionaries, and which did not yet have a permanently established hierarchy.

6. Facultas dispensandi in matrimoniis tam saecularibus quam regularibus in utroque foro concedantur, ubi non erunt eposcopi; ubi vero erunt, in foro conscientiae tantum, et quod tam episcopi quam missionarii huiusmodi facultatem a Sede Apostolica habentes in dispensatione concedenda teneantur inserere facultatis praedictae articulum cum expressione temporis ad quod concessa fuit.

Rule 7 provided means of action in respect to those places and circumstances which fell outside the contingencies enumerated in the previously given six rules.

7. Ab his tamen regulis, quia propter diversitatem regionum et casuum non semper poterunt observari, huic Congregationi super facultates missionariorum, SSm̃o annuente, retinendas, licebit recedere prout opus fuerit.

The five formulas were composed with consideration of the following three factors, viz: 1) the state of religion in the various countries; 2) the distance and the consequent difficulty of recourse to the Holy See; and 3) the distinctions in office and power on the part of those to whom the faculties were to be granted.[9]

In this regard they were designated by Roman numerals, I to V. Formula I was designed for issuance to bishops of Asia, Africa, and the Americas; Formula II, for the bishops in those parts of Europe which were under the rule of infidels, and were distant from the Holy See; Formula III, for issuance to the apostolic muncios and bishops in the neighboring parts of Europe where heresies had taken root; Formula IV, for mission prefects; and Formula V, for missonaries.[10]

---

[9] Vermeersch, "Commentaria"—*Periodica*, XI (1922), (41).
[10] Vermeersch, "Commentaria"—*Periodica*, XI (1922), (41).

The territory which now comprises the United States of America was administered according to several of the formulas, depending upon the country from which the missionaries came. Formula IV of the post-Code faculties has its source mainly in Formula I of the faculties of 1637, which was the formula used for the bishops in the Americas.[11]

Five additional Formulas had also been written by Secretary Ingoli to demonstrate the use of the rules and the five original forms. These latter five did not, however, receive any formal approbation at the time of the approval of the others. They were designated as Formula VI, for use in Ireland; Formula VII, VIII, and IX for issuance to missionary prefects in various parts of northern Europe, and Formula X, for use in France.[12]

Article 2

Changes in the Faculties Prior to the Code of Canon Law

With a few minor changes the original formulas remained in use until January 1, 1920, at which time revised formulas were approved by Pope Benedict XV (1914-1922) in an audience granted to the Secretary of the Congregation for the Propagation of the Faith on February 6, 1919, and thereupon were put into use.[13] Another period of transition which affected jurisdiction in the United States took place in 1908 when the United States were removed from the status of mission lands, taken from the jurisdiction of the Congregation for the Propagation of the Faith, and placed under that of the Sacred Consistorial Congregation.[14] The faculties granted to

[11] Briefly, catholicity in the United States of America grew out of the missionary activity of the European countries which colonized the newly discovered continent. Of these countries, France and Spain were Catholic and considered the establishment of the Church as an integral part of their colonization program. Consequently, missionary activity was largely the work of priests from these nations. Cf. Shea, *History of the Catholic Church in the United States,* (4 vols., New York, 1886-1892), *French Colonies,* I, bks. 3 and 6; *Spanish Colonies,* I, bks. 2 and 5; *English Colonies,* I, bks. 1 and 4; II, 50; 540 ff.

[12] Vermeersch, "Commentaria"—*Periodica* XI (1922), (42); Putzer, *Commentarium in Facultates Apostolicas* (4. ed., Neo-Eboraci, 1897), p. 3; henceforth cited as *Commentarium.*

[13] Vermeersch, "Commentarium"—*Periodica* XI (1922), (70).

[14] Pius X, Const. "Sapienti Concilio", 29 iun. 1908, I, *Sacrae Congregationes,* Fc—*Congregatio de Propagande Fide.* 2: "*Itaque a iurisdictione Congregationis de Propaganda Fide exempta et ad ius commune deductas decernimur in America—provincias ecclesiasticas dominii Canadensis,* Terae

bishops in the United States remained in effect, however, until December 31, 1912, after which date they were to be obtained through the Apostolic Delegate.[15]

Of the five original formulas the first four, viz: Formulas I, II, III, and IV, were considered ordinary by reason of the persons to whom they were issued. Formula V remained more flexible and adjustable for concession to missionary prefects and other superiors. For bishops of the United States faculties were issued according to Formula I. However, all five formulas had undergone some few changes, and other faculties, called extraordinary, had been added to the original grants. The extraordinary faculties were designated by the letters of the alphabet, both small and capital, and were drawn up and issued during the latter half of the nineteenth century. Of these the bishops in the United States received Formulas C, D, and E, approved in audience by Pope Pius IX (1846-1878) on the dates of January 4, 1863; July 26, 1863; and March 1, 1864, respectively.[16]

The changes in Formula I which had taken place during the intervening years, that is, between their approval in 1637 and the year 1897, were few indeed when one considers the length of time and the variety of circumstances in which the use of the formula prevailed. The extraordinary faculties of Formulas C, D, and E, were grouped under one form, viz: Formula T, about the year 1905.[17]

In the copies of the faculties used by Putzer (1863-1904) in his revision of the work of Konings (1821-1884) a number of changes are noticed as compared with the original forms approved in 1637.[18]

Article 6 of Formula I was altered to read:

> Dispensandi in 3° et 4° consanguintatis et affinitatis gradu simplici et mixto tantum, et in 2°, 3°, et 4° mixtis, non tamen in 2° solo quoad futura matrimonia; quo vero ad praeterita

Novae Foederatorum Civitatum seu *Statuum Unitorum.*"—*Acta Apostolicae Sedis,* (Romae, 1909—), I (1909), 12.

[15] S. C. C., letter of October 21, 1909; issued as a circular letter to American bishops by the Office of the Apostolic Delegate—*The Ecclesiastical Review* (originally *The American Ecclesiastical Review, Philadelphia,* 1889-1943; since January, 1944, *The American Ecclesiastical Review,* Baltimore, 1944—), XLI (1909), 741. (*Hereafter cited Ecclesiastical Review*).

[16] Vermeesch, "Commentarium"—*Periodica,* XI (1922), (67-68).

[17] *Ecclesicastical Review,* XL (1909), 494.

[18] Putzer, *Commentarium,* p. 144.

etiam in 2° solo, dummodo nullo modo attingat primum gradum, cum his qui ab haeresi vel infidelitate convertuntur ad fidem catholicam, et in praefatis casibus prolem susceptam declarandi legitimam."[19]

In article 7 the word *"iustitiae"* was altered to read *"iusti,"* a change which Feije (1820-1894) said was caused by the misreading *"iustit.,"* an abbreviation of *"iustitiae."*[20] Article 16 was necessarily rearranged in view of the change brought about in the legislation, according to the Bull *"Apostolicae Sedis"* of Pope Pius IX.[21] In 1842, according to Putzer,[22] article 21 was entirely rewritten to read:

"Tenendi et legendi, non tamen aliis concedendi, praeterquam, ad tempus tamen, iis sacerdotibus, quos praecipue idoneos atque honestos esse sciat, libros prohititos, exceptis operibus Dupuy, Volney, M. Reghellini, Pigault-Le Brun, De Potter, Bentham, J. A. Dulaure, Fetes et Courtisanes de la Grece, Novelle di Casti, et aliis operibus de obscoenis et contra religionem ex professo tractantibus."

An addition was made to article 23, not so much by way of extending or enlarging the faculty of allowing bination as granted to the bishops, but rather through an interpretation of that faculty. Indication was made of the need of care and vigilance, and of the necessity of a grave cause attendant on the delegation of the faculty;

" . . . Caveat vero ne praedicta facultate seu dispensatione celebrandi bis in die aliter quam ex gravissimis causis et rarissime utatur, in quo graviter ipsius conscientia oneratur. Quod si hanc eandem facultatem alteri sacerdoti iuxta potestatem inferius apponendam communicare, aut causas ea utendi alicui, qui a Sancta Sede hanc facultatem obtinuerit, approbare visum

---

[19] Putzer, *Commentarium,* p. 274, n. 114; Baart, *Legal Formulary,* (2 ed., New York, 1898), p. 234.

[20] Feije, *De Impedimentis et Dispensationibus Matrimonialibus,* (3. ed., Lovanii, 1885), n. 615; (*hereafter cited De Impedimentis*).

[21] *Fontes,* n. 552.

[22] Commentarium, n. 157, p. 265; Baart, *Legal Formulary,* p. 240.

fuerit, serio ipsius conscientiae iniungitur, ut paucis dumtaxat iisque maturioris prudentiae ac zeli et qui absolute necessarii sunt, nec pro quolibet loco, sed ubi gravis necessitas tulerit, et ad breve tempus eamdem communicet aut respective causas approbet."[23]

The faculty of dispensing from fast and abstinence, as contained in article 27, was changed by the addition of a phrase concerning its application and use: "Non tamen per generale indultum, sed in casibus particularibus." As in article 23 given above, this addition was appended for the sake of interpretation.[24]

Formula I in its entirety contained twenty-nine articles of distinct faculties. Not all of these, however, contained grants of power. Eleven conceded the power of granting dispensations from certain enactments of ecclesiastical law, the majority of which were concerned with the sacrament of matrimony. Of the remaining articles two contained the grant of power to absolve from censures; three of them concerned the bestowal of indulgences; eight conferred privileges; two dealt with the delegation or communication of the faculties to other priests of the diocese; one governed the appointment of regulars as pastors or assistants, and the final article determined the limits of the faculties along with the added caution that the faculties were to be granted absolutely gratis. Article 10 governed the use of the powers conceded in articles 6, 7, 8, and 9, and thus, though the formula of faculties contained 29 articles, only 28 of these granted a power.

The extraordinary faculties which were granted with Formulas C, D, and E did not revoke, but rather enlarged, the previous faculties granted under Formula I. The extraordinary faculties contained twenty-four articles in all, twelve in Formula C, eight in Formula D, and four in Formula E. Considered collectively, eleven of the concessions concerned the granting of dispensations of which Formula C contained two, Formula D comprised five, and Formula E included four. Formula D contained one article which granted the power to absolve from any ecclesiastical penalty incurred by

---

[23] Putzer, *Commentarium*, p. 268, n. 159; Baart, *Legal Formulary*, p. 240.
[24] Putzer, *op. cit.* p. 292, n. 169; Baart, *opp. cit.* p. 240.

reason of the impediment those to whom the dispensations were given. There were four articles in Formula C concerning the erection of the Way of the Cross and Confraternities, and regarding matters dealing with the grant of indulgences and special blessings. Two articles granted privileges, both in Formula C, which also contained an article on the delegating of the powers contained in the faculties to priests of the diocese. Formula D likewise contained an article on delegation, but it was lacking in Formula E. The bishops were granted also the privilege of ordaining priests *"ad titulum missionis,"* a faculty of great importance in the United States at that time. Similar to Formula I the extraordinary faculties were also granted gratis.

In addition there were also faculties issued by the Sacred Penitentiary for use in the internal forum. They were contained in a booklet known as *"Pagella Facultatem S. Poenitentiariae."* Putzer was of the opinion that the *Pagella* was not issued to bishops of the United States.[25]

Article 3
Concession of the Faculties

The issuance of the faculties by the Holy Office grew out of custom rather than legislation. This fact was to be expected, however, since the Holy Office enjoyed seniority in years and more extensive jurisdiction than the Congregation for the Propagation of the Faith. When missionaries applied to the latter Congregation for faculties they were referred to the Holy Office, and this practice remained until the year 1765, during which year moves were initiated to alter the situation. Under the new practice faculties were issued by the Pope through audiences granted to the Secretary of the Congregation for the Propagation of the Faith. The length of time necessary to complete such a change in procedure was indicated by the fact that as late as 1790 the Congregation was still referring missionaries to the Holy Office.[26]

The task of preparing each manuscript of faculties was assigned

[25] *Commentarium,* n. 251, p. 432.

[26] Vermeersch, "Commentarium"—*Periodica,* XI, (1922), (66). Vermeersch cited the work *Nota d'Archivo,* of Franciscus Bernardus Rosi, an author of the 19th century.

to the Secretary of the Pontifical Commission for the composition of the faculties. For a long period they were issued in manuscript form. Printing of the formulas was recommended by Pope Urban VIII. The reasons for such action were indicated by Vermeersch as being: 1) the easier reproduction of the formulas; 2) the lesser consumption of time for the issuing of the formula; 3) the greater security against all danger of forgery; and 4) their readier transmission to the various territories.[27]

There seems to have been neither a standard nor a required form designated for use by bishops in requesting the faculties or their renewal. The usual procedure in requesting the faculties seems to have consisted in the use of a mandate whereby the Secretary of the Congregation for the Propagation of the Faith was authorized to petition the Pope either for the grant or for the renewal of the faculties. The petition could also be made by a bishop in person, but this means was rarely employed.[28]

Since bishops in the United States obtained their faculties through the Vicar Apostolic in London until the appointment of Bishop Carroll in 1790, there was no change effected in their regard when the task of issuing the faculties was transferred from the Holy Office to the Congregation for the Propagation of the Faith. From 1790 until 1912 bishops of the United States obtained their faculties through this Congregation, and consequently the Secretary of the Congregation, acting on mandate, presented their petition to the Pope.

After 1912 the same procedure prevailed except that the faculties were obtained from the particular Congregation to whose competency the subject-matter of the petitioned faculties pertained. This procedure was followed until 1923, when Pope Pius XI, (1922-1939) in the Motu Proprio *Post Datam,* of April, 1923, consigned to the Sacred Consistorial Congregation the duty of the issuing of faculties to Ordinaries not subject to the Congregation for the Propagation of the Faith, which change included the Ordinaries of the United States.[29]

---

[27] Vermeersch, "Commentarium"—*Periodica,* XI, (1922), (67). This author cited Mss. from the *Acta S. Cong. de Prop. Fide.*

[28] Wernz, *Ius Decretalium,* IV, n. 622, 99.

[29] *AAS,* XV (1923), 193 -1941. For the text of the faculties used by the

The participation of the vicar general in the use of the Apostolic Faculties was a much disputed point. The common opinion, however, was that the vicar general did not, by virtue of his office, enjoy any of the powers conceded in the faculties, and hence could use them only when he was specifically empowered by means of an act of delegation to do so.[30] The controversy was settled by a letter issued by the Holy Office on February 21, 1888, in which it was stated that the term "Ordinary" included also the vicar general. Thus, by reason of his office, the vicar general participated in those Apostolic Faculties of the bishop which for their use did not require the episcopal character. No delegation of faculties to the vicar general was necessary.[31]

Article 4
Cessation of the Faculties

The period of time or the number of cases for which the faculties were valid was determined in the preface of the indult. The usual period of use for faculties issued to bishops in the United States was five or ten years, but periods of longer or shorter duration were sometimes prescribed.[32] In some of the extraordinary faculties issued after 1863, a definite number of cases was indicated, and in this manner the faculties' duration was determined. In such instances, however, the faculties, though given for a definite number of cases, expired with the date set in the indult regardless of whether the number of cases had or had not been called into use for the application of the faculty given.[33]

In all instances, as far as the bishops in the United States were concerned according to Putzer, who cited as his authority the Sec-

various Congregations, cf. Gasparri, *Tractatus Canonicus de Matrimonio* (ed. nova, 2 vols., Romae: Typis Polyglottis Vaticanis, 1932), II, Allegatum V; Vermeersch—Creusen, *Epitome Iuris Canonica* (3 vols., Vol. I. 6. ed., 1937; Vol. II, 5 ed., 1943; Vol. III, 5 ed., 1936, Romae—Mechliniae: H. Dessain), I, n. 874, p. 654. (Hereafter cited *Epitome*).

[30] Reiffenstuel, *Ius Canonicum Universum*, 4 vols., Venetiis, 1735), lib. I, tit. XXIX, n. 126 sqq.; lib. IV, App. n. 34; Schmalzgrueber, *Ius Ecclesiasticum Universum*, (5 vols. in 12, Romae, 1843-1845), lib. I, tit. IV, n. 33; lib. IV, tit. XXVIII, nn. 18 sqq.; Smith, *Elements of Ecclesiastical Law*, (5. ed., 3 vols., New York, 1883) I, nn. 627-629.

[31] *Collect.* (1893), n. 1685.

[32] Wernz, *Ius Decretalium*, IV, n. 621.

[33] *Collect.* (1893), n. 1238.

retary of the Congregation for the Propagation of the Faith, the beginning of the period was computed from the day on which the faculties had been issued in Rome.[34] In other parts of the world which came under the jurisdiction of the Sacred Congregation for the Propagation of the Faith the period of duration was computed as beginning on the day on which the faculties were received by the ordinary.[35] In instances wherein the faculties expired before a request for their renewal had been submitted, the bishop acted validly if the neglect to petition their renewal had not been culpable.[36]

Since it is clear that the concessions were made freely by the Pope, it was within his power to revoke them. While theoretically this was true, the practical application or use of that power was not contemplated. Whether the laws in relation to which the faculties had been given would resume their binding force once the faculties were revoked, especially in consideration of the difficulty of communication and the presence of other contingencies attendant on a given case, likewise raised a question. A general act of revocation was not sufficient, as is apparent from the response of the Holy Office, given February 1, 1781, in which it was declared that faculties granted through the Sacred Penitentiary and the Sacred Congregation for the Propagation of the Faith were not affected by a general revocation of privileges.[37]

Since the faculties were necessary instruments of administration in most cases, it seems that a bishop was not free to decline their acceptance or to forego their application and use, at least those faculties which were not concerned with personal privileges. That is to say, that a bishop could conceivably withhold his acceptance or forego the use of the faculty which granted him personally the privilege of the portable altar, but very probably he had no like freedom in relation to the imparted faculty of granting absolution from reserved censures.[38]

The faculties did not expire upon the death of the Pope who

---

[34] *Commentarium*, n. 39, p. 52.

[35] *Acta Sanctae Sedis*, (41 vols., Romae, 1865-1908), XXIV, (1891), 146; *Collect.* (1893), nn. 100-146.

[36] *ASS, XXIV*, (1891), 393; *Collect.* (1893), n. 148.

[37] Putzer, *Commentarium*, n. 41, p. 55.

[38] Reiffenstuel, *Ius Canonicum Universum*, lib. V, tit. 33, nn. 188-190.

granted them, for they were given after the manner of privileges, unless, as annotated in the faculties themselves, their duration was fixed by the terms indicated in the concession. No petition was necessary for their renewal in case of the death of the reigning Pope.[39] It was held, however, that the faculties ceased with the death of the bishop to whom they had been granted.[40]

In the United States special provision for counteracting this possible eventuality was made by the II Plenary Council of Baltimore (1866).[41] The legislation advised that a bishop should, before death, subdelegate his faculties to a priest, in order that the diocese should not be without their potential use. In case such action had not been taken, the Metropolitan or Senior Suffragan was to see to it that faculties were provided for the diocese by means of subdelegation. This legislation of the Council was submitted in the form of a difficulty to the Holy See, but no response was received; consequently, the practice in the United States followed the pattern indicated in the Council. The question was repeated in the X Provincial Council of Baltimore (1869), and the response was that the successor of a bishop, either deceased or transferred, had the same faculties as the bishop whom he succeeded, including those granted in Formulas C, D, and E.[42]

Smith (1845-1895) observed that the response applied only to the Baltimore province, since the Council was a provincial one and not plenary in character.[43] This conclusion hardly seems justified in view of the fact that responses from the Sacred Congregation were the sole means available for an official interpretation of the faculties. When such responses were issued, it was considered that they had equal application for all the dioceses which came under the juris-

---

[39] Reiffenstuel, *Ius Canonicum Universum*, lib. V, tit. 33, n. 167; Putzer, *Commentarium*, n. 37, p. 50.

[40] S. Poenit., 3 apr. 1886—*Ecclesiastical Review*, III, (1892), 153; Benedictus XIV, *De Synodo Dioecesana*, (2 vols., Prati, 1844), lib. II, cap. 9, n. 3.

[41] II Plenary Council of Baltimore (1866), nn. 96, 97, 98—*Acta et Decreta Sacrorum Conciliorum Recentiorum, Collectio Lacensis*, (7 vols., Friburgi Brisgoviae, 1870-1890), III, cols. 428, 429; hereafter cited *Coll. Lac.*

[42] X Provincial Council of Baltimore, (1869), response recorded: " . . . administrator, sede vacante, donetur facultatibus extraordinariis contentis sub formulis C. D. et E., exceptis iis quae characterem (episcopalem) requirunt." *Coll. Lac.*, III. col. 599.

[43] *Elements of Ecclesiastical Law*, I. n. 638.

diction of the Congregation, unless the opposite was explicitly stated.

Article 28 of Formula I explicitly mentioned the death of a bishop as a condition precedent to the subdelegation of these faculties. Thus it appears that no difficulty should have arisen on this point. All controversial arguments touching on the power of the bishop to subdelegate the faculties, or on the type of power he used under the faculties, that is, whether ordinary or delegated, or on the manner in which the faculties were granted by the Holy See, or also on related points in this matter, were answered by the Sacred Congregation which controlled the concession and use of the faculties. The mind of the Holy See and its current practice seem clear from the wording of the letter issued by the Holy Office on February 20, 1888, in which it was stated that the bishop could subdelegate the faculties of giving dispensations to any priest whom he deemed qualified as an agent to exercise them.[44] In the same letter the vicar general, the vicar capitular and the legitimate administrator of a diocese were included in the term, "Ordinary."

The position held by the earlier writers, including Pope Benedict XIV (1740-1758), was reversed by a decree of the Holy Office which declared that all faculties automatically pass to the successor of a bishop. Thus the question in relation to the successor of the bishop during the vacancy of the episcopal see was settled.[45] The same legislation was incorporated into the Code of Canon Law in cannon 66 § 2.

Article 5

Subdelegation of the Faculties

Whether or not bishops could subdelegate the powers contained in the faculties was a question of paramount importance from the very beginning of their use. The purpose of the faculties, as set forth by the Secretary of the Commission, R. D. Franciscus Ingoli,[46] was to facilitate the administration of those dioceses which found communication with Rome difficult by reason of distance or in view of other hampering conditions existing in those regions. So it seems

---

[44] *Collect.* (1893), n. 1685, " . . . Ordinarii dispensare valeant sive per se sive per ecclesiasticam personam sibi bene visam."

[45] S. C. S. Off., 20 nov. 1897—*ASS*, XXX, (1897), 627.

[46] Praefatio R. D. Franciscus Ingoli, S. C. de Propaganda Fide Secretarii, in Formulas Facultatum—*Collect.* (1893), n. 89.

that, since the purpose of the faculties was the facilitation of church administration, the Holy See stood in favor of the possible subdelegation of the faculties by the bishop to his priests, inasmuch as they were his necessary assistants in ministering to the needs of the faithful.

Provision for subdelegation or communication [47] of the faculties was made within the indult, in article 28 of Formula I. In this article was contained the faculty of communicating the powers conceded by Formula I, namely to worthy priests who were working in the diocese of the bishop. The concession was restricted to those of the faculties which did not require the episcopal character in the administration of them. The class of priests to whom the faculties could be communicated was very clearly stated. It was sufficient that they be working in the diocese; there was no need for them to be priests who belonged to the diocese. [48]

The wording of article 28, Formula I, indicated that the faculties could be communicated habitually, since it was not prescribed that they be communicated for each single case. No such provision for communication was made in Formula C, but in both Formula D (article 8) and Formula E (article 4) the permission to subdelegate was given. It may, however, be reasonably concluded that, since subdelegation of some of the faculties was almost a necessity in the United States in view of the extent of the dioceses and the inadequate means of communication, the principle regarding possible subdelegation as contained in Formulas I, D, and E, applied also to Formula C.

Article 6
Interpretation of the Faculties

As to interpretation and use of the faculties, the Congregations themselves were from their foundation the first source of rules and guidance, and the supreme authority in the solution of doubts and

---

[47] The terms delegation and communication are used as synonyms by most authors when they speak of faculties . Putzer insisted that, in an absolute sense, a distinction should be made, but that with reference to faculties, the term communication, when used in a wide sense, comprehended also subdelegation or delegation.—*Commentarium*, nn. 28-32, pp. 40-44.

[48] S. Cong. de Prop. Fide, 14 maii 1838—*Collectanea S. Congregationis de Propaganda Fide*, (2 vols., Romae: Typographia Polyglotta S. C. de Propaganda Fide, 1907), n. 35; hereafter cited as *Collect.* (1907).

controversies.[49] In order to facilitate reference to the letters, decrees and responses of the S. Congregation concerning the use of the faculties, two collections of the documents were published and authenticated for use in those countries which came under the jurisdiction of the two Congregations. The first work arranged according to subject-matter and with an analytical index, was published by the Congregation for the Propagation of the Faith in 1893, and the second, arranged in chronological order, was published in 1907 by the same Congregation. These collections from the time of their publication governed the use of the faculties up to the publication of the present Code of Canon Law, and also the new Formulas of Faculties effective from 1918 to 1923.[50]

Prior to the publication of the above mentioned works, private sources were relied upon, namely, the *Nota d'Archivo sulle formule di facolta ordinarie, by Franciscus Bernardini Rossi, archivist,* dated 1866; a manuscript signed, Redatta dal Prof. D. Francisco Rossi, archivista, (usually considered as one work together with the former, since the author was the same), and a collection named *Collecta iussu SS. D. N. PP Benedicti XIV,* and dated 1821.[51]

In addition to the responses and decrees of the Congregations thus collected, much interpretation was taken from the approved authors or commentators on Decretal law, such as Reiffenstuel (who treated *ex professo* the faculties issued to German bishops in the Appendix of Tom. IV), Schmalzgrueber, Wernz, and others. In the United States, both the work of Anthony Konings, *Commentarium in Facultates Apostolicas* (1884), and the revised editions of this work under the same title by Joseph Putzer, were used extensively in the interpretation and use of the faculties. On the part of the commentators particular attention was necessarily paid to the exact wording of the Formulas themselves. In nearly all cases chances for misunderstanding were few, not only because of the great effort

---

[49] Monin, *De Curia Romana,* pp. 12-17; 64-70.

[50] A much more recent work for use in the mission countries was published in 1939; *Sylloge praecipuorum documentorum recentium Summorum Pontificum et S. Congregationis de Propaganda Fide necon aliarum SS. Congregationum Romanarum ad usum Missionariorum,* Typis Polyglottis Vaticanis, 1939.

[51] Vermeersch, "Commentarium"—*Periodica,* XI, (1922), p. (40) n. 1: p. (60).

and skill that were employed in the composition of the original Formulas, but also in view of the vigilance exercised by the Congregations to whose care the issuance of the faculties was committed.

The controversies that did arise, such as were noted in the previous articles dealing with the concession and the cessation of the faculties, were the result of the introduction of the new institute of Apostolic Faculties into Canon Law. The institute of habitual faculties was a new entity; none of the concepts previously used seemed to fit this institution exactly. Thus, new concepts and new rules became necessary, to say nothing of the new terminology, and a certain lapse of time was necessary for the forming of the concepts and of a crystallized expression for them.

One example of this difficulty is easily seen in the treatment given by Reiffenstuel. He wrote that the faculties could not be considered as privileges, since they were without the note of perpetuity, which note was essential to the concept of privileges.[52] Hence the vicar general could not without a special mandate use the faculties of dispensing. Reiffenstuel consequently called the faculties quasi-privileges, which accordingly were not interpretable at all times according to the principles of interpretation applied to privileges.

Another example is found in Wernz, who wrote that the faculties had to be interpreted according to the proper meaning of their text, not indeed strictly as a dispensation, but liberally as a privilege, that is, comprehensively but not extensively. He cited Scherer (1845-1918) as holding the opposite view, that is, that the faculties had to be taken according to the proper meaning of their text, but also in the strict sense.[53] Further, Wernz at the same time directed attention to the sources of the faculties as guides for their correct interpretation and proper use. Moreover, while in the Formulas themselves the administrative power there conceded was referred to as extraordinary, Feije, in treating of the matrimonial dispensations which could be granted in virtue of the concessions made in the

[52] *Ius Canonicum Universum*, lib. IV, A; nn. 33 sqq. " . . . vocamus quasi tale, quia proprie privilegium non est; cum istud, juxta dicenda infra, ex natura sua debeat esse perpetum . . . " Reiffentsuel cited Sanchez, Barbosa, and others who supported this view.

[53] *Ius Decretalium*, IV, n. 620, 101: " . . . Facultates dispensandi super impedimentis matrimonialibus, quamvis sint favorabiles, nec strictae interpretationis ad instar dispensationum, sed potius late . . . ad instar privilegiorum."

Formulas of extraordinary faculties, called that dispensatory power *"quasi-ordinary"* for the reason that the power, though it was attached to the office of the bishop, became usuable only with the permission of the Holy See.[54]

In spite of the apparent disagreement among the commentators, there were general rules which were acknowledged as applicable in all cases. In the case of doubt concerning the rightful use of the faculties the decision always rested with the Congregation which enjoyed jurisdictional competence relative to the matter in doubt. It was not rare for decisions given by the Congregations to contradict opinions formerly supported as tenable, and to disavow solutions formerly held to be even mandatory.[55]

Those for whom the faculties could and should be applied were definitely held to be simply those who by baptism were members of the Church, to the exclusion of those who were incapable of receiving benefits from the Church in consequence of their contraction of a censure or of some other disqualification by way of penalty. This exclusion naturally did not stand in the way of the use of the faculties for absolving from the censure itself.[56]

Bishops were confined to the use of the faculties in their own territory and for their own subjects. However, within their territory the faculties could in general be used also for *"vagi"* and *"peregrini"*; and outside their territory they could be used for persons properly subject to the bishop. Ordinarily the subject, but not necessarily the bishop, had to be within the diocese when use was made of the faculties in favor of the subject.[57] An exception to this principle was made in regard to the United States.[58]

The granting of dispensations in virtue of the faculties was regulated by the practice of the Roman Curia.[59] Particular attention was directed to the necessity of a sufficient cause for the dis-

---

[54] *De Impedimentis*, n. 697.

[55] Reiffenstuel, *Ius Canonicum Universum*, lib. IV, Appendix, nn. 34 sqq; *Collect.* (1893). n. 1685.

[56] C. 1, X, *de rescriptis, I, 3, in VI°*; Putzer, *Commentarium*, n. 46, p. 63.

[57] S. C. S. Off., 2 maii 1877—*Collect.* (1893), n. 158.

[58] S. C. S. Off., 20 dec. 1894—cited by Putzer, *Commentarium*, n. 57, p. 76.

[59] Ferraris, *Prompta Bibilotheca, Canonica, Iuridica, Moralis, Theologica necnon Ascetica, Polemica, Rubricistica, Historica*, (ed. novissima 9 vols., Romae, 1885-1899), I, *Beneficium*, IX, n. 8; hereafter cited as *Prompta Bibiliotheca.*

pensation at the time of its concession. The nature of the needed cause was sometimes indicated within the faculties themselves, as in article 4 of Formula I, where the words *"ex rationabili causa"* were used. In other places, such as article 6, Formula D, there were contained explanatory phrases whose import was to be followed in the issuing of the dispensations. After 1877, bishops in the United States followed an Instruction, issued by the Sacred Congregation for the Propagation of the Faith, on May 9, 1877, which treated of the causes for dispensation from diriment impediments in relation to the sacrament of matrimony.[60] Causes admitted by the Sacred Penitentiary were listed in a response issued through the Holy Office in 1754.[61]

No standard formularies were prescribed by the Congregations for use by the bishops in granting dispensations, or in submitting questions to the Holy See for solution. There were available, however, many recommended and sample formularies as found in the works of recognized authors.[62]

Thus, up to the time that the present Code became binding law on May 19, 1918,[63] the interpretation of the Apostolic Faculties of bishops was governed by the following norms, set down here in the order of their importance: 1) the wording of the text of the indult; 2) the instructions, decrees, and responses of the Sacred Congregations; and 3) the common opinions of the recognized jurists. The Code of Canon Law incorporated many of the powers which formerly were granted only in the faculties, and consequently, after May 19, 1918, such powers became subject to the same rules of interpretation to which the Code itself is subject. But such powers as were not incorporated in the Code were cancelled, except the faculties concerning the granting of matrimonial dispensations, which were designated as continuing in force, but which for their use and application were subject to the prescripts contained in the

---

[60] S. Cong. de Prop. Fide, Instr. super dispensationibus matrimonialibus, 9 maii 1877—*Collect.* (1907), n. 1470.

[61] S. C. S. Off., 26 sept. 1754—*Fontes*, n. 806, *Collect.* (1907), n. 393.

[62] E. g., Gasparri, *Tractatus Canonicus de Matrimonio*, Putzer, *Commentarium.*

[63] Benedictus XV, const. *"Providentissima Mater Ecclesia"*, 27 maii 1917.— *Codex Iuris Canonici Pii X Pontificis Maximi iussu digestus Benedicti Papae XV auctoritate promulgatus*, (Romae: Typis Polyglottis Vaticanis, 1917, [reimpressio, 1934].

canons of Book III, Title VII, of the Code of Canon Law.[64] New faculties were written and put into use March 17, 1922,[65] and these are the habitual faculties spoken of in canon 66, § 1, where it is stated that they are to be considered as *"privilegia praeter ius."* They are thus given the status of a recognized and necessary institute in the present discipline of the Church.

---

[64] S. C. Consist., decr. *"Proxima sacra,"* 25 ap. 1918—*AAS*, X (1918), 190-192. For English translation cf. *Ecclesiastical Review*, LXVI, (1922), 630. No list of faculties was issued at that time. Cf. *Il Monitore Ecclesiastico* (Romae, 1876—), Ser. 4, Vol. V (1923), 200. Volume LXV in the entire series).

[65] Pius XI, motu propr. *"Post datam"*, 20 apr.. 1923—*AAS*, XV (1923), 193-194.

CANONICAL COMMENTARY

CHAPTER V

INTRODUCTION

ARTICLE I

PRELIMINARY NOTIONS

The Quinquennial Faculties of Formula IV, granted to the Ordinaries in North and South America and the adjacent islands, are issued each five years, computed according to the prescript of canon 340.[1] Since 1923, the faculties have been issued in one Formula, designated as Formula IV, by the Sacred Consistorial Congregation.[2] They are granted, upon petition ,to those included under the term "Ordinary" in canon 198, § 1, that is, to residential bishops, abbots, or prelates *nullius* and the vicars general of these officers, vicars, prefects, and administrators apostolic, and all those who during a vacancy succeed or are appointed to replace the above mentioned officers.[3]

Any exception to the rule mentioned above is in the text of the faculties themselves, where special considerations attached by the competent Congregation are found. Many of the faculties contained in the Formulas of 1637 [4] are not at present contained in the Code of Canon Law, and although the principles used in the composition of the Formulas today remain the same as those formerly employed, the material content differs to some extent. The faculties are given a definite canonical status in canon 66, which states in paragraph 1 that such habitual faculties are privileges outside the law.[5]

[1] In the United States these periods coincide with those years whose final number is either four (4) or nine (9), as 1944, 1949.

[2] Cf. Motu prop., "*Post datam*" of Pope Pius XI, 20 apr. 1923—*AAS*, XV (1923), 193-194.

[3] The Major Religious Superiors of exempt clerical orders do not receive Formula IV of the faculties. Such faculties as they do receive are granted through the Sacred Congregation of Religions.

[4] Vermeersch, "Commentaria"—*Periodica*, XI (1922), (41).

[5] Canon 66, § 1, Facultates habituales quae conceduntur vel in perpetuum vel ad praefinitum tempus aut certum numerum casuum, accensentur privilegiis praeter ius.

Article 2

General Rules of Interpretation

A. The Ordinaries of Canon 198, § 1.

Ordinaries to whom the Quinquennial Faculties are issued are to be understood as those named in paragraph 1 of canon 198.[6] Thus, the determining note is the possession of ordinary jurisdiction, on the part of the person receiving the faculties, in regard to territory or persons.[7] The type of jurisdiction used in the exercise of the major portion of the faculties is known as non-judicial or voluntary, and may be used in favor of an Ordinary's subjects, either within his proper territory or outside of it, or, in some cases, in favor of non-subjects; i. e., when they are actually within the proper territory of the Ordinary.[8] Some exceptions are noted to the rule of the canon, which exceptions are indicated in the text of the faculties or in notations appended by the Congregations enjoying jurisdiction in the matter concerned. These exceptions are discussed in the commenting on the respective faculties in the subsequent articles of this dissertation.

The term residential bishop, *Episcopus residentialis,* in canon 198, § 1, excludes titular bishops,[9] since titular bishops do not enjoy ordinary jurisdiction in their dioceses.[10] Bishops appointed as coadjutors or auxiliaries may also assist in the rule of a diocese. These bishops are grouped in three general classifications by the Code of Canon Law,[11] that is to say, coadjutor bishops given to the

---

[6] Canon 198 § 1: In iure nomine Ordinarii intelliguntur, nisi quis expresso excipiatur, praeter Romanum Pontificem, pro suo quisque territorio Episcopus residentialis, Abbas vel Praelatus *nullius* eorumque Vicarius Generalis, Administrator, Vicarius et Praefectus Apostolicus, itemque ii qui praedictis deficientibus interim ex iuris praescripto aut ex probatis constitutionibus succedunt in regimine, pro suis vero subditis Superiores maiores in religionibus clericalibus exemptis.

[7] Vromant, *Facultates Apostolicae quas Sacra Congregatio de Propaganda Fide delegare solet Ordinariis Missionum, Commentaria in Formulam Tertiam,* Museum Lessianum—Section Théologique, n. 16 (Louvain; Editions du Museum Lessianum, 1926), n. 17, p. 12. (Hereafter cited *Facultates Apostolicae*).

[8] Cf. canon 201, § 3.

[9] Cf. canon 334, § 1.

[10] Cf. canon 348, § 1: Titular bishops may, however, enjoy the use of the faculties by reason of some other office of which they are the incumbent.

[11] Canon 350, § 2: Coadiutor dari solet personae Episcopi cum iure successionis; sed nonnumquam datur quoque sedi.

§ 3: Coadiutor, datus personae Episcopi sine iure successionis speciali nomine dicitur *Auxiliaris.*

person of the bishops: 1) with the right of succession; 2) without the right of succession; and 3) coadjutor bishops given to the episcopal see.[12]

Coadjutors do not enjoy the Quinquennial Faculties by virtue of their appointment, and their exercise of the powers contained in the Faculties depends upon their letters of appointment and their commissions from the reigning bishop to whom they are appointed.[13] Those coadjutors, however, who are given the right of succession acquire at the moment of their succession to the rule of the diocese the powers contained in the Quinquennial faculties.[14]

Abbots and prelates *nullius* are explicitly mentioned in canon 198, § 1, and enjoy ordinary jurisdiction within the limits of their subjects and territory.[15]

Vicars general likewise are named in both canons 66, § 2, and 198, § 1; hence, by virtue of their office they enjoy the same faculties as are granted to their Ordinaries, provided that the faculties are not granted to the bishop personally, as is stated in some of the texts, and that, in other cases, the vicars general have the character of the episcopacy where it is required by the nature of the faculty.[16] It follows that, since the vicar general enjoys the use of the faculties by reason of his office, and since the faculties are granted by the Holy See, the bishop has not the power to restrict or limit the powers of the faculties with regard to their use by the vicar general.[17]

It must be borne in mind, however, that the office of vicar general ceases upon the death, removal, or resignation of the bishop according to canon 371. The faculties of the vicar general cease with the cessation of his office. In case the faculties are revoked from a particular bishop, the vicar general of that bishop continues to enjoy the faculties unless the revocation explicitly mentions that the vicar general also loses the faculties, since the vicar general enjoys the faculties from his office and not through the medium of the bishop.

Canon 66, § 2, also states that these faculties do not cease in the

---

[12] Lynch, *Coadjutors and Auxiliaries of Bishops*, The Catholic University of America, Canon Law Studies, n. 238 (Washington, D. C.: The Catholic University of America Press, 1947), p. 35.

[13] Cf. canons 351, §§ 1, 2, 3, and 4; 352.

[14] Cf. canon 66, § 2.

[15] Cf. canon 323, § 1.

[16] Cf. canon 66, § 2.

[17] Cf. canon 60, § 1.

case of the diocese's becoming vacant, even though the bishop to whom they were granted has already begun to use them.[18] In this case they are, by the law of canon 66, § 2, extended to the one who succeeds the bishop in the rule of the diocese. Book II, Part I, Title VIII, Chapter 7, canons 429-444, of the Code of Canon Law regulates the succession of rule in a diocese which becomes vacant. In some cases the direct intervention of the Holy See interrupts the procedure as outlined in the above mentioned canons. In the ordinary procedure the rule of the diocese, and the powers of the faculties pass from the original Ordinary to the cathedral chapter, the diocesan consultors in the United States, thence to the vicar capitular or administrator, and on to the new residential bishop. The bishop enjoys the faculties from the moment he takes canonical possession of the diocese, according to the procedure of canon 334, § 3.

The procedure of succession in regard to abbots and prelates *nullius* is outlined in canon 327, § 1 and § 2, which states that, unless the constitutions rule otherwise, religious abbots and prelates *nullius* are succeeded by the chapter of religious and, in the case of seculars, the chapter of canons, which chapters are in turn required to appoint a vicar capitular to assume the government until the election of another abbot or prelate. In the case of the abbacy's or prelacy's becoming impeded, the rule of canon 429, which indicates the procedure to be following in the case of vacant dioceses, obtains.

The use of the faculties by the cathedral chapter, by the religious chapter and by the chapter of canons, presents the question of whether the faculties are enjoyed by the group as a group, by the individuals of the group as individuals, or by any one of the body as being representative of the chapter.[19] The wording of canon 431, § 1, indicates that the rule of the diocese devolves upon the cathedral chapter as the chapter, that is, as a moral person,[20] hence not upon

---

[18] Cf. canon 66, § 2.

[19] In the United States the diocesan consultors act in place of the cathedral chapters. Cf. canon 423. The consultors act as a chapter and in the same manner as a chapter, that is, as a group rather than as individuals. Cf. canon 427.

[20] Cf. canon 391, § 1: Chelodi, *Ius Canonicum de Personis*, (3. ed., curavit Pius Ciprotti, Vicenza: Societa Anonima Tipographica Adesi, 1942), n. 204, p. 318. (Hereafter cited *De Personis.*)

the individuals of a body, as such. It seems then that the faculties likewise, since they are instruments used in the government of the diocese, are transmitted to the group as a whole and must be used by them acting as a unit. Thus, no individual of the chapter enjoys the faculties personally, nor any representative of the chapter, unless that representative be delegated by the chapter. The vicar capitular, as constituted by the chapter, enjoys the use of the faculties.[21] The chapter cannot retain any of the powers of the faculties or limit these powers in any way.[22]

Thus, canon 198, § 1, in conjunction with canon 66, § 2, clearly suggests those who may be expected to receive the Quinquennial Faculties. The Holy See is under no obligation to extend the faculties to these Ordinaries, but the administration of the affairs of the Church in the territories or with respect to the subjects under the jurisdiction of those known as Ordinaries in the above mentioned canon often requires the powers of the faculties and they may be granted.[23]

B. Subdelegation of the Faculties by the Ordinaries.

Subdelegation of the powers contained in the faculties by an Ordinary to a priest for use within the scope of the jurisdiction of the Ordinary [24] is governed by the prescripts of canon 199, § 2.[25] In some cases subdelegation of the faculties is expressly prohibited; or the powers of the faculties are of such a nature that they cannot be subdelegated to a person lacking the episcopacy. These exceptions are pointed out in the treatment of the individual faculties that follows.

As a general rule priests using the powers of the Quinquennial

---

[21] Cf. canon 66, § 2.

[22] Canon 437: In Vicario constituendo nullam sibi iurisdictionis partem Capitulum retinere potest, nec gerendo muneri tempus praefinire aliasve restrictiones praestituere.

[23] Religious Ordinaries as mentioned in canon 198, § 1, are treated *ex professo* by Keene, *Religious Ordinaries and Canon 198*, The Catholic University of America Canon Law Studies, n. 135 (Washington, D. C.: The Catholic University of America Press, 1942). Cf. pp. 1-3.

[24] Cf. canon 201.

[25] Canon 199, § 2: Etiam potestas iurisdictionis ab Apostolica Sede delegata subdelegari potest sive ad actum, sive etiam habitualiter, nisi electa fuerit industria personae aut subdelegatio prohibita.

faculties by reason of subdelegation from an Ordinary cannot again subdelegate the powers they have received.[26]

C. Persons in Whose Favor the Powers of the Faculties May Be Used.

In order that persons may benefit from the use of the Quinquennial Faculties they must first be subjects of the Catholic Church, a bond which is established by valid baptism, according to the prescript of canon 87.[27] The bond must be presently existing between the person and the jurisdiction of the Church and free from impairment by an obstacle such as heresy, apostasy or schism or by a punishment inflicted by the Church.[28] Moral persons, recognized as such by the Church,[29] may also be the beneficiaries of acts performed in virtue of the powers delegated in the Quinquennial Faculties.

In view of the fact that the powers contained in the faculties are delegated by the Holy See, the prescription of canon 36, § 2, is to be observed. Thus, those persons, whether moral or physical, who are under the censures of excommunication, interdict or suspension are prevented from receiving favors granted through the powers of these faculties.[30] Exceptions to the above mentioned rules are found in the faculties such as the faculty to bless objects of piety which may be used to bless articles presented by non-Catholics, and in the powers conceded by the Sacred Penitentiary. These exceptions are discussed in the treatment of the particular faculties in which they occur.

In the use of the faculties, either in person or by means of a subdelegate, an Ordinary may be limited either in regard to territory

[26] Canon 199, § 5: Nulla subdelegata potestas potest iterum subdelegari, nisi id expresse concessum fuerit.

[27] Canon 87: Baptismate homo constituitur in Ecclesia Christi persona cum omnibus christianorum iuribus et officiis, nisi, ad iura quod attinet obstet obex, ecclesiasticae communionis vinculum impediens, vel lata ab Ecclesia censura.

[28] Cf. Cappello, *Summa Iuris Canonici in usum Scholarum Concinnata*, (3 vols., Romae: apud Aedes Universitatis Gregorianae, 1936-1939), I, 3. ed., n. 184, p. 204; Beste, *Introductio in Codicem*, (Editio altera, Collegeville, Minnesota: St. John's Abbey Press, 1944), p. 131.

[29] Canon 99: In Ecclesia praeter personas physicas, sunt etiam personae morales, publica auctoritate constitutae, quae distinguuntur in personas morales collegiales et non collegiales, ut ecclesiae, Seminaria, beneficia, etc.

[30] Cf. canons 36, § 2; 2265, and 2283.

or with respect to persons. The bond of non-juridical jurisdiction. or of voluntary jurisdiction, is required to be existing between the Ordinary as grantor and the subject as grantee for the valid use of the powers conceded in the Quinquennial Faculties, unless the contrary appears from the text or nature of the various faculties.[31]

Thus, an Ordinary may use the powers of the faculties, with some exceptions, in favor of his subjects, either within or outside his territory, and in favor of *vagi* within his territory.[32] Whether or not the faculties may be used in favor or *peregrini* depends upon the nature and text of the respective faculty itself. Exceptions to the above mentioned rules and the scope of the application of the faculties in particular cases are treated in the discussions of the individual faculties that follow.

Two groups of persons present general exceptions to the rules shown above: Religious and Oriental Catholics. In regard to religious, the prescripts of canon 500 are to be followed for the determining of the proper Ordinary of the person or community in question. A treatment of this precedure of determination in found in Chapter V of this work.

In regard to the use of the faculties in favor Oriental Catholics the competency of the various Sacred Congregations which issue the faculties, insofar as it extends to Oriental Catholics, needs be determined. Authors writing *ex professo* on the subject conclude that the faculties from the Sacred Congregation of the Holy Office, because of the extraordinary jurisdiction of that Congregation, may be used in favor of the Oriental subjects of a Latin ordinary by that ordinary. In the cases of the faculties from the remaining Congregations, however, an extension of the Faculties must be obtained from the Sacred Congregation for the Oriental Church in order that they may be validly used in favor of the Oriental Catholics within the jurisdiction of a Latin ordinary.[33] Thus, it may safely be con-

---

[31] Canon 201, § 3: Nisi aliud ex rerum natura aut ex iure constet, potestatem iurisdictionis voluntariam seu non-iudicalem quis exercere potest in proprium commodum, aut extra territorium existens, aut in subditum e territorio absentem.

[32] Cf. canon 94, § 2.

[33] Plöchl, "Quinquennial Faculties extended by the S. Congregation for The Oriental Church to Latin Ordinaries," *The Jurist*, (Washington, D. C.: The Catholic University of America 1941—), (1946), 73; Marbach, *Marriage Legislation for the Catholics of the Oriental Rites in the United*

cluded that an ordinary may use the faculties conceded by the Holy Office in favor of those Oriental Catholics who are his subjects and have no ordinary proper to their rite in the United States. In order, however, to make the same use of the faculties from the other Sacred Congregations the ordinary must first petition and receive an extension of the faculties from the Sacred Congregation for the Oriental Church.

ARTICLE 3

GENERAL RULES OF INTERPRETATION AND APPLICATION

The Quinquennial Faculties of Ordinaries are to be interpreted liberally, *late*; that is, in the most comprehensive manner that is compatible with the proper meaning of the text.[34] The conditions contained in the text of the faculties must be considered in the light of canon 39.[35] In some cases provisions are required which do not affect the validity of an action. The distinctions are treated in the discussion of the particular faculties that follows. In the consideration of individual faculties, the extent of the jurisdiction of the Sacred Congregation which issues the faculty must also be considered. This aspect of the faculties' use is also discussed in the treatment that follows.

An Ordinary who has received these faculties, as also the subdelegate of the Ordinary, is understood to receive with the faculties all the powers necessary for the attainment of the end envisioned by the concession.[36] In the use of the faculties, however, the prescript of canon 44, § 1 and § 2, must be observed,[37] as well as that of canon

States and Canada, The Catholic University of America Canon Law Studies, n. 243 (Washington, D. C.: The Catholic University of America Press, 1946), pp. 221-229; Duskie, *The Canonical Status of the Orientals in the United States,* The Catholic University of America Canon Law Studies, n. 48, (Washington, D. C.: The Catholic University of America, 1928), pp. 178-180.

[34] Cf. canon 200, § 1: Van Hove, *De Privilegiis, De Dispensationibus,* Commentarium Lovaniense in Codicem Iuris Canonici, Vol. I, Tom. V (Mechliniae-Romae: H. Dessain, 1939), p. 161; Vermeersch-Greusen, *Epitome,* I, n. 183, p. 159.

[35] Canon 39: Conditiones in rescriptis tunc tantum essentiales pro eorundem validitate censentur, cum per particulas *si, dummodo,* vel aliam eiusdem significationis exprimuntur.

[36] Cf. canon 200, § 1.

[37] Canon 44, § 1: Nemo gratiam a proprio Ordinario denegatam ab alio Ordinario petat, nulla facta denegationis mentione; facta autem mentione,

204, § 2.[38] Hence application to the Ordinary for a favor to be granted in virtue of the Quinquennial Faculties does not invalidate action in the case on the part of a subdelegate of the Ordinary. The subdelegate, however, should not undertake action in the matter without a grave and urgent reason, and should at once inform his Superior of the action he has taken.

Canon 44 directs that no one may, without making mention of denial, seek from another Ordinary a favor which has been denied by his own proper Ordinary, and that the former shall not grant such a favor without first obtaining from the proper Ordinary of the person the reasons for the refusal. The procedure outlined in paragraph 1 of canon 44 does not, however, pertain to the valid use of an Ordinàry's power. Even though favors are granted contrary to the presecipt of the canon, the favors are validly given.

The rule of canon 44 differs in regard to vicars general. In paragraph 2 of the canon it is stated that a favor asked of the vicar general cannot be validly obtained from the bishop unless mention is made of the refusal on the part of the vicar general. If, however, the favor is first refused by the bishop it cannot later be obtained from the vicar general even if mention is made of the refusal on the part of the bishop.

In regard to dispensations granted in virtue of the faculties, the legislation of canons 84, § 1 and § 2, are to be observed in regard to the presence of a sufficient cause in each case.[39] It is apparent that dispensations granted by virtue of these faculties are invalidly granted unless given with sufficient and adequate cause. The doubt mentioned in canon 84, § 2, is concerned with the sufficiency of the cause, that is, the gravity of the cause in relation to the law from

---

Ordinarius gratiam ne concedat, nisi habitis, a priore Ordinario denegationis rationibus.

§ 2: Gratia a Vicario Generali denegata et postea, nulla facta huius denegationis mentione, ab Episcopo impetrata, invalida est; gratia autem ab Episcopo denegata nequit valide, etiam facta denegationis mentione, a Vicario Generali, non consentiente episcopo, impetrari.

[38] Canon 204, § 2: Attamen rei ad Superiorem delatae ne se immisceat inferior, nisi ex gravi urgentique causa; et hoc in casu statim Superiorem de re moneat.

[39] Canon 84, § 1: A lege ecclesiastica ne dispensetur sine iusta et rationabili causa, habita ratione gravitatis legis a qua dispensatur; alias dispensatio ab inferiore data illicita et invalida est.

§ 2: Dispensatio in dubio de sufficientia causae licite petitur et potest licite et valide concedi.

which the dispensation is being granted. The admissible causes and their sufficiency in regard to particular cases is treated in the discussion of the particular faculties which follows.

Favors granted in the use of these faculties may be granted with or without the intervention of an executor. If an executor is employed, he will act either as a necessary (*necessarious*) or as a voluntary (*voluntarius*) agent in the conferral of the favor.[40] The *exsecutor necessarius* is the mere minister of the favor; by his action he simply gives effect to the favor already granted. In this case the executor has no power to deny the favor, unless one or the other of the essential conditions set in canon 54, § 1, is not fulfilled. Hence he may deny the favor only in those cases in which 1) it is plainly evident that either a suppression of facts or a statement of a falsehood has rendered the rescript null; 2) the conditions demanded in the rescript have not been complied with, and this fact is known to the executor; and 3) the executor judged that the concession, because of the unworthiness of the petitioner, would cause scandal to others.[41]

The *exsecutor voluntarius,* is described in paragraph 2 of canon 54 as given above. In this case the granting of the favor is referred to the executor himself, who is to grant or refuse the favor according to his own judgment. The executor is given the faculty, the power, to concede the favor sought by the petitioner and is, in the matter concerned, a delegate of his Superior. Hence, in those faculties in

---

[40] Canon 54, § 1: Si in rescripto committatur merum exsecutionis ministerium exsecutio rescripti denegari non potest, nisi aut manifeste pateat rescriptum vitio subreptionis aut obreptionis nullum esse, aut in rescripto apponantur conditiones quas exsecutori constet non esse impletas, aut qui rescriptum impetravit adeo, iudicio exsecutoris, videatur indignus ut aliorum offensioni futura sit gratiae concessio; quod ultimum si accedat, exsecutor, intermissa exsecutione, statim ea de re certiorum faciat rescribentum.

§ 2: Quod si in rescripto concessio gratiae exsecutori committatur, ipsius est pro suo prudenti arbitrio, et conscentia gratiam concedere vel denegare.

[41] Cf. O'Neill, *Papal Rescripts of Favor,* The Catholic University of America Canon Law Studies, n. 57 (Washington, D. C.; The Catholic University of America, 1930), pp. 167-176; Van Hove, *De Rescriptis,* Commentarium Lovaniense in Codicem Iuris Canonici editum a magistris et doctoribus Universitatis Lovaniensis, Vol. I. Tomus IV, Mechliniae-Romae; H. Dessain, 1936), nn. 255-259, pp. 237-240; (Hereafter cited *De Rescriptis.*) Cicognani, - O'Hara, - Brennan, *Canon Law,* (2. ed. revised, 1935, Westminster, Maryland: The Newman Bookshop, 1946), 750.

which a subdelegation of them is forbidden the use of an *exsecutor voluntarius* is not permitted.[42]

A person commissioned as the executor of a rescript is bound by the terms of his commission, according to the prescript of canon 55.[43]. That is to say, he must, under pain of acting invalidly, take care that the essential conditions [44] are fulfilled and the substantial form of procedure is observed.[45] Rescripts pertaining to the external forum should be executed in writing.[46] The directive of canon 56 does not, however, pertain to the valid execution of a rescript.[47]

The granting of the favors contained in the Quinquennial Faculties may be effected either in writing or orally. It seems advisable, however, that such concessions be made in writing, especially when they are concerned with the external forum.[48] Written documents of the Ordinary, composed in the Curia as official documents are acceptable as established evidence in the external forum.[49] Execution of the rescripts of the Ordinary, issued in virtue of these faculties, should be effected in writing, when the rescripts pertain to the external forum.[50] In the issuance of the above mentioned rescripts, it is desirable to follow the curial style and practice of the Roman Curia as a guide.[51]

The Ordinary, in his use of the powers conceded in the faculties, is not considered as an executor of favors granted by the Holy See, but rather as the possessor of the privilege of acting in given cases,

---

[42] O'Neill, *Papal Rescripts of Favor*, p. 168.

[43] Canon 55: Exsecutor procedere debet ad mandati normam, et nisi conditiones essentiales in litteris appositas impleverit ac substantialem procedendi formam servaverit, irrita est exsecutio.

[44] Cf. canon 39.

[45] Cf. O'Neill, *Papal Rescripts of Favor*, p. 179. Adhering to the substantial form of procedure does not indicate necessarily that a fixed formula is to be used. The requisite substantial form of procedure will be learned from the nature of the favor granted, from the rules concerning the particular matter contained in the Code of Canon Law, or from the directions contained in the rescript.

[46] Canon 56: Exsecutio rescriptorum quae forum externum respiciunt, scripto facienda est.

[47] Cf. Van Hove, *De Rescriptis*, n. 264, p. 244.

[48] Special rules are attached to the Faculties of the Sacred Penitentiary which are discussed in Chapter XI.

[49] Cf. canon 1814.

[50] Cf. canon 56.

[51] Cf. Motry, *Diocesan Faculties*, p. 29.

with the power or jurisdiction necessary in those cases.[52] A distinction is made between the Ordinary as the possessor of the privileges of the faculties, and the voluntary executor of a papal rescript.[53] Rescripts issued in virtue of the faculties are among those documents mentioned in canon 375, § 1, which are to be recorded in the Diocesan Archives.[54]

Article 4

Cessation and Revocation of the Faculties

In the terms of the rescript of delegation which prefaces the *pagella* of the faculties it is stated that they are issued for a term of five years, as explained in the introduction of this work. The term, according to current practice, begins on January 1st and ends with December 31st, five years later.[55] Subdelegates of an Ordinary are limited by the same term, that is, the period of subdelegation cannot continue longer than the period for which the Ordinary possesses the power which he is subdelegating. Hence the subdelegation of the faculties to priests must be renewed if they are subdelegated habitually, as is permitted in some cases, with each new delegation received by the Ordinary.[56]

Accordingly, the Quinquennial Faculties cease with the expiration of the period for which they are granted. Canon 208, § 1, states other modes in which faculties may cease, namely by exhaustion of the number of cases for which the faculties were granted,[57] by the cessation of the final cause of the delegation by an explicit revocation on the part of the delegator, and by the renunciation of the grantee.[58]

---

[52] Cf. canon 66, § 1.

[53] Cf. Roelker, *Principles of Privilege According to the Code of Canon Law*, The Catholic University of America Canon Law Studies, n. 35 (Washington, D. C.: The Catholic University of America, 1926), p. 21; O'Neill, *Papal Rescripts of Favor*, p. 176.

[54] Cf. Louis, *Diocesan Archives*, The Catholic University of America Canon Law Studies, n. 137 (Washington, D. C.,: The Catholic University of America Press, 1941), pp. 48-50.

[55] The faculties currently in force are issued for the period beginning on January 1st, 1944; they expire after December 31st, 1949.

[56] Vromant, *Facultates Apostolicae*, n. 32, p. 25; Vermeersch, "Commentaria"—*Periodica*, XI, (1922), (79).

[57] None of the faculties currently in force are limited as to the number of cases for which they may be used.

[58] Canon 207, § 1: Potestas delegata exstinguitur, expleto mandato; elapso

The final or motive cause for which the Quinquennial Faculties are issued is, as is demonstrated in the historical section of this dissertation, to facilitate the administration of the affairs of the Church. Any termination of the final cause would have to be made known by an official statement from the Holy See. In the case of a subdelegate of an Ordinary, the final cause could very easily cease. In such a case the subdelegation is considered terminated.[59]

Revocation of the faculties may be made by the Sacred Congregation which issued that particular faculty. It is doubtful whether an Ordinary could refuse to accept the faculties, or renounce them once they are accepted.

An Ordinary may refrain from the use of those faculties which contain personal privileges. His action, however, does not prevent the privileges from passing to his successor in the manner outlined earlier in this work. In regard to those faculties which contain concessions to be dispensed in favor of others, the rule of canon 72, §3, indicates that the Ordinary is not free to renounce or refuse them.[60] The office of Ordinary is connected necessarily with territory or subjects, and at least indirectly, if not also directly, the faculties are issued to the Ordinary because of the place, territory, or subjects. Hence it seems that the Ordinary is not free to renounce, reject, or remit those faculties which contain privileges to be used in favor of his subjects or territory.[61]

A further distinction is necessary as to the duration of the favor involved between the powers conceded to the Ordinary by the faculties, the powers of a subdelegate of the Ordinary and the

---

tempore aut exhausto numero casuum pro quo concessa fuit; cessante causa finali delegationis; revocatione delegantis delegato directe intimata aut renuntiatione delegati deleganti directe intimata et ab eodem acceptata; non autem resoluto iure delegantis nisi in duobus casibus de quibus in canon 61.

[59] A priest stationed in a distant part of the diocese could be a subdelegate of his Ordinary, the cause of his subdelegation being the distance involved and the difficulty of communication. Should that priest be transferred to the Cathedral city, the cause of his subdelegation would cease, and according to the rule of canon 207, § 1, his subdelegation would cease also.

[60] Canon 72, § 3: Concessio alicui communitati, dignitati locove renuntiare privatis personis non licet.

[61] Refusal on the part of the Ordinary to use the Faculties does not, then, result in the termination of those Faculties; Motry, *Diocesan Faculties*, p. 39.

favors extended to the subjects of the Ordinary in the use of the powers conceded in the faculties. The same norms of termination do not apply in these respective cases. Some of the grants made in virtue of these faculties are limited in time by the text of the rescript, e. g., the permission which may be given to read and retain certain forbidden books. Others are perpetual by their nature e. g., the sanation of marriages. Still others present the question of how long the grant may be extended to a community or person, in view of the fact that the faculties are issued for a period of five years duration, e. g., the privilege of anticipation of the Divine Office.

In those cases wherein the text of the faculty or the nature of the matter concerned imposes a limitation as to time, there is no difficulty. However, in the remaining cases it seems that extended favors may be considered in two groups, viz., as true priviliges or as dispensations which extend over a period of time. In the event that the concessions granted are privileges, they will not necessarily cease with the termination of the five year period of the Quinquennial Faculties, that is, unless such a condition is contained in the grant.[62] Should such favors be granted, however, in the form of dispensations which are effective as often as the cause is present, they cease, not only in the manner of cessation imposed on privileges,[63] but also by the cessation of the cause for which they were granted.[64]

Dispensations granted in virtue of the Quinquennial Faculties may also be revoked by the grantor, provided that a sufficient cause for the revocation exists and the dispensation in question has not yet been used.[65]

---

[62] Canon 73: Resoluto iure concedentis, privilegia non exstinguuntur, nisi data fuerint cum clausula; *ad beneplacitum nostrum*, vel alia aequipollenti.

[63] Cf. canon 72-78.

[64] Canon 86: Dispensatio quae tractum habet successivum, cessat iisdem modis quibus privilegium, nec non certa ac totali cessatione causae motivae; Reilly, *The General Norms of Dispensation*, p. 137.

[65] Cf. Reilly, *The General Norms of Dispensation*, p. 127.

CHAPTER VI

FACULTIES FROM THE HOLY OFFICE

ARTICLE I

PERMISSION TO READ AND RETAIN PROHIBITED BOOKS

"Concedendi, non ultra triennium, licentiam legendi ac retinendi, sub custodia tamen ne ad aliorum manus preveniant, libros prohibitos et ephemerides exceptis operibus haeresim vel schisma ex professo propugnantibus, vel etiam ipsa religionis fundamenta evertere nutentibus nec non operibus de obscoenis ex professo tractantibus, singulis christifidelibus sibi subditis, nonnisi tamen cum delectu et iusta ac rationabili causa (cf. can. 1402, § 2, *Cod. I. C.*), iis scilicet tantum, qui eorumdem librorum et ephemeridum lectione sive ad ea impugnanda sive ad proprium legitimum munus exercendum, vel iustum studiorum curriculum peragendum, vere indigeant.

ADNOTANDUM, — *Recensita facultas Episcopis conceditur per se ipsos personaliter exercenda, seu nemini deleganda; et graviter onerata ipsorum conscientia super reali omnium memoratarum conditionum concursu.*"[1]

The faculty broadens the powers given Ordinaries by canon 1402, which limits dispensatory action to cases involving only single books and urgent cases. The power of the Ordinary is extended by the faculty to grant the benefit of a dispensation enduring over a period of three years, and with reference to all books except those explicitly excluded by the terms of the faculty. Books and periodicals treating *ex professo* of heresy or schism flaunting obsenity and those

[1] Canon 1402, § 2: "Quod si generalem a Sede Apostolica facultatem impetraverint suis subditis permittendi ut libros proscriptos retineant ac legant, eam nonnisi cum delectu et iusta ac rationabili causa concedant."

which seek to overthrow the foundations of religion are excluded by the terms of the faculty.

Ordinaries may grant permissions in virtue of this faculty to their own subjects only. Subjects of an Ordinary can both receive and use the permission outside the territory of their Ordinary, since its grant requires only the bond of voluntary jurisdiction.[2] The faculty cannot be used by an Ordinary in favor or *peregrini* while they are within his territory; however, *vagi* can receive the permission granted in the use of this faculty from the Ordinary of the place in which they are living.[3]

With regard to Oriental Catholics, it seems that, since they are subject to the laws concerning the prohibition of books,[4] they can be the recipients of this permission. Those Orientals who have a proper Ordinary of their rite in the United States may receive the permission from that Ordinary; those who do not have such an Ordinary, from the Latin Ordinary to whom they are subject.

The three years for which the permission may be granted is to be computed according to the rule of canon 34, § 3, 2°, that is to say, the three year period which starts with the beginning of a given day comes to a close three years later at the start of the day which marks the recurring date. The permission thus granted, which became operative with the beginning of January 1, 1946, expires at the beginning of January 1, 1949.[5]

The annotation attached to the faculty states that it is the command of the Holy Office that this faculty be used by the bishop only and that it may not be subdelegated. It is evident that the term "bishop", in this instance includes also the vicar general; the restriction as placed is directed against the delegation of the faculty, *seu nemini deleganda* . . .[6] even though subdelegation of the faculty

[2] Cf. canon 201, § 3.

[3] Cf. canon 94, § 2.

[4] Sacred Congregation for the Oriental Church, Declaration, May 26, 1928 —Bouscaren, *Canon Law Digest*, (2 vols., Milwaukee: The Bruce Publishing Co.), II, canon 1396; *AAS*, XX (1928), 195:—"Libra ab Apostolcia Sede damnati ubique locorum et in quodcunque vertantur idioma prohibiti censeantur."

[5] Canon 34, § 3, 20: Si terminus a quo coincidat cum initio diei, eg., duo vacationum menses a die 15 augusti, primus dies ad explendam numerationem computetur et tempus finiatur incipiente ultimo die eiusdem numeri.

[6] In this the power of the faculty differs from the concession of power granted in canon 1402, § 1. The latter power can be delegated.

is prohibited, the faculty passes to the successor of the bishop, since there is nothing in the text to indicate that the Holy Office wishes to exclude the transfer of the faculty by succession as well as by subdelegation.[7]

Certain precautions and conditions must be observed in the use of the faculty. These are enumerated within the text of the faculty itself. The just and reasonable cause is to be determined by the grantor from the text of the petition. The petition should state clearly the petitioner's state in life, the nature of his work, and the reason or reasons why he feels that he needs the dispensation. In effect the granted dispensation relaxes the petitioner from compliance with the common law of the Church. If the dispensation were granted without a sufficient cause, the grant would be invalid.[8] But the presence of some doubt concerning the sufficiency of the reasons alleged permits both the valid and the licit use of the faculty for the granting of the desired dispensation.[9]

Article 2

Matrimonial Dispensations: Impediments of Mixed Religion and of Disparity of Cult *"ad cautelam"*

"Dispensandi, iustis gravibusque accedentibus causis, cum subditis etiam extra territorium, aut non subditis intra limites proprii territorii, super impedimento mixtae religionis, et, si casus ferat, etiam super disparitate cultus, ad cautelam; quoties prudens dubium oriatur de collatione baptismi partis acatholicae; quatenus ante nuptias pars acatholica ad veram religionem adduci aut catholica ab ipsis nuptiis absterreri nequiverit, dummodo prius regulariter, ad praescriptum *Cod. I. C.* can. 1061, § 2, cautum omnino sit conditionibus ab Ecclesia requisitis, et ipse *Excmus P. D. Ordinarius moraliter certus sit easdem impletum iri,* scilicet: ex parte nupturientis acatholici de amovendo a parte catholica perversionis periculo, et ab utroque contrahente de universa prole utruisque sexus in catholicae religionis sanctitate omnino baptizanda et educanda; decla-

[7] Cf. canon 66, § 2.
[8] Cf. canon 84, § 1.
[9] Cf. canon 84, § 2.

rata insuper parti catholicae obligatione, qua tenetur, prudenter curandi conversionem coniugis ad fidem catholicam.

"Nupturientes autem moneantur se, ante vel post matrimonium coram Ecclesia initum, ministrum quoque acatholicum ad matrimonialem consensum praestandum vel renovandum adire non posse, ad mentem *Cod. I. C.* can. 1063, § 1, sub poena excommunicationis latae sententiae Ordinario reservatae a parte catholica incurrendae, iuxta can 2319, § 1, n. 1°, stricte caeteroquin servatis quae de parochi in casu agendi ratione statuta sunt in can. 1063, § 2.

"Quod si partes actu in concubinatu vivant, provideatur opportunis modis ut scandalum, si adsit, removeatur et pars catholica ad gratiam Dei recipiendam rite disponatur, praevia eius absolutione ab excommunicatione contracta, si forte matrimonium attentatum fuerit coram ministro acatholico, eique impositis congruis poenitentiis salutaribus; si autem ex illicita unione iam nata sit proles, partes moneantur de gravi obligatione iuris divini curandi, pro posse, eius catholicam educationem et (si casus ferat) conversionem, baptismum; a parte autem catholica exquiratur obligationis implendae explicita promissio."

This faculty is concerned with the prohibitive impediment of mixed religion as treated in canon 1060 of the Code of Canon Law.[10] The faculty is not concerned with the powers of dispensation conceded by the Code of Canon Law in extraordinary cases, such as are envisioned in canons 1043, 1045, and 81. The powers of the faculty are for use in those cases which are not extraordinary, and which otherwise would require recourse to the Sacred Congregation of the Holy Office.

The text both of canon 1060 and of the faculty is clear in stating

[10] Canon 1060: Severissime Ecclesia ubique prohibet ne matrimonium ineatur inter duas personas baptizatas, quarum alter sit catholica, alter vero sectae haereticae seu schismaticae adscripta; quod si adsit perversionis periculum coniugis catholici et prolis, coniugium ipsa etiam lege divina vetatur.

The impediment is treated *ex professo* by Schenk, *The Matrimonial Impediments of Mixed Religion and Disparity of Cult*, the Catholic University of America Canon Law Studies, n. 51 (Washington, D. C.: The Catholic University of America, 1929), pp. 78 ff.

that it is concerned only with those cases in which a Catholic wishes to contract marriage with a person who is a member of a heretical or a schismatical sect, and who is either baptised or doubtfully baptised. Those who have apostatized from the Catholic Church and have enrolled in a heretical sect do not appear to be included under the specific prohibition enacted in canon 1060, and therefore, are not included among those for whom the faculty may be used.[11] Those who profess themselves aethists, provided they have received either a valid or a doubtfully valid baptism, are considered as heretics.[12] Apostates, although they have publicly denied their faith, are not contemplated in the wording of canon 1060, and consequently do not come under the terms which allow the application of this faculty for them.[13] The cases wherein the non-baptism of the non-Catholic party is certain, neither canon 1060 nor this faculty applies. Such cases are treated in the following Article.

The jurisdiction conceded in the faculty is both personal in regard to the proper subjects of an Ordinary and territorial in regard to all those who reside within the territory of an Ordinary. The faculty may be used in favor of all such persons—provided that all the other conditions are fulfilled—who are either subject to the Ordinary or who reside within the limits of his territorial jurisdiction. Both *vagi* and *peregrini* are therefore included as possible subjects of the faculty.

A grave and just cause is required before the power of dispensing can be used. Dispensations granted without cause by virtue of this faculty are invalidly granted.[14] The Ordinary may, however, act when a doubt regarding the sufficiency of the represented cause

[11] Cf. Schenk, *The Matrimonial Impediments of Mixed Religion and Disparity of Cult*, pp. 85-91; Infants baptised in the Catholic Church but reared in a false religion are considered heretics—ibid.

[12] Commissio ad Codicis Canones Authentice Interpretandos (hereafter cited Com. Interp.) 30 iulii, 1934—*AAS*, XXVI (1934), 494; Bouscaren, *The Canon Law Digest*, II, canon 1965; Beste, *Introductio in Codicem*, p. 546.

[13] Cf., canon 1065; Heneghan, *The Marriages of Unworthy Catholics*, canons 1065 and 1066, The Catholic University of America Canon Law Studies, n. 188, (Washington, D. C.: The Catholic University of America Press, 1944,) pp. 82 ff.

[14] Cf. canons 1061, § 1, 1°; Reilly, *The General Norms of Dispensation*, 110; Cappello, *Tractatus Canonici—Moralis de Sacramentis*, (3 vols., in 6, Romae: Marietti, 1932-1939), III, n. 309. (Hereafter cited *De Sacramentis*.)

exists. Whether he may act when the doubt regards the very existence of a cause is disputed, however, it appears that any doubt as to the very existence of a cause as just and reasonable gives rise necessarily to a doubt concerning the validity of any dispensation granted in virtue of this faculty; hence, in such cases an Ordinary cannot act by virtue of the powers conceded in this faculty.[15] The responsibility of determining both the sufficiency and the existence of the represented cause pertains to the Ordinary, or his subdelegate, who is petitioned for the granting of the dispensation.

In addition to a just and grave cause,[16] other concomitant provisions must be fulfilled prior to the use of this faculty. An attempt to bring the non-Catholic party into the true faith is to be made both by the pastor and the Catholic party, and some instruction must be given.[17] In the event that conscientiously made attempts fail to bring about the conversion of the non-Catholic party, then the Catholic party is to be dissuaded from entering the marriage (" . . . *quatenus ante nuptias pars acatholica ad veram religionem adduci aut catholica ab ipsis nuptiis absterreri nequiverit,* . . . ") It is only after these provisions have been fulfilled that the dispensation may be asked for. As is evident from the nature of these provisions, the obligation of procurring the fulfillment of them pertains to the pastor of the parties. The mention of these obligations in the text of the faculty indicates that it is an obligation of the Ordinary, or his subdelegate, to ascertain whether or not the above mentioned provisions have been fulfilled. The provisions do

---

[15] Cf. canon 84, § 1: Van Hove, *De Privilegiis, De Dispensationibus,* n. 477, p. 437 ;Reilly, *The General Norms of Dispensation,* p. 114; De Smet, *De Sponsalibus et Matrimonio,* 4 ed., inde a Codice Altera (Brugis: Beyeart), 1927, n. 812. Authors concede, however, that an Ordinary may dispense by reason of the legislation of canon 15: Leges, etiam irritantes et inhabilitantes, in dubio iuris non urgent; in dubio autem facti potest Ordinarius in eis dispensare, dummodo agatur de legibus in quibus Romanus Pontifex dispensare solet; cf. Van Hove, *loc. cit.,* and Reilly, *loc. cit.*

[16] For a list of acceptable causes, cf. *Collect.* (1893), n. 1470; *S. Dataria Apostolica, ASS,* XXXIV (1901), 34-35; O'Mara, *Canonical Causes for Matrimonial Dispensation,* The Catholic University of America Canon Law Studies, n. 96, (Washington, D. C.: The Catholic University of America, 1935), pp. 72-130; Ayrinhac-Lydon, *Marriage Legislation in the New Code of Canon Law,* (Benziger: New York, 1946), n. 102. (Hereafter cited *Marriage Legislation*). Feije, *De Impedimentis,* p. 601.

[17] Cf. canon 1033.

not, however, pertain to the validity of the dispensations granted in virtue of this faculty.[18]

A dispensation is never to be granted in virtue of this faculty unless the proper promises, *cautiones,* have been obtained from the parties and there is a moral certainty of their fulfillment in the mind of the grantor of the dispensation.[19] The promise should, in ordinary circumstances, be exacted in writing; this regulation does not, however, pertain to the valid use of the faculty. The promises may be made orally.[20] The term *"non dispensat"* of canon 1061, § 2, is clear; a lack of the promises themselves, or the lack of moral certitude regarding their fulfillment on the part of the Ordinary would render invalid a dispensation granted in virtue of this faculty.[21] The matter of the *cautiones* is clearly stated in canon 1061 and in the text of the faculty; namely,)1 the removal of all danger of perversion from the Faith with regard to the Catholic party, and 2) the solemn promise of both parties that the children of the union will be baptized and educated in the Catholic Faith.[22]

The legislation of canon 1063, § 1, is repeated in the text of the faculty.[23] The obligation of reminding the parties of the prohibition contained in this canon, as it is repeated in the text of the faculty, pertains to the grantor of the dispensation. The admonition to the parties may, however, be contained in the text of the rescript issued for the concession of the dispensation, or, as is frequently the practice, the parties may be asked to agree, prior to their marriage, that they will refrain from either giving or renewing their matrimonial consent before a non-Catholic minister. The

[18] Cf. canon 39.

[19] Cf. canon 1061, § 1.

[20] Cf. canon 1061, § 2.

[21] S. Off. 14. ian, 1932; *AAS,* XXIV, (1932) 25; Bouscaren, *The Canon Law Digest,* I, canon 1061; Vermeersch-Creusen, *Epitome,* II, n. 331, p. 232; Woywod, *A Practical Commentary on the Code of Canon Law* (9. printing, revised by Callistus Smith, 2 vols., New York: Joseph F. Wagner, 1945), I, 615. (Hereafter cited *The Code of Canon Law*).

[22] A printed form containing these promises is usually a part of the petition for the dispensation; signed by both parties and witnessed by the pastor, or his substitute, it is submitted with the petition.

[23] Canon 1063, § 1: Etsi ab Ecclesia obtenta sit dispensatio super impedimento mixtae religionis, coniuges nequeunt, vel ante vel post matrimonium coram Ecclesia initum, adire quoque, sive per se vel per procuratorum, ministrum acatholicum uti sacris addictum, ad matrimonialem consensum praestandum vel renovandum.

Catholic party is to be reminded of the punishment inflicted by the Church on those of the faithful who give their matrimonial consent before non-Catholic ministers.[24] If, in the judgment of the pastor, or his substitute, it is certain that the provisions of canon 1063, § 1, will not be fulfilled, then he is to act in the manner described in paragraph 2 of the same canon.[25] The above mentioned provision does not affect the validity of dispensations granted in virtue of this faculty.[26]

The vicar general, by virtue of his office, enjoys this faculty. But the same obligation that rests on the bishop rests also upon him, namely, of seeing that the conditions and the provisions are duly fulfilled.[27] The Ordinary may also subdelegate this faculty to any of his priests for use under the same conditions.[28] But the faculty cannot again be subdelegated by these priests who have received it through an act of subdelegation from the Ordinary.[29]

The final paragraph of this faculty indicates the procedure to be followed in those cases in which the parties of the marriage are already living in concubinage. Care should be taken to remove any and all scandal, if such scandal should exist, and the Catholic party should be reconciled with the Church in order to become disposed for the reception of the favors of the Church. In cases in which marriage had already been attempted before a non-Catholic minister, the Catholic party should first be absolved from the excommunication incurred, and a salutary penance imposed. In regard to the promises concerning the rearing of children which may be born to the union, the procedure outlined above obtains also in these cases. In regard to children already born to the parties, both parties should be reminded of their obligation to baptize and educate these children in the Catholic faith, even to the extent of converting them from a false religion. An explicit promise that this action concerning the children already born to the union will be effected should be exacted from the Catholic party.

---

[24] Cf. canon 2319, § 1, 1°.

[25] Canon 1063, § 2: Si parochus certe noverit sponsos hanc legem violaturos esse vel iam violasse, eorum matrimonio ne assistat, nisi ex gravissimis causis, remoto scandalo et consulto prius Ordinario.

[26] Cf. canon 39.

[27] Cf. canons 66, § 2, and 368, § 2.

[28] Cf. canon 199, § 2.

[29] Canon 199, § 2, § 5.

Dispensations granted in the use of this faculty may be granted in *forma gratiosa,* that is, directly to the parties who presented the petition, or in *forma commissoria,* that is, through the agency of an executor. In either case the dispensation should be granted in writing, [30] and mention should be made of the fact that it was granted in virtue of this Apostolic Faculty.[31] In practice, the one who grants the dispensation through the use of this faculty is generally dependent upon the pastor (or his substitute) of the parties for the information and assurances necessary for the use of the faculty. No fixed formula is prescribed either in the petition for the dispensation or in the granting of the dispensation; hence, any procedure which fulfills the conditions and provisions as set forth in the text of the faculty will suffice.

Further instructions relative to the use of this faculty are contained in the text of the faculty which follows, and are discussed in the closing paragraphs of the following Article.[32]

---

[30] Cf. canon 56.

[31] Cf. canon 1057.

[32] The following sample formulas contain all the necessary elements.

Petition for a dispensation in:

1. Mixed religion.
2. Mixed religion and Disparity of Cult *ad cautelam.*

Your Excellency:

I, ...N. N...................., A Catholic of..............................parish, Diocese of.., desiring to contract marriage with ....N. N................, a non-Catholic, baptized in the.................................. sect, humbly petition Your Excellency to grant a dispensation from the impediment of.. The Canonical reasons are ....

Signed..

Catholic Party.

....

I, the undersigned priest, hereby attest: That I have duly instructed the parties according to canon 1033 and (Diocesan Law); that the required agreement given in writing on the reverse side of this application, along with this application, was signed in my presence; and that, from my knowledge of the parties, I am morally certain that this agreement will be faithfully kept. There is not present any foreseeable danger of perversion. Both parties have given due assurance that there will be no other marriage ceremony either before or after the Catholic ceremony.

Signed, Rev...

Office..

....

MARRIAGE AGREEMENT

We, ...N. N............. and ....N. N.............., hereby mutually promise that all the children of our marriage shall be baptized and reared solely in the Roman Catholic Religion. I,........N. N........., the non-Catholic party further promise not to interfere in any way with the faith of the

Article 3
Matrimonial Dispensations:
Disparity of Cult

"Dispensandi, iustis gravibusque accedentibus causis, cum subditis etiam extra territorium, aut non subditis intra limites proprii territorii, super impendimento disparitatis cultus (excepto tamen casu matrimonii cum parte mahumetana); quatenus sine contumelia Creatoris id fieri possit et ante nuptias pars non baptizata ad veram religionem adduci aut catholica ab ipsis absterreri nequiverit, dummodo prius regulariter, ad praescriptum *Cod. I. C.* can. 1061, § 2, cautum omnino sit conditionibus ab Ecclesia requisitis, et *ipse Excm̃us P. D. Ordinarius moraliter certus sit easdem impletum iri,* scilicet: ex parte nupturientis non baptizati de amovendo a parte catholica perversionis periculo et ab utroque contrahente de universa prole utriusque sexus in catholicae religionis sanctitate omnino baptizanda et educanda; declarata insuper parti catholicae obligatione,

---

said............N. N............., the Catholic party, and promise not to interfere in any way with the exercise of..religion.

Signed..

L. S. ....

Witnessed:.. Dated:..

Parish:..

The following is a sample rescript used in the granting of the abovementioned dispensation:

Diocese of..

City of..

Rev. Domino..:

Attenta causa canonica quam in litteris, diei........... mensis.................., A. D..............., Nobis exposuisti, Nos, vigore Facultatis Nobis ab Apostolica Sede per Sacram Congregationem Sancti Officii concessae, dispensamus super Impedimento

1) Mixtae religionis,
2) et ad cautelam Disparitatis cultus,

inter............N. N............., Catholicum (am), et ....N. N.............(dubie) baptizatum (am) existente; dummodo cautiones canonicae subsignatae sint earumque implementum sit moraliter certum. Servatis in reliquo de iure servandis.

....

L. S. Episcopus

....

Delegatus Vicarius Generalis

Datum.........................., die...................., mensis........................... A. D...............

qua tenetur, prudenter curandi conversionem coniugis ad fidem catholicam.

"Nupturientes autem moneantur se, ante vel post matrimonium coram Ecclesia initum, ministrum quoque falsi cultus ad matrimonialem consensum praestandum vel renovandum adire non posse, ad mentem *Cod. I. C.* can. 1063, § 2. Quod vero attinet ad legitimationem prolis, prae oculis habeatur can. 1051.

"Quod si partes actu in concubinatu vivant, provideatur opportunis modis ut scandalum, si adsit, removeatur et pars catholica ad gratiam Dei recipiendam rite disponatur; si autem ex illicita unione iam nata sit proles, fiat monitio et exigatur promissio ut supra, n. 2.

"In reliquis, quod refertur ad publicationes, interrogationes de consensu et sacros ritus, sive agatur de impedimento mixtae religionis sive disparitatis cultus, serventur praescripta *Cod. I. C.* cann. 1026, 1102, 1109; et huiusmodi nuptiis celebratis, sive in proprio, sive in alieno territorio, R.P.D. Ordinarius invigilet ut coniuges promissiones factas fideliter impleant.[33]

This faculty is concerned with the diriment impediment of disparity of cult as existing between Catholics and non-baptized persons, according to canon 1070.[34] Apart from the case which involves a validly baptized heretic's or schmatic's conversion to the Church, the impediment of disparity of cult does not exist unless one of the parties of the marriage was baptized in the Catholic

[33] Prior to July 1, 1946, the granting of a dispensation for marriages between Catholics and Jews as well as for marriages between Catholics and Mohammedans was withheld from the scope of this faculty. The Ordinary may now dispense even in the case of marriages between Catholics and Jews by virtue of the current amended faculty. Cf. Letter to the Ordinaries of the United States from the Apostolic Delegate to the United States, May 19, 1946; *The Jurist*, VI (1946), 424.

[34] Canon 1070, § 1: Nullum est matrimonium contractum a persona non baptizata cum persona baptizata in Ecclesia catholica vel ad eandem ex haeresi aut schismate conversa.

Schenk (*The Matrimonial Impediments of Mixed Religion and Disparity of Cult, pp. 98 ff.*) treats of this impediment *ex professo*.

Church, and the other was not baptized. The impediment does not affect those who have received baptism in non-catholic sects.[35]

The fact of non-baptism on the part of the non-Catholic party is required for the use of this faculty. An unsoluble doubt concerning either the validity of a non-Catholic baptism known to have been received or regarding the very reception of baptism obstructs the use of this faculty, and requires the use of the faculty dealing with the impediment of mixed religion, in which case the possible granting of a dispensation from the impediment of disparity of cult (*ad cautelam*) is provided for.

What has been said in the foregoing article with regard to the faculty of dispensing from the impediment of mixed religion concerning the provisions under which dispensations may be granted, regarding the *cautiones* to be obtained, the admonitions to be given the parties of the marriage, and the subdelegation of the faculty, may also be predicated of the faculty for dispensing from the impediment of disparity of cult. Likewise this faculty is enjoyed by the vicar general.

Some few differences are noted in the text of the respective faculties, however. In the text of the faculty affecting the impediment of disparity of cult, use of the faculty in cases of marriages between Mohammedans and Catholics is prohibited. This exception is explicitly stated so that the use of the faculty in defiance of the prohibition is invalid.[36] As noted above, prior to July 1, 1946, the above mentioned prohibition applied also to Jews.

Another provision, over and above those, the observance of which is required in the faculty permitting dispensation from the impediment of mixed religion, is stated in the text of the faculty affecting the impediment of disparity of cult, namely; "when this (dispensing) can be done without irreverence to the Creator" *"quatenus sine contumelia Creatoris id fieri possit . . ."* An interpretation of this provision issued prior to the Code by the Sacred Congregation of the Propagation of the Faith,[37] indicated that especially to be considered were 1) the danger of perversion of the Catholic party; 2) the

[35] Cf. S. C. S. Off., resp., 1 apr. 1922; Bouscaren, *Canon Law Digest*, I, canon 1070.

[36] Cf. Canon 67.

[37] *Collect.* (1893), n. 1261.

education of any children which might be born of the union; 3) the possibility of conversion to the Faith of the non-Catholic party. In view of the fact that these considerations are incorporated in the text of the faculty, it appears that in those cases in which there exists danger of irreverance to the Creator the powers of this faculty cannot be validly used.[38]

As in the faculty discussed in the foregoing article of this work, moral certitude of the fulfillment of this condition is provided for by the *cautiones*, required for the valid use of this faculty. It seems, therefore, that the phrase, *quatenus sine contumelia Creatoris id fieri possit . . .*, desires to emphasize the necessity of the *cautiones* and of the moral certitude on the part of the Ordinary regarding their fulfillment. In the practical use of the faculty the Ordinary is dependent upon the pastor (or his substitute) preparing the parties for marriage. Through the pastor there is offered to the Ordinary the means of determining whether the provisions and conditions of the faculties have received proper attention. In practice the admonitions which are to be given in regard to the legislation of canon 1063, § 1, form part of the obligation of the pastor.

In the event that illegitimate children have already been conceived of or born to the parties, such children are in accordance with the norm of canon 1051 rendered legitimate in status through the dispensation from disparity of cult granted by the Ordinary in virtue of this general quinquennial faculty, provided that they are not of one or the other of the two groups barred in canon 1051 from thus reaping the benefit of legitimation.[39]

The publication of the banns in mixed marriages is to be omitted according to the norm of canon 1026. Furthermore, no liturgical ceremony is to be observed or permitted in the celebration of the marriage. The giving and receiving of the matrimonial consent should take place outside the Church. The restrictions, however, may be mitigated somewhat by the Ordinary.[40]

---

[38] Cf. canon 39.

[39] Canon 1051: Per dispensationem super inpedimento dirimente concessam sive ex potestate ordinaria, sive ex potestate delegata per indultum generale, non vero per rescriptum in casibus particularibus, conceditur quoque eo ipso legitimatio prolis, si qua ex iis cum quibus dispensatur iam nata vel concepta fuerit, excepta tamen adulterina et sacrilega.

[40] Cf. canons 1102, § 2; 1109, § 3.

Just as the Ordinary is dependent upon the pastors, or their substitutes, for the proper execution of the pre-requisites of the granting of the dispensation, so also is he dependent upon them in great part in the fulfillment of his obligation to attend to the faithful execution of the promises made by the parties. The sample form of application for the dispensation of the rescript granting the dispensation, and of the promises exacted from the parties, as given in the preceding article concerning the impediment of mixed religion, can also be used in those cases which involve the impediment of disparity of cult.

Article 4
The Granting of a *Sanatio in Radice*: In Cases Involving the Impediments of Mixed Religion and Disparity of Cult

"Sanandi in radice matrimonia attentata coram officiali civili vel ministro acatholico a suis subitis etiam extra territorium, aut non subditis, intra limites proprii territorii, cum impedimento mixtae religionis aut disparitatis cultus, dummodo consensus in utroque coniuge perseveret, isque legitime renovari non possit, sive quia pars acatholica de invaliditate matrimonii moneri nequeat sine periculo gravis damni aut incommodi a catholico coniuge subeundi; sive quia pars acatholica ad renovandum coram Ecclesia matrimonialem consensum, aut ad cautiones praestandas, ad praescriptum *Cod. I. C.* can. 1061, § 2, ullo modo induci nequeat; dummodo:

1° moraliter certum sit partem acatholicam non esse impedituram baptismum et catholicam educationem universae prolis forte nasciturae;

2° pars catholica explicite promittat se, pro posse, curaturam esse baptismum et catholicam educationem universae prolis forte nasciturae, et (si casus ferat) etiam conversionem, baptismum, catholicam educationem prolis iam natae;

3° partes, ante attentatum matrimonium, sive privatim sive per publicum actum, set non obstrinxerint ad educationem acatholicam prolis;

4° neutra pars sit actu demens;

5° pars saltem catholica sit sanationis conscia eamque petat;

6° nullus aliud obstet canonicum impedimentum dirimens, super quo Ipse Ordinarius dispensandi aut sanandi facultate non polleat.

"Ipse autem excmus Episcopus P. D. serio moneat partem catholicam de gravissimo patrato scelere, salutares ei poenitentias imponat et, si casus ferat, eam ab excommunicatione absolvat iuxta C. I. C. can. 2319, § 1, simulque declaret ob sanationis gratiam a se acceptam, matrimonium effectum esse validum, legitimum et indissolubile iure divino, et prolem forte susceptam vel suscipiendam, legitiman esse; eique insuper in mentem revocet obligationem qua tenetur prudenter curandi conversionem coniugis ad fidem catholicam.

"Cum autem de matrimonii validitate et prolis legitimatione in foro externo constare debeat, Excmus P. D. Episcopus mandet ut singulis vicibus documentum sanationis cum attestatione peractae executionis diligenter custodiatur in Curia locali, nec non curet, nisi pro sua prudentia aliter iudicaverit, ut in libro baptizatorum paroeciae, ubi pars catholica baptismum recepit, transcribatur notitia sanationis matrimonii, de quo actum est, cum adnotatione diei et anni."

"Mens autem S. Officii est ut Episcopus hanc facultatem sanadi matrimonia in radice per se ipse personaliter exerceat, scilicet nemini subdeleget.[41]

Those in whose favor the faculty may be used are the same as those mentioned in the preceding faculties, as treated in this chapter, concerning dispensations from the matrimonial impediments of mixed religion and disparity of cult. This faculty is restricted in its use, however, to those cases in which an attempted marriage is

[41] This text of the faculty is the revised text, effective July 1, 1946. Considerable change in the wording of the faculty was made at that time. A copy of the faculty as it existed prior to this revision may be found in Beste, *Introductio in Codicem*, Appendix, *Allegatum*, I, p. 975.

invalid by reason of defect of canonical form in addition to the presence of either the impediment of mixed religion or of disparity of cult. Marriages which are invalid simply by reason of the non-observance of the canonical form are excluded by the text of the faculty.[42]

The use of the faculty in the cases of marriages between Mohammedans and Catholics presents a difficulty, for in the text it is stated that there must not be present any other diriment impediment from which the bishop has not the power to dispense, . . . *dummodo aliud non obstet canonicum impedimentum dirimens super quo Ipse dispensandi aut sanandi facultate non polleat.* In the faculty discussed in Article 3 of this Chapter the granting of a dispensation from the diriment impediment of disparity of cult existing between Catholics and Mohammedans is prohibited.[43] Thus, the question arises whether Mohammedans are excluded from the scope of this faculty with regard to the sanation of marriages invalid by reason of defect of canonical form concomitant with the impediments either of mixed religion or of disparity of cult. That is to say, does the impediment of disparity of cult as existing between a Mohammedan and a Catholic constitute another impediment, *aliud impedimentum dirimens,* from which the Ordinary cannot dispense, and which, therefore, obstructs the use of this faculty?

In answer to this the text of the preceding faculty is to be considered. The exception made in regard to Mohammedans is stated clearly, *excepto tamen casu matrimonii cum parte mahumetana.* The Ordinary cannot dispense in those cases which involve the marriage of a Catholic with a Mohammedan. Thus there exists between Catholics and Mohammedans a diriment impediment from which the Ordinary cannot dispense, and consequently the Ordinary cannot use the powers conceded in this faculty in order that he may sanate those marriages between Catholics and Mohammedans which are invalid because of the diriment impediment of disparity of cult and in consequence of the non-observance of the canonical form.[44] But in view of the fact that the Ordinary can now dispense

[42] Cf. canon 67.

[43] The prohibition concerning Jews is not contained in the revised formula issued July 1, 1946.

[44] Prior to July 1, 1946, the foregoing conclusion applied also to marriages between Catholics and Jews which were invalid because of the diriment

from the impediment of disparity of cult as existing between Catholics and Jews, it may be concluded that he can also sanate those marriages between Catholics and Jews which are invalid because of the impediment of disparity of cult and as a result of the non-observance of the required canonical form.[45]

Several conditions are required for the valid use of the faculty. Considerable amplification and explanation of the conditions is made in the July 1, 1946, text as compared with the text in effect prior to that date. As has been stated above, the faculty may be used only in those marriages which are invalid by reason of defect of canonical form, that is to say, marriages in which one of the parties is a Catholic bound to the canonical form of the Church,[46] and in which the impediment either of mixed religion or of disparity of cult is existing at the time when the sanation is petitioned. Marriages invalid solely in consequence of the lack of canonical form cannot be validly healed by virtue of this faculty.[47]

The first mentioned condition of the faculty is that the matrimonial consent on the part of both parties persevere. The consent spoken of in the faculty must, as is apparent, be a true matrimonial consent,[48] persevering on the part of both parties at the moment the sanation is granted.[49] Secondly, it is postulated that the above mentioned consent cannot be legitimately renewed because 1) the non-Catholic party cannot be informed of the invalidity of the marriage in question apart from the simultaneous subjection of the

impediment of disparity of cult and the non-observance of the requisite canonical form. There does not seem to be sufficient latitude in the text of the faculty for the doubt suggested by Harrigan, *The Radical Sanation of Invalid Marriages*, The Catholic University of America Canon Law Studies, n. 116, (Washington, D. C.: The Catholic University of America, 1938) p. 154, the existence of which doubt would permit the use of the faculty in those cases in which the Ordinary cannot dispense from the impediment of disparity of cult.

[45] Prior to July 1, 1946, Jews were under the same exception as Mohammedans are in the present. Hence, prior to that date sanatons could not be given by the Ordinary in marriages between Jews and Catholics which were invalid because of the impediment of disparity of cult and in consequence of the lack of canonical form in the contracting of the union.

[46] Cf. canon 1099.

[47] Cf. canon 67.

[48] Cf. canon 1081 and following.

[49] Cf. Harrigan, *The Radical Sanation of Invalid Marriages*, p. 95. Harrigan, *The Radical Sanation of Invalid Marriages* (The Catholic University of America Canon Law Studies, n. 116, Washington, D. C.: The Catholic University of America 1938), p. 95.

Catholic party either to grave harm or to serious inconvenience, . . . *gravis damni aut incommodi* . . . , or 2) the non-Catholic party cannot in any manner be induced to renew the matrimonial consent according to the proper form of the Church, or to give the promises required by canon 1061, § 2. An interview with the Catholic party must reveal the presence of the above given conditions. There is nothing in the text of the faculties to indicate that this preliminary investigation cannot be attended to by the pastor (or his substitute) of the Catholic party. The conditions, as stated, are postulated for the valid use of the faculty. The wording of the faculty does not permit its use in cases in which it is the Catholic party who is ignorant of the invalidity of the marriage.[50]

Further conditions pertaining to the valid use of the faculty are enumerated in the revised text under the numbers 1 to 6. Number 1 required that moral certitude be established to the effect that the non-Catholic party is not opposed to and will not impede the baptism and education of all the children of both sexes which may be born to the union in the future.

The method of establishing this necessary certainty will vary with the circumstances of individual cases.

Number 2 provides that an explicit promise be exacted from the Catholic party to the effect that the said party will provide, insofar as possible, for the baptism and education in the Catholic faith of all the children of both sexes which may be born and, in cases wherein the need exists, the Catholic party is to promise to the effect the conversion, baptism, and education of all the children already born to the parties.[51]

Number 3 of the conditions provides that before their attempt at marriage the parties must not have bound themselves, either publicly or privately, in any agreement which would require the non-Catholic education of their children. As is apparent from the context of the above mentioned conditions, they are closely related, and the investigation of one lends itself to the establishment of the remaining two. In the use of the faculty the Ordinary is dependent upon the pastor (or his substitute) of the Catholic party for the

---

[50] Cf. No. 5, as treated in the following text.

[51] Cf. canon 1013, § 1.

information necessary for the verification of the foregoing conditions.

Number 4 of the conditions postulates that neither of the parties be insane, *neutra pars sit actu demens.* Obviously a person permanently and perpetually insane could be no party to a marriage, even in the process of sanation.[52] In those cases in which one of the parties in insane but at times enjoys lucid intervals, it appears that a sanation can be granted, provided that it be granted at a time when the person is experiencing a lucid interval, since the consent postulated for the use of this faculty is sufficient if it perseveres at the time the sanation is conceded.[53]

Number 5 presents another condition essential for the valid use of the faculty. At least the Catholic party must have knowledge of the sanation and of the need for it, and likewise, must petition it. The faculty cannot be validly used in those cases in which both parties are ignorant of the invalidity of their attempted marriage, or in cases in which the Catholic party is the one ignorant of the invalidity.[54] The petition for the sanation must be made by the Catholic party.[55] This condition does not, it seems, prohibit the transmission of the petition to the Ordinary through the agency of the pastor of the Catholic party. The requirement is satisfied if the petition is signed by the Catholic party, although an exception may be permitted in this regard if the pastor or his substitute clearly establishes in the petition that it is made at the request of the Catholic party.[56]

Number 6 of the conditions required for the valid use of this faculty is that there be no other extant diriment impediment to the marriage, with reference to which the Ordinary has not the power

[52] Cf. Harrigan, *The Radical Sanation of Invalid Marriages*, p. 93.

[53] "However, in view of the fact that civil divorce is quite easily obtained because of the insanity of one of the parties, it is questionable whether the Church would be willing to grant radical sanation in such cases [cases in which the insane party enjoys lucid intervals] as these."—Harrigan, *The Radical Sanation of Invalid Marriages*, p. 93.

[54] Cf. mention of this condition in the preceding text.

[55] Cf. canon 37: The rule of this canon does not permit action contrary to the terms of the condition as stated in the text of the faculty.

[56] Harrigan, (*The Radical Sanation of Invalid Marriages*, p. 188, Appendix II, B) gives a sample form of petition to the Ordinary for the radical sanation of a marriage invalid by reason of defect of form and the impediment of either mixed religion or disparity of cult.

of granting a dispensation or of supplying a sanation.[57] The wording of this condition is clear: In those cases in which there exists another diriment impediment, such as sacred orders or solemn vows, the Ordinary cannot grant a radical sanation validly. This faculty must be considered together with the faculty of healing invalid marriages as granted to the Ordinaries by the Sacred Congregation of the Sacraments, which is treated in the Chapter following.[58]

The instructions to be given by the Most Reverend Bishop as mentioned in the second paragraph of the faculty are postulated for the licit use of the power; the discharge of the instructions does not pertain to the validity of the sanations granted in virtue of this faculty. The admonition of the Catholic party and the imposition of a suitable penance, while clearly the task of the Most Reverend Bishop, may nevertheless be administered through a third party, such as the pastor of the Catholic party. There is nothing in the text of the faculty to forbid this procedure. The requirement is that the admonition and penance proceed from the Most Reverend Bishop himself. In those cases wherein the need is present, absolution from the excommunication incurred by the Catholic party in consequence of the law enacted in canon 2319, § 1, 1°, should be given to the granting of the sanation.[59]

The effect of the sanation should be announced by the bishop. The Catholic party who is aware of the invalidity of the marriage should be informed of the effects of the dispensation. These effects are enumerated in the text of the faculty as 1) the rendering of the marriage as valid, lawful, and indissoluble, and 2) the legitimation of children already born to the parties as also the legitimacy of the children which may be born of the union. Further, the Catholic

[57] Cf. supra, p. 55, for treatment of the prohibition concerning marriages between Catholics and Mohammedans.

[58] The condition under which the faculty is to be used, as they are treated above, are those which are contained in the July 1, 1946, text of this faculty. The text as issued is effective, provided that no other changes are made before then, until January 1, 1949. Previous to July 1, 1946, the conditions pertaining to the valid use of this faculty were stated as follows: *casibus exceptis: 1° in quo pars acatholica adversatur baptismo vel catholicae educationi prolis utriusque sexus natae vel nasciturae; 2° in quo ante attentatum matrimonium, sive privatim sive per publicum actum, partes se obstrinxerunt educationi non catholicae prolis, uti supra: dummodo aliud non obstet canonicum impedimentum dirimens, super quo Ipse dispensandi aut sanandi facultate non polleat.*

[59] Cf. canon 2265, § 2; Van Hove, *De Rescriptis*, n. 110.

party should be reminded of his or her duty to care, to the best of his or her ability, for the Catholic baptism and education of the children, and to work prudently toward the conversion of the non-Catholic party.

The Most Reverend Bishop is also directed carefully to preserve the document of sanation in the diocesan curia, in order that proof of the validity of the marriage and legitimacy of the children may, if need arise, be proved at any future date. It is left to the prudent judgment of the Most Reverend Bishop whether or not he should direct that the usual notations be made in the baptismal record of the Catholic party.[60] In view of the obligation as stated in the canons, it appears that to omit the directing of these notations, the bishop must have a comparatively sufficient reason since omission of the notations is, in effect, a dispensation from the rules of canons 470, § 2, and 1103, § 2.[61]

The notation attached to the text of the faculty states that it is the mind of the Holy Office that this faculty be used only by the Most Reverend Bishop himself, that is to say, that the faculty be subdelegated to no one.[62]

The use of the word *episcopus* does not indicate, however, that the Holy Office intended to exclude the vicar general. It is apparent from the phrase, *scilicet nemini subdeleget,* that the vicar general enjoys the use of this faculty equal with, and with the same obligations as the bishop.[63] Subdelegation is strictly forbidden, and consequently sanations granted by one subdelegated by either the Bishop or the vicar general are invalid. This prohibition will require, in some cases, the grant of the sanation with the pastor (or his substitute) of the Catholic party as the executor of the rescript, that is, in *forma commissoria necessaria.* In the use of this procedure the bishop must exercise due care to avoid any form of subdelegation. The pastor will accordingly be made the necessary

---

[60] Cf. canons 470, § 2; 1103, § 2.

[61] Cf. canon 84, § 1.

[62] Formerly, prior to 1934, pastors could be subdelegated. Cf. Bouscaren, *Canon Law Digest*, I, canon 66; Doheny, *Canonical Procedure in Matrimonial Cases*, Vol. II, *Informal Procedure* (Milwaukee, Wisconsin: The Bruce Publishing Co., 1944) pp. 25, 26.

[63] Cf. canons 66, § 2, and 368, § 2.

executor.[64] If he were made the voluntary executor in the execution of the rescript, his assignment would, contrary to the manifest mind of the Holy Office, involve an attempted act of subdelegation.[65] The executor is, in all these cases, bound by the legislation of canons 54, § 1, and 55.

ADNOTANDA.—1. *In singulis praefatis sive sanationibus sive dispensationibus concedendis, Episcopus vel Ordinarius expressam faciat mentionem Apostolicae delegationis* (*Cod. I. C.* can. 1057).

2. *Ordinarius in fine cuislibet anni referat ad S. Congregationem S. officii de numero et specie dispensationum vigore praesentis Indulti elargitarum.*

This final notation appended to the text of the faculties from the Holy Office is a reminder of the legislation of canon 1057.[66] In view of the nature of the canon mentioned and the text of the notation, the rule does not seem to apply to those concessions which are granted in virtue of the faculty which authorizes the bishop to permit the reading and the retaining of forbidden books. The Ordinary is further required to report, at the end of each year, the number and kinds of dispensations and sanations granted by virtue of these faculties. It appears that the number of permissions granted in virtue of the faculty which authorizes the bishop to permit the reading and the retaining of forbidden books should be included in this report, since no exception is made in regard to that faculty, and since the grants of permissions do come under the general title of dispensations.[67]

---

[64] Cf. canon 54, § 1.

[65] Cf. Van Hove, *De Rescriptis*, nn. 129, 130.

[66] Canon 1057: Qui ex potestate a Sede Apostolica delegata dispensationem concedunt, in eadem expressam pontificii indulti mentionem faciant.

[67] Cf. canon 86.

CHAPTER VII.

FACULTIES FROM THE SACRED CONGREGATION OF THE SACRAMENTS

INTRODUCTION

The faculties issued by the Sacred Congregation of the Sacraments deal with the granting of dispensations from matrimonial impediments and with the concession of sanations for certain invalid marriages. Appended to the transcript of the faculties are certain conditions, the first two of which are of such a nature that their discussion prior to the treatment of the faculties themselves seems desirable. The third will be treated subsequently to the consideration of the individual faculties granted by the Sacred Congregation.

ADNOTANDA.—1. *Ordinarius recensitis facultatibus, sive per se sive per alias idoneas ecclesiasticas personas ad hoc specialiter deputandas, uti poterit in matrimoniis contrahendis et nulliter contractis cum suis subditis ubique commorantibus et aliis omnibus in proprio territorio actu degentibus, facta in unoquoque casu expressa mentione huius Apostolicae delegationis ad norman canonis* 1057.

2. *In usu earundem facultatum prae oculis habeantur quae in* can. 1048 *ad* 1054 *statuta reperiuntur.*

3. *Ordinarius, in fine cuiuslibet anni referat ad Sacram Congregationem Sacramentorum, per tramitem S. Congregationis Consistorialis, de numero et specie dispensationum quas vigore praesentis Indulti ipse fuerit elargitus.*

In regard to the rules set forth in number 1 of these notations, the term *Ordinarius* includes also the vicar general, who enjoys these faculties by reason of his office.[1] Other worthy ecclesiastical persons may be subdelegated, even habitually, if the Ordinary so

[1] Cf. canons 66, § 2; 378, § 2.

desires,[2] according to the terms of the text. It seems, however, that the mind of the Sacred Congregation is against indiscriminate delegation, that is, the subdelegation of all or even a major portion of the priests of the diocese, as is implied in the use of the words, *idoneas ecclesiasticas personas ad hoc specialiter deputandas.* Both the Ordinary and his delegate are required to make explicit mention of the Apostolic delegation in each use of the faculty.[3]

Unless the contrary is stated in the text of the individual faculties, they may be used also in the convalidation of marriages. In what manner this applies will become apparent from the discussion of the first of the faculties in the first article of this Chapter. The faculties may be used according to the rules as given in the general norms regarding interpretation, as treated previously, that is to say, for the subjects of the Ordinary, either within or outside the territory of the Ordinary, and for non-subjects within the proper territory of the Ordinary.[4]

Number 2 of the notations reminds persons acting in virtue of these faculties that the rules of canons 1048 to 1054 inclusive are to be observed. The rule of canon 1048[5] states that the Ordinary is not to dispense from an impediment in a given case by virtue of these faculties if a petition has already been sent to the Holy See for the dispensation that is required. He may, however, according to canon 204, § 2, even then dispense from the impediment if a grave and urgent cause exists; in such a case he must notify the Holy See of his action at once.

Canon 1049, § 1, permits the use of the faculties in those cases which involve a multiplicity of the same impediment in any one case, and canon 1049, § 2, in those cases which involve a number of impediments even of a public character.[6]

---

[2] Cf. canon 199, § 2.

[3] Cf. canons 1057; 200, § 2.

[4] Cf. Chapter V, Article 2, C.

[5] Canon 1048: Si petitio dispensationis ad Sanctam Sedem missa sit, Ordinarii locorum suis facultatibus, si quas habeant, ne utantur, nisi ad norman can. 204, § 2.

Canon 204, § 2: Attamen rei ad Superiorem delata ne se immisceat inferior, nisi ex gravi urgentique causa; et hoc in casu statim Superiorem de re moneat.

[6] Canon 1049, § 1: In matrimoniis sive contractis sive contrahendis, qui gaudet indulto generali dispensandi super certo quodam impedimento,

Canon 1050 prescribes that an Ordinary who has a general indult to dispense from one or more public impediments must apply to the Holy See for the dispensation from all the impediments present in any single case, if there exists in that case some impediment from which he has not the power to dispense. In those cases, however, in which the impediments from which he has the power to dispense are discovered after application has been made to the Holy See for dispensation, the Ordinary may use that power only after dispensation has been received from the Holy See.[7]

Canon 1051 deals with the legitimation of the children. It states that in the case of diriment impediments the dispensations granted in virtue of power delegated through a general indult have the effect of making the children legitimate *ipso facto*. (The same is not true of dispensations which are granted in virtue of a power conferred by special rescript.) The children must be the children of the parties requesting the dispensation. But the benefit of legitimation is denied when the offspring is conceived in adultery or sacrilege.[8]

The legislation of canon 1052 concerns itself with the impediments of consanguinity and affinity and the attendant errors in the computation of the degree of relationship. Such errors do not invalidate the dispensations which are granted, provided that no degree of relationship exists closer than the degree described in the petition for the dispensation or in the grant of the latter. The

---

potest, nisi in ipso indulto aliud expresse praescribatur, super eo dispensare etiamsi idem impedimentum multiplex sit.

§ 2: Qui habet indultum generale dispensandi super pluribus diversae speciei impedimentis, sive dirimentibus sive impedientibus, potest dispensare super iisdem impedimentis, etiam publicis, in uno eodemque casu occurentibus.

[7] Canon 1050: Si quando cum impedimento seu impedimentis publicis super quibus ex indulto dispensare quis potest, concurrat aliud impedimentum super quo dispensare nequeat, pro omnibus Sedes Apostolica adiri debet; si tamen impedimentum seu impedimenta super quibus dispensare potest, comperiantur post impetratam a Sancta Sede dispensationem, suis facultatibus uti poterit.

[8] Canon 1051: Per dispensationem super impedimento dirimente concessam sive ex potestate ordinaria, sive ex potestate delegata per indultum generale non vero per rescriptum in casibus particularibus, conceditur quoque eo ipso legitimatio prolis, si qua ex iis, cum quibus dispensatur iam nata vel concepta fuerit, excepta tamen adulterina et sacrilega.

computation of the degrees of relationship will be treated in the discussion of the faculty which concerns these impediments.[9]

The effect of a dispensation obtained from the Holy See in the cases of a *ratum et non consummatum* marriage, and the permission given by the Holy See to a party to remarry in the event of the presumed death of the former spouse, are treated in canon 1053. Such dispensations and permissions always contain a dispensation from the impediment of *crimen,* as described in canon 1075, § 1.[10]

The effect of the legislation of canon 1054 is of paramount importance in the use of faculties which are concerned with dispensations from matrimonial impediments of minor degree. The canon states that even though the represented cause is false or some pertinent factor be concealed, the dispensation which is granted for matrimonial impediment of minor degree remains valid; the same is true even though the single advanced final cause is false.[11]

In view of the legislation of canon 84, § 1, an Ordinary must have reason for considering the cause put forth as true and sufficient at the time when he grants the dispensation; otherwise, as canon 84, § 1, states, he acts invalidly. Should the Ordinary later learn that the represented cause in consequence of which he granted the dispensation was false, or that pertinent facts were concealed, the dispensation nevertheless is valid, according to canon 1054. However, if the Ordinary is aware of the falsity of the cause prior to the grant of the dispensation, he cannot act lawfully in granting the dispensation.

The contents of the third section of the notations is more appropriately considered at the end of this Chapter.

Article I
Matrimonial Dispensations:
Impediments Enacted in Canons 1042 and 1058

"Dispensandi iusta et rationablili ex casua super matri-

---

[9] Canon 1052: Dispensatio ab impedimento consanguinitatis vel affinitatis, concessa in aliquo impedimenti gradu, valet, licet in petitione vel in concessione error circa gradum irrepserit, dummodo gradus revera exsistens sit inferio, aut licet reticitum fuerit aliud impedimentum eiusdem speciei in aequali vel inferiore gradu.

[10] Cf. canon 1053.

[11] Canon 1054: Dispensatio a minore impedimento concessa, nullo sive obreptionis sive subreptionis vitio irritatur, etsi unica causa finalis in precibus exposita falsa fuerit.

monialibus impediments minoris gradus, quae in can. 1042 recensentur, necnon super impedimentis impedientibus, de quibus in can. 1058, ad effectum tantum matrimonium contrahendi."

This faculty is concerned with the granting of dispensations from the diriment matrimonial impediments of minor degree, [12] as they are listed in canon 1042, § 2, [13] and from prohibitive impediments listed in canon 1058, § 1. [14] Use of the faculty in regard to the impediments listed in canon 1058, § 1, is restricted, however, to the granting of dispensations for the exclusivce purpose of contracting marriage, *ad effectum tantum matrimonium contrahendi.* As was stated previously, the power inherent in this faculty may be used not only with reference to marriage yet to be contracted, but also in relation to previous unions invalidly contracted . . . *uti poterit in matrimoniis contrahendis et nulliter contractis* . . . .

A just and reasonable cause is required for the use of this faculty. The presence of such a cause pertains to the valid use of the power. [15] This is to say that the Ordinary must have a reasonable and just cause for granting the dispensation, even though the cause or causes as advanced in the petition should later prove to have been false. [16]

1.

Consanguinity in the Third Degree Collaterally Computed

The impediment of consanguinity, as stated in the Code of Canon

[12] The distinction made between minor and major grade impediments by canon 1042, pertains principally to the act of dispensing from those impediments. Matrimonial impediments of the minor grade are more easily subject to dispensation and hence require less gravity or seriousness in the cause for which the dispensation is granted. Cf. Vermeersch—Creusen, *Epitome*, II, n. 302, p. 212; canon 1054.

[13] Canon 1042, § 2: Impedimenta gradus minoris sunt:
1. Consanguinitas in tertio gradu lineae collateralis;
2. Affinitas in secundo gradu lineae collateralis;
3. Publica honestas in secundo gradu;
4. Cognatio spiritualis;
5. Crimen ex adulterio cum promissione vel attentatione matrimonii etiam per civilem tantum actum.

[14] Canon 1058: Matrimonium impedit votum simplex virginitatis, castitatis perfectae, non nubendi, suscipiendi ordines sacros et amplectendi statum religiosum.

[15] Cf. canon 84, § 1: See authors listed on p. 72, Chapter VI, Article 2.

[16] Cf. canon 1054.

Law, invalidates marriages between persons who are collaterally related within the third degree or closer.[17] Consanguinity in the direct line invalidates marriage, in any and every degree, ascending or descending.[18] A multiplication of the impediment in the present law is had only as often as there is a multiplication of the common ancestry of the parties.[19] The existence of this factor of multiplicity does not, however, bar the use of this faculty.[20] The present law concerning the impediment of consanguinity is more clearly and definitely outlined than the pre-Code legislation. As a consequence the faculties issued to Ordinaries for use under the Code are also more clearly and simply stated.[21]

The presence or absence of the impediment of consanguinity should stand revealed through the prenuptial investigation.[22] In the event that blood relationship is found to exist between the parties contemplating marriage, the degree of that relationship can best be computed and demonstrated by means of a chart which recounts and lists all the ancestors of the parties concerned. Although, it is not required that such a chart accompany the petition for a dispensation, the chances of error are reduced if that procedure is followed.[23] Dispensations given in virtue of this faculty from the impediment of consanguinity in the third degree computed collaterally are invalid if, either by intention or through error, the com-

---

[17] Canon 1076, § 2: In linea collaterali irritum est usque ad tertium gradum inclusive, ita tamen ut matrimonii impedimentum toties tantum multiplicetur quoties communis stipes multiplicatur.

[18] Canon 1076, § 1: In linea recta consanguinitatis matrimonium irritum est inter omnes ascendentes et descendentes tum legitimos tum naturales.

[19] Cf. canon 1076, § 2.

[20] Cf. canon 1049, § 1.

[21] Cf. Putzer, *Commentarium*, nn. 114, 222, 240, 241. Prior to the Code of Canon Law the impediment of consanguinity extended to the fourth degree of collateral relationship. Cf. Vermeersch—Creusen, *Epitome*, II, n. 353, p. 249.

[22] Cf. canon 1020; S. C. de Sacr. instr., 29 iun 1941—*AAS*, XXXIII (1941), 297 FF.; Bouscaren, *The Canon Law Digest*, II, canon 1020.

[23] Typical graphs are furnished in nearly all manuals on matrimonial law. Cf. Wahl, *The Matrimonial Impediments of Consanguinity and Affinity*, The Catholic University of America Canon Law Studies, n. 90 (The Catholic University of America; Washington, D. C., 1934), p. 5; Payen, *De Matrimonio in Missionibus ac Potissimum in Sinis Tractatus Practicus et Casus* (altera editio, 3 vols., Zi-Ka-wei; in Tpyographia T'OU-SE-WE 1935-1936), I. nn. 1428 ff., pp. 1038 ff. Petrovits, *The New Church Law on Matrimony* (2. ed., Philadelphia: John Joseph McVey, 1926), n. 328; De Smet, *De Sponsalibus et Matrimonia*, n. 599, p. 524.

putation should describe the impediment as being of the third degree when in fact the impediment arises from a closer degree of relationship.[24] An erroneous computation does not give rise to invalidity in such a dispensation, provided that no relationship closer than the third degree is actually existing.

As is stated above, a multiplicity in the impediment of consanguinity does not prevent the use of this faculty provided that the relationship does not exist in any degree closer than the third degree collaterally computed. Thus, in those cases in which parties are related in the third collateral degree touching the second or first degree, it appears that this faculty cannot be used validly.[25] In those cases which involve the fourth or the fifth degree of collateral relationship in one of the branches of the family tree, but only the third degree in the other lineal branch, the use of this faculty is in no way indicated as necessary.[26]

2.
Affinity in the Second Degree Collaterally Computed, and Public Decency in the Second Degree.

Use of the faculty to dispense from the impediment of affinity in the second degree computed collaterally,[27] and from the impediment of public decency in the second degree,[28] is governed by the same procedure as that relating to the faculty concerning the impediment of consanguinity as treated above. It is to be noted here that in regard to the impediment of public decency the use of the faculty to dispense from the impediment in the first degree is

[24] Cf. canons 67; 1052.

[25] Cf. canon 67; Article 2 of this Chapter.

[26] Cf. canon 96, § 3.

[27] Canon 1077, § 1: Affinitas in linea recta dirimit matrimonium in quolibet gradu; in linea collaterali usque ad secundum gradum inclusive.
2: Affinitatis impedimentum multiplicatur:
1° Quoties multiplicatur impedimentum consanguinitatis quo procedit;
2° Iterato successive matrimonio cum consanguineo coniugis defuncti.

[28] Canon 1078: Impedimentum publicae honestatis oritur ex matrimonio invalido, sive consummato sive non, et ex publico vel notorio concubinatu; et nuptias dirimit in primo et secundo gradu lineae rectae inter virum et consanguineas mulieris, ac vice versa.

invalid.[29] It may be noted further that, according to a response given by the Pontifical Commission for the Interpretation of the Code, merely civil marriages entered into by person bound by the form, do not give rise to the impediment of public decency in itself, but only when considered as consummated, that is, as public concubinage.[30]

As in the impediment of consanguinity, the grantor of the dispensation is dependent upon the prenuptial investigation for an accurate discription of the bonds of blood or affinity existing between the parties. A clear, simple and accurate chart of the relationship should accompany the petition for a dispensation. Errors in the computation of the degree or of the multiplicity of the impediments are to be considered as are errors in connection with the impediment of consanguinity.[31]

The legislation of canons 1048 to 1054 inclusive applies to the use of this faculty.[32]

3.

Spiritual Relationship.

The impediment of spiritual relationship[33] is considered as existing between the baptised person, and the person who performs the baptism and the sponsors.[34] The existence of the impediment of spiritual relationship between the minister and the subject in the case of a conditional baptism is doubtful in fact, and accordingly the powers of this faculty are not needed, since canon 15 enables the Ordinary to grant a dispensation in such an event, as long as there

---

[29] Cf. canon 67.

[30] Com. Interp. resp. 12 mart. 1929 — *AAS*, XXI (1929), 170; Bouscaren, *The Canon Law Digest*, I, 517, canon 1078.

[31] Cf. canon 1052.

[32] Cf. treatment given these canons above, pp. 71 ff.

[33] Canon 1079: Ea tantum spiritualis cognatio matrimonium irritat, de quo in can. 768.

768: Ex baptismo spiritualem cognationem contrahunt tantum cum baptizato baptizans et patrinus.

[34] Canon 763, § 2: Iterato baptismo sub conditione, neque patrinus qui priori baptismo adfuit, neque qui posteriori, cognationem spiritualem contrahit, nisi idem patrinus in utroque baptismo adhibitus fuerit.

When the impediment of spiritual relationship certainly exists, the powers of this faculty are to be used. The powers of the faculty are not needed in cases wherein a doubt obtains as to the existence of the impediment. In such cases canon 15 gives the Ordinary all necessary powers.

is question simply of a law from which the Roman Pontiff customarily dispenses.[35]

4.

CRIMEN.

In regard to the impediment of *crimen* the use of the faculty is limited to the specific category of the impediment as it is described in paragraph 1 of canon 1075. There it is stated that a valid marriage cannot be contracted between persons who, while bound by a valid marriage, have committed true adultery and have entered into a mutual promise of marrying, or have attempted marriage even by means of a civil union.[36] The impediment as described in paragraphs 2 and 3 of canon 1075 is excluded from the scope of this faculty.[37] Further treatment is given the impediment of crime as described in the second and third sections of canon 1075 in the faculties from the Sacred Penitentiary, which are treated in the final Chapter of this dissertation.

As regards the impediments treated above in this Article, the grantor of the dispensations from the impediment of crime is dependent upon the prenuptial investigation for the knowledge of the existence and extent of this impediment. The fact that the impediment is occult does not prevent the use of the faculty for dispensing from it, even though the impediment be one of several existing in any given case.[38]

Ignorance on the part of either or both of the parties does not excuse from the impediment.[39]

---

[35] In dubio autem facti potest Ordinarius in eis (legibus) dispensare, dummodo agatur de legibus in quibus Romanus Pontifex dispensare solet.

[36] Canon 1075: Valide contrahere nequent matrimonium:

1° Qui, perdurante eodem legitimo matrimonio adulterium inter se consummarunt et fidem sibi mutuo dederunt de matrimonio ineundo vel ipsum matrimonium, etiam per civilem tantum actum, attentarunt. Cf. Donohue, *The Impediment of Crime*, The Catholic University of America Canon Law Studies, n. 69; (Washington, D. C.: The Catholic University of America, 1931) which treats of the subject *ex professo*; De Smet, *De Sponsalibus et Matrimonio*, n. 658; Ayrinhac — Lydon, *Marriage Legislation*, n. 152.

[37] Canon 1075, 2°: Qui, perdurante pariter eodem legitimo matrimonio, adulterium inter se consummarunt eorumque alter coniugicidium patravit;

3°: Qui mutua opera physica vel morali, etiam sine adulterio, mortem coniugi intulerunt.

[38] Cf. canon 1049, § 1, § 2.

[39] Cf. canon 16, § 1.

It is the duty of the priest preparing the couple for marriage to take care that no impediment be overlooked. In regard to the presence of the impediment of *crimen* the directives of the Instruction issued by the Sacred Congregation of the Sacraments on prenuptial investigation give the norms to be followed.[40]

Any extension of the faculties beyond the limits set by the text of the faculty itself results in the invalid use of the power. A delegate who exceeds the bounds of his authority acts invalidly.[41]

Simple Vows.

The impediment of simple vows, as listed in canon 1058, is among the impediments for which a dispensation may be granted in virtue of the powers conceded in this faculty.[42] The text of the faculty makes no distinction between the first and second paragraphs of the above mentioned canon; therefore, it may be concluded that both are included. Determination of the type of vow involved in any given case depends upon the classification as given in canon 1308.[43]

In regard to dispensations from simple vows, the faculty states that such dispensations can be given only for the purpose of contracting marriage, *ad effectum tantum matrimonium contrahendi.* Canon 67 forbids the extension of the faculty to other cases.

Article 2

Matrimonial Dispensations From the Impediments of Consanguinity, Affinity, and Public Decency in the More Proximate Degrees.

"Dispensandi ex gravi urgentique causa, quoties periculum sit in mora et matrimonium nequeat differri usque dum dispensatio a Sancta Sede obtineatur super impedimentis infra recensitis:

[40] S. C. de Sacr. instr. 29 iun 1941 — *AAS,* XXXIII (1941), 297 ff.; Bouscaren, *The Canon Law Digest,* II, canon 1020.

[41] Cf. canons 203, § 1; 67.

[42] Canon 1058, § 1: Matrimonium impedit votum simplex virginitatis, castitatis perfectae, non nubendi, suscipiendi ordines sacros, et amplectendi statum religiosum.

§ 2: Nullum votum simplex irritat matrimonium, nisi irritatio speciali Sedis Apostolicae praescripto pro aliquibus statuta fuerit.

[43] Cappello, *De Sacramentis,* III, pars 1, n. 292; De Smet, *De Sponsalibus et Matrimonio,* p. 429.

a) consanguinitatis in secundo aut in tertio cum primo mixtis, dummodo nullum exinde scandalum aut admiratio exoriatur;
b) Consanguinitatis in secundo lineae collateralis gradu;
c) affinitatis in primo lineae collateralis gradu aequali vel mixto cum secundo;
d) publicae honestatis in primo gradu, dummodo nullum subsit dubium quod coniux esse possit proles ab altero contrahentium genita."

Grave and urgent reasons are required for the valid use of this faculty, more grave than the causes for which the faculty treated in Article 1 may be used, as is evident from the nature of the impediments and the tenor of canon 84, § 1.[44] The list given, or suggested, by the Apostolic Datary, and cited by the authors, enumerates those causes which may be considered grave, and in any given case may be considered as a sufficient reason for the granting of a dispensation by virtue of this faculty.

In addition to the factor of gravity the note of urgency must also be present in the cause. What may constitute urgency in any particular case is described in the next clause of the text of the faculty, i. e., *quoties periculum sit in mora et matrimonium nequeat differri usque dum dispensatio a Sancta Sede obtineatur,* that is, whenever there is danger in delay and the marriage cannot be postponed until a dispensation is obtained from the Holy See. The existence of these conditions depends upon the circumstances surrounding the contemplated marriage in the judgment of the Ordinary, who in turn is dependent upon the facts presented by the pastor preparing the parties for the marriage.[45] Dispensations granted in the absence

[44] In regard to acceptable causes see authors listed in Chapter VI. Article 2, especially O'Mara, *Canonical Causes for Matrimonial Dispensations*, pp. 72 — 130.

[45] The time for a response from Rome to a submitted application is computed as from 40 to 50 days for the places outside Europe. Cappello, *Summa Iuris Canonici*, I, n. 125, footnote 11. The time will vary in some degree in various sections of the United States, and has been shortened somewhat since the date of Capello's writing. In practice the experience of the curia considering the case suffices for a safe norm. The use of *Air Mail* does not appear to be required as it is, at present, not considered to be the usual means of communication.

of such a cause which is at once both grave and urgent are invalid, as is apparent from the text of the faculty as written by the Sacred Congregation of the Sacraments, and of the law of canon 84, § 1.[46]

The clause, *dummodo nullum exinde scandalum aut admiratio exoriatur*—provided that there arise no scandal or wonderment therefrom—expresses a condition which pertains to the valid use of the faculty[47] to dispense from the impediment described under number 1. A dispensation given in those cases in which scandal or wonderment is forseen to arise from it is invalidly granted. The determination regarding the absence of scandal or wonderment in any given case rests with the judgment of the Ordinary, who in turn is dependent upon the pastor for a statement of the circumstances. Since the foregoing conditions pertain to the validity of the dispensation, it follows that the pastor's opinion on the matter with his statement of the facts should be contained in the peition for the dispensation.[48]

Numbers 2 and 3 of the text of the faculty contain no such conditions. Computation of the impediments of both consanguinity and affinity as described in the faculty, will follow the method indicated in Article 1 of this Chapter. Similarily an accurate and clear description of the relationship, by means of a graph, should accompany the petition for the dispensation, since no extension of the faculty beyond the listed impediments is permitted.[49]

The impediment of public decency, *publica honestas,* is treated in number 4 of the faculty. The dispensation from the impediment as in number 1, is subject to a condition which pertains to the valid use of the dispensatory power, viz., *dummodo nullum subsit dubium quod coniux esse possit proles ab altero contrahentium genita;* provided there be no doubt that one of the parties is not the offspring of the other. As a consequence the petition for the dispensa-

---

[46] The note of urgency may vary widely even within the same given cause; e. g., in the cause *copula iam habita,* the case is obviously more urgent if pregnancy results than if that condition did not result.

[47] Cf. canon 39.

[48] In cases involving doubts of fact concerning the above mentioned condition the powers conceded in canon 15 are to be used, and in consequence this faculty is then not needed.

[49] Cf. canon 67.

tion should contain such an exposition of the circumstances as will obviate the above mentioned doubt.[50]

The faculty granted in paragraph two of the text of faculties issued by the Sacred Congregation of the Sacraments is, for certain occasions, extended for use in dispensations from the same impediments that are discussed above. This further extension of the faculty appears in paragraph three of the rescript.

> "Dispensandi tempore et in actu Sacrae Pastoralis Visitationis aut Sacrarum Missionum, et non ultra, super omnibus impedimentis supra memoratis cum iis qui in concubinatu vivere reperiuntur."

The impediments concerned are those enumerated above, viz., 1) consanguinity in the second or third degree touching the first, provided that there be no scandal or wonderment arising from the use of the faculty in this regard; 2) consanguinity in the second degree of the collateral line; 3) affinity in the first degree of the collateral line; and 4) public decency in the first degree, provided that there be no doubt that one of the parties is not the offspring of the other.

The pastoral visitation spoken of in the faculty is that visitation which the Ordinary is required by law to make at least every five years.[51] The visit of the Ordinary to a parish for the purpose of inspecting the parochial records, as he is directed to do in the Instruction issued by the Sacred Congregation of the Sacraments, June 29, 1941,[52] does not seem to be included in the term *Sacrae Pastoralis Visitationis* of the faculty, hence the use of the faculty on the occasion of the above mentioned visit would imply an extension of the power conceded and this would connote an invalid use of

---

[50] Marriage is never permitted if a doubt as described in the faculty exists. Canon 1076, § 3: Numquam matrimonium permittatur, si quod subsit dubium num partes sint consangiuneae in aliquo gradu lineae rectae aut in primo gradu lineae collateralis.

[51] Cf. canon 343, § 2: Slafkosky, *The Canonical Episcopal Visitation of the Diocese*, The Catholic University of America Canon Law Studies, n. 142, (Washington, D. C.: The Catholic University of America Press, 1941) treats of the subject *ex professo*.

[52] *AAS* XXXIII (1941), 297 ff.; Bouscaren, *The Canon Law Digest*, II, canon 1020; paragraph 11, n. f. The Instruction directs that the visitation be made every six months or at least once each year.

that power.[53] If the task of the pastoral visitation is delegated, the delegate does not enjoy the powers of this faculty by virtue of this delegation for the visitation, but must, if he proposes to use the powers, have received an express delegation from the Ordinary.

Use of the faculty during the period of mission, *Sacrarum Missionum,* is also permitted. The missions spoken of are those mentioned in canon 1349, § 1.[54] Although the canon states that these missions should be given at least once in ten years, they may be given oftener, and as often as they are given the faculty can be used.

Dispensations can be granted in virtue of this faculty only in those cases in which the parties are actually living in concubinage.[55] This condition is necessary for the valid use of the faculty.[56] In cases in which the concubinage is either public or concurrent with an invalid marriage, whose status of invalidity was occasioned either by reason of the nonobservance of the requisite canonical form or in consequence of the existence of a publicly known impediment, care should be exercised to make certain that any penalties contracted by the parties be remitted before a dispensation is granted.[57]

Article 3

Faculty of Granting a Sanation of Marriage.

"Sanandi in radice matrimonia nulliter contracta ob aliquod ex impedimentis iuris ecclesiastici maioris vel minoris gradus, exceptis iis provenientibus ex sacro presbyteratus ordine et affinitate in linea recta, matrimonio consummato, si magnum adsit incommodum requirendi a parte, ignora nullitatis matrimonii, renovationem consensus, dummodo tamen prior maritalis consensus perseveret et absit periculum divortii; monita tamen parte

---

[53] Cf. canon 203, § 1.

[54] Canon 1349, § 1: Ordinarii advigilent ut, saltem decimo quoque anno sacram, quam vocant, missionem, ad gregem sibi commissum habendam parochi curent.

[55] Cf. Chapter VI, Article 2; the fact of the concubinage alone constitutes a sufficient cause for the granting of the dispensation.

[56] Cf. canon 39.

[57] Cf. canons 2319, 1°; 2357, § 2: Heneghan, *The Marriages of Unworthy Catholics, Canons* 1065 *and* 1066, pp. 113, 114.

> conscia impedimenti de effectu huius sanationi sit debita facta adnotatione in libro baptizatorum et matrimoniorum."

The term "impediments" as used in the faculty is to be interpreted in the broad sense, [58] that is, as inclusive of all the impediments of ecclesiastical law except those which are explicitly mentioned as being excluded in the text of the faculty, viz., the impediments arising from the sacred priesthood or from affinity in the direct line when the marriage which gave rise to the impediment has been consummated. [59] In addition, the impediments of mixed religion and disparity of cult are beyond the scope of this faculty, since exclusive competency in regard to these impediments, pertains to the Holy Office. Likewise excluded, by their very nature and implicitly also by the context of the faculty, are the matrimonial impediments of divine law.

Cases permitting the use of the faculty are those in which there is great inconvenience, *magnum incommodum,* standing in the way of requiring a renewal of consent from the party to the marriage contract who is ignorant of its nullity. The presence of the great inconvenience is to be determined by the judgment of the Ordinary, and is dependent upon the facts and circumstances of each individual case. The text of the faculty, by implication, limits its use to those cases in which one of the parties is ignorant of the nullity of the marriage contract. Extension of the power of the faculty to those cases in which both parties are in ignorance of the nullity seems a violation of the rule of canon 67, and therefore seems to imply an invalid use of the power. Ignorance of the existence of the impediment is not required, however, and the power of sanation could be used to heal those marriages in which one of the parties knew of the material existence of the impediment, but was unaware of the nullity of the marriage. [60]

Two conditions are required for the valid use of the faculty, viz., 1) the previously exchanged matrimonial consent must continue to exist; and 2) there must be no apparent danger of divorce. The

---

[58] Cf. canon 67; 200, § 1.

[59] Thus the impediment arising from the reception of the sacred orders of subdiaconate and diaconate is within the scope of this faculty.

[60] Cf. Harrigan, *The Radical Sanation of Invalid Marriages,* p. 157.

matrimonial consent originally given is held to perserve until evidence of its revocation is present.[61] The Ordinary is dependent, in most cases involving the use of this faculty, upon the circumstances of the case as presented by the pastor, or of some other priest, who is acquainted with those circumstances to determine whether or not the danger of divorce, spoken of in the faculty, is present. It seems that the term *divortii* is inclusive of the separation of the parties, whether this be effected by means of a civil divorce or simply through the parties living apart without the benefit of any legal process. In cases wherein this danger is apparent, the faculty cannot be used validly.

The text of the faculty which follows upon the part which considers the power of effecting a sanation of the marriage states that the party who knows of the nullity of the marriage is to be informed of the fact of sanation and its effects. Further, the proper entries are to be made in the matrimonial registers of the parish in which the sanation takes place and in the baptismal registers which contain the record of the baptism of the parties. A record of the sanation is also to be preserved in the diocesan archives. In this matter the faculties require the same procedure as is required by the Holy Office.

Number 3 of the notations appended to the text of the faculties from the Sacred Congregation of the Sacraments [62] directs the Ordinary to report yearly to the Sacred Congregation of the Sacraments the number and kinds of dispensations granted in virtue of this faculty. This report is to be submitted through the Sacred Consistorial Congregation. Since the rule of the Congregation makes no mention of desiring to know whether the dispensations were granted by the Ordinary himself, by the vicar general, or by a subdelegated person, there need be no mention of this fact; a report of only the number and kinds is required.

---

[61] Cf. canon 1093.

[62] Cf. Introduction of this Chapter.

CHAPTER VIII.

FACULTIES FROM THE SACRED CONGREGATION OF THE COUNCIL

The faculties issued by the Sacred Congregation of the Council are divided into five paragraphs, numbered accordingly, and are treated individually in the discussion that follows. Competence in the matters with which the faculties deal pertains to the Sacred Congregation of Religious when these matters are considered from the point of view of membership in a religious institute.[1] There are no special instructions to be considered in the use of these faculties. The rules as set forth in Chapter I are the guiding principles.

Article i

The Reduction of Mass Obligations.

> "Reducendi per quiquennium, ob diminutionem redituum, perpetua Missarum onera ad rationem eleemosynae in dioecesi legitime vigentis, quoties nemo sit qui de iure teneatur et utiliter cogi queat ad eleemosynae augmentum, et sub lege ut de Missarum ita reductarum satisfactione a singulis celebrantibus Curia diocesana quovis anno legitime doceatur."

The five year period named in the faculty refers to the period over which a reduction in the number of Masses of a perpetual foundation may be made. It is measured according to the rules of canon 34, § 3, 2°.[2] Thus, if the number of Perpetual Mass obligations

---

[1] Cf. canons 250; 251, § 1; "Responsio", Special Commission of Cardinals, March 24, 1919; *AAS*, XI (1919), 251 Bouscaren, *The Canon Law Digest*, I, canon 251; Coronata, *Interpretatio Authentica Codicis Iuris Canonici et circa Ipsum Sanctae Sedis Iurisprudentia* (Romae; Marietti, 1940), p. 54. Hereafter cited as *Interpretatio Authentica*.

[2] Canon 34, § 3, 2°: Si terminus a quo coincidat cum initio diei, ex. gr., *duo vacationum menses a die 15 augusti*, primus dies ad explendam numerationem computetur et tempus finiatur incipiente ultimo die eiusdem numeri.

were reduced by virtue of this faculty over a period of five years beginning January 1st, 1947, the reduction would cease on December 31st, 1952, but would include the day of the 31st . There is nothing in the text of the faculty which indicates that each reduction of Mass obligations must cover a period of five years, for the term is simply given as the maximum. Reductions for lesser terms will in some cases be both useful and advisable and cannot be held to be violations of canon 67 which prohibits the restriction of the general indult. The reduction of Mass obligations effected in virtue of this faculty does not necessarily terminate with the expiration of the faculty itself. For example, if the Mass obligations of a particular foundation were reduced by virtue of this faculty in the last few days of the faculty's duration, the reduction is nevertheless valid for five years.[3]

The reason for which perpetual Mass obligations may be reduced in number is set forth in the faculty. The consideration is that of a diminished revenue. This revenue refers to the income deriving from the invested funds of the foundation. Whether or not the decrease is sufficient to warrant the reduction in the number of founded Masses is left to the judgment of the Ordinary. The tenor of canon 84 seems to indicate that the decrease in revenue must be such as to cause grave inconvenience to the beneficiary of the foundation. The reduction is to be made to correspond to the retention of that number of Mass obligations for which the available revenue will suffice according to the established stipend in the diocese.[4] Further reduction is outside the scope of this faculty. In those cases wherein such a kind of reduction would not suffice to obviate the attendant difficulty of insufficient income, a transfer of some of the Masses may be considered, which transferral is treated in the following Article.

Perpetual Mass Obligations are those which arise from a foundation or bequest as enduring either for an indefinite or at least for a long period of time.[5] The period which is considered sufficient to

---

[3] Cf. canon 73.

[4] The diocesan Mass stipend may be fixed either by the Ordinary or by custom. Cf. canon 831, § 1 and § 2.

[5] Miller, *Founded Massess According to the Code of the Canon Law*, The Catholic University of America Canon Law Studies, n. 34, (Washington, D. C.: The Catholic University of America, 1929, 2.

be included within the notion of perpetual is judged as from forty to fifty years.[6] In the event that the duration of the obligation is not fixed in the terms of the foundation, no period of years need expire before the power of this faculty may be used. From their beginning such foundations are considered perpetual.

The use of the faculty is permitted only in those cases wherein there is no one who can be considered as lawfully bound to augment the stipend named in the foundation. The faculty may be used, however, even in these cases, if it is found impracticable to persuade the person to exercise his power if he could be bound to augment the stipend. Consultation of the terms of the foundation will reveal whether these conditions are present.

The faculty states that priests celebrating Masses which have been reduced in number in virtue of this faculty be required to report to the diocesan curia the fact regarding the satisfaction of the obligations. This report is to be submitted annually.

Article 2

The Transfer of Mass Obligations Within the Diocese

> "Transferendi per quinquennium intra fines diocesis onera Missarum in dies, ecclesias vel altaria alia a fundatione statuta, dummodo adsit vera necessitas nec divinus cultus idcirco minuatur aut populi commoditati praeiudicium inferatur, exceptis tamen legatis quae in certis locis adimpleri facile possunt per eleemosynae augmentum, et cauto ut de translatarum Missarum satisfactione quovis anno Curia dioecesana a singulis celebrantibus legitime doceatur."

The period for which the transfer of Mass obligations may be

[6] Blat, *Commentarium Textus Codicis Iuris Canonici* (5 vols. in 6, Romae: Collegio Angelico, 1919 - 1927), III, P. II, p. 461; Vermeersch - Creusen, *Epitome*, II, p. 865. These authors, in offering their determination of the period of time involved, are commenting on the words *perpetuum vel diuturnum* of canon 1544, § 1. Even though the text of the faculty uses only the word *perpetua,* nevertheless, any Mass obligation established according to the rule of canon 1544, § 1, could be the object of the faculty's use, and it seems therefore, in keeping with the mind of the Sacred Congregation of the Council to include the concept of Mass obligations of long duration within the meaning or scope of the word *perpetua*.

effected in virtue of this faculty is measured in the same manner as described in Article I of this Chapter, and is limited to the same duration, namely, five years. As in the case of the reduction of perpetual Mass obligations, not each transfer need be made for a period of five years, for that is simply the maximum time allowed. Transfers of shorter duration may be effected if desired by the Ordinary. The perpetual transfer of Mass obligations is excluded by the text of the faculty, although successive applications of the power delegated in this faculty to one and the same foundation is not prohibited, and in some cases may in effect become a tantamount to a perpetual transfer, and that, considered as a whole, the repeated periods of the transfer of the Mass obligations may outlive the temporal term of the foundation itself.[7]

The text is clear in its statement that any transfer of Mass obligations when made in virtue of the faculty must be made within the diocese. Such transfers are limited by the faculty to the alteration of the days, churches or altars as listed in the rescript. In view of the rule of canon 67 it appears that any alteration in the terms of the obligations other than those mentioned in the faculty is an unlawful alteration. In those cases in which alterations are effected in all the conditions named, that is to say, when the day, church and altar are all changed, a proportionately more grave cause is required for the transfer.[8] A change in the hour on a specified day appears to be contained within the notion of "day", and consequently, the effecting of such a change seems not forbidden, although a foundation which specifies the hour at which Mass is to be celebrated seems hardly acceptable as a reasonable provision in a foundation.

The real necessity required by the text of the faculty must be regarded as an essential condition for the valid use of the faculty.[9] What may constitute a real necessity in individual cases will necessarily vary with the circumstances, and for the most part remains to be determined by the judgment of the Ordinary.[10] Miller accepts

---

[7] This conclusion presumes that the foregoing faculty is renewed with each renewal of the Quinquennial Faculties as a whole.

[8] Cf. canon 84, § 1.

[9] Cf. canon 39.

[10] Cf. canon 84, § 1. The factor of a due proportion in relation to the necessity is required.

the statement of Gasparri, "The one and only cause for a transfer [of Mass obligations] is that the Masses cannot be celebrated in that church or on that altar, because of lack of priests." [11]

While it is true that Gasparri treated of a transfer effected by the direct action of the Holy See and in regard to Masses requested by the founder out of special devotion or regard for the people of a particular community, nevertheless, it seems that in the same case he would have held an Ordinary in the use of this faculty to the same interpretation of real necessity. A better norm seems furnished in the opinion of Vermeersch, who stated that a real necessity exists when there is no other way of obtaining the good desired. [12]

A further provision, namely, that there be no diminution of divine worship or inconvenience to the people, is also required for the valid use of the faculty. Certainly the transfer of a founded Mass which would deny the opportunity of daily Mass to a group of people or which would impose upon them unreasonable difficulties in assisting at Mass, would be an invalid transfer. However, the fact of the diminution of divine worship or of an imposed inconvenience is left to the judgment of the Ordinary, whose judgment is to be made with the fact in mind that any deliberate act contrary to this proviison in the faculty is an invalid act. The proportionate cause required in canon 84, § 1, is, in this regard, to be considered in the light of paragraph 2 of the same canon. [13] Obligations of Masses founded by legacies are excepted from the use of this faculty when they can be easily fulfilled in consequence of an increased stipend. Mere inconvenience on the part of the celebrant and other similar reasons are not sufficient causes fo rthe use of this faculty in the transfer of Mass obligations of this category.

---

[11] *Founded Masses According to the Code of Canon Law*, p. 78.

[12] *Epitome*, II, n. 936, p. 585; Keller, *Mass Stipends*, (The Catholic University of America Canon Law Studies, n. 27, Washington D. C.: The Catholic University of America, 1925), p. 77, lists as causes sufficient for the permanent transferral of founded Mass obligations; the danger of a haphazard celebration in one church along with the greater certitude of celebration in another church; the rejection of the foundation by the priest named in the will of the founder; the lack of priests; the expulsion of the religious from the church or the monastery where the Mass was founded.

[13] Canon 84, § 2: Dispensatio in dubio de sufficientia causae licite petitur et potest licite et valide concedi.

As in the faculty treated in Article 1 of this Chapter, an annual report of the satisfaction of the transferred Mass obligations is to be made to the diocesan curia.

Article 3

The Transfer of Surplus Mass Obligations.

> "Transferendi per quinquennium exuberantia Missarum onera etiam extra diocesim, cauto tamen ut quam maximus Missarum numerus intra fines dioecesis celebretur atque adamussim serventur praescripta Codicis Iuris Canonici circa cautelas adhibendas in Missis committendis."

The period of five years mentioned in this faculty is measured according to the norms of canon 34, § 3, 2°, a discussion of which is given in Article 1 of this Chapter.

The surplus Mass obligations are those which accrue from foundations, or result from offerings made for the benefit of a pious cause (*intuitu causae piae*) in such a manner that they are attached to a place, which involve conditions that prevent their transfer, which it is forbidden to transfer in view of some prohibition made by the Ordinary, or which have come into the possession of the Ordinary in keeping with the norm of canon 841. In other words, All Mass obligations which cannot be transferred according to the acts permitted by the Code of Canon Law [14] are potentially contained in the subject matter of this faculty.

Two provisions are required of the Ordinary in the use of the faculty, which provision, however, are not stated in such a manner as to pertain to the valid use of the faculty. [15] First, as many of the Masses as possible should be celebrated within the diocese, [16] and second, the provisions of the Code of Canon Law should be exactly observed in the transfer of Mass obligations and of the stipends attached to them. [17]

---

[14] Cf. canons 836; 838; 841.

[15] Cf. canon 39.

[16] Cf. canon 215, § 2.

[17] Canons 827; 839; 840, § 1 and § 2: Keller, *Mass Stipends*, pp. 145-152; Miller, *Founded Masses According to the Code of Canon Law*, p. 78.

Article 4

The Anticipation of Matins and Lauds in the Private Recitation of the Divine Office.

"Permittendi ut privata Matutini cum Laudibus recitatio anticipari possit ab hora prima post meridiem, quoties adsit rationabilis causa."

The obligation of reciting the Divine Office, incumbent upon all clerics in major orders except those who have been relieved of the obligation through the application of canons 213 or 214, is a daily obligation and therefore to be fulfilled each day according to the canonical notion of what constitutes a day as given in canon 32, § 1, [18] that is, 24 hours measured from midnight to midnight. The obligation is one of a private nature and required the private recitation of the prayers. Choral recitation is required of some religious orders, over and above the obligation of canon 135. [19] The anticipation of Matins and Lauds from two o'clock in the afternoon of the preceding day has been recognized as a privilege enjoyed by all in the private recitation of the Divine Office. [20]

The use of the faculty requires a reasonable and proportionate cause, which allows for almost any cause that is not merely fictitious or imaginary. Examples of sufficient causes include: anticipation for the sake of greater devotion, the duties of one's assignment such as studies, instructions, etc., or any cause which would result in the greater spiritual or corporal good either of the priest or of those committed to his care. [21]

The hour of one o'clock in the afternoon may be taken according to any of the several customs of the possible computation of time

[18] Canon 32, § 1: Dies constat 24 horis continuo supputandis a media nocte. Cf. Dube, *The General Principles for the Reckoning of Time in Canon Law*, The Catholic University of America Canon Law Studies, n. 144 (Washington, D. C.: The Catholic University of America Press, 1941), pp .127, 145 ff.

[19] Cf. canon 610, § 1 and § 3.

[20] S. R. C., decr., 12 maii 1905—*ASS*, XXVII (1905, 712; Gardellini, *Decreta Authentica Congregationis Sacrorum Rituum ex actis eiusdem collecta*, (3. ed., 4 vols., cum appendictibus, Romae: 1856-1887), n. 4158; (hereafter cited *Decret. Auth.*) Vermeersch, *Theologiae Moralis, Principia-Responsa-Consilia*, 3 ed., 4 vols., Romae, 1933-1937.

[21] Cf. Putzer, *Commentarium*, n. 173.

according to the rule given in canon 33, § 1.[22] The private recitation of the Divine Office is distinguished, in the faculty as in the canons, from the public recitation in choir, as is practiced in some religious orders. The obligation enacted in canon 135 is of a private nature, and similarly the faculty to anticipate Matins and Lauds is of a private nature. The faculty cannot be used to extend the privilege of anticipating to those who recite the Divine Office in choir. The recitation of the Divine Office by several persons in common does not necessarily constitute a choral recitation, and therefore, does not obstruct the use of this faculty.[23]

Article 5
The Alienation of Ecclesiastical Property

"Permittendi alienationem bonorum ecclesiasticorum usque ad summam capitalum 10,000 dollariorum pro Statibus Americae Foederatis et ditione Canadensi; et 15,000 *pesos* pro America Meridionali aliisque regionibus; hoc vero quatenus necessitas adsit et tempus non suppetat recurrendi ad S. Sedem, edocta, statim ac effecta fuerit alienatio, eadem S. Sede de alienatione ita peracta."

The alienation of ecclesiastical property may be understood either in the strict meaning of alienation, that is, as an act of completely relinquishing all right of ownership,[24] or in the broader sense, that is, as comprehending any transaction in which the rights of ownership are diminished or jeopardized to any extent.[25] The broader meaning of the term alienation is the meaning considered in the treatment of the subject in law, and hence is the sense in

---

[22] Cf. Dube, *The General Principles for the Reckoning of Time in Canon Law*, pp. 145 ff.

[23] Cf. Augustine, *Liturgical Law*, (St. Louis: Herder, 1931), p. 173.

[24] Heston, *The Alienation of Church Property in the United States*, The Catholic University of America Canon Law Studies, n. 132, (Washington, D. C.: The Catholic University of America Press), 1941, p. 69. (Hereafter cited *The Alienation of Church Property*.)

[25] Heston, *The Alienation of Church Property*, p. 70; Doheny, *Practical Problems in Church Finance*, (Milwaukee: The Bruce Publishing Co., 1941) pp. 21, 22; Vermeersch-Creusen, *Epitome*, II, n. 851, p. 596; Ayrinhac, *Administrative Legislation in The New Code of Canon Law* (New York: Banziger Brothers, 1930) n. 359. Hereafter cited *Administrative Legislation*.

which the term is to be understood in the text of the faculty, [26] that is, as comprehensive of any transaction in which the ownership enjoyed by the Church, or by any legitimately constituted body within the Church, may become less stable or jeopardized.

Ecclesiastical goods, as contemplated in the faculty, are to be interpreted according to the meaning given in canon 1497, § 1 and § 2, which defines ecclesiastical goods as temporal corporeal goods, whether movable or immovable, and also incorporeal, which belong to the universal Church, or to some juridical entity in the Church. Also included within the definition of ecclesiastical goods are those which are considered sacred by reason of their being destined for divine service through an act either of blessing or of consecration, and those which are regarded as precious by reason of their artistic, material or historical value.[27]

The faculty speaks of ecclesiastical goods in a capital sum (usque ad summam capitalem) that is, ecclesiastical property or goods which are invested or stably fixed in such a manner as to constitute part of the fixed holdings of the Church or of a moral person within the Church.[28] Thus, funds preserved in the accounts of the Church which are to be used in the ordinary maintenance and operation of the affairs of the Church are not considered as capital sums. It is only when these funds, or property, or the income of such holdings, become invested or fixed in such a manner as to contribute to the stability of the Church, that they are considered as capital sums and governed by the rules concerning alienation.[29]

The value of ecclesiastical property which the Ordinary may alienate in virtue of this faculty is, in the United States and Canada, ten thousand dollars. Authors writing *ex professo* on the subject of alienation are in agreement on the conclusion that the sum is

---

[26] Ferraris, *Prompta Bibliotheca*, s. v. *Alienatio*, art. III; Doheny, *Practical Problems in Church Finance*, p. 22.

[27] Canon 1497, § 1: Bona temporalia, sive corporalia, tum immobilia tum mobilia, sive incorporalia, quae vel ad Ecclesiam universam et ad Apostolicam Sedem vel ad alium in Ecclesia personam moralem pertineant, sunt bona ecclesiastica.

§ 2: Dicuntur sacra, quae consecratione vel benedictione ad divinum cultum destinata sunt; pretiosa, quibus notabilis valor sit, artis vel historiae vel materiae causa.

[28] Cf. Doheny, *Practical Problems in Church Finance*, pp. 40-66.

[29] Cf. Doheny, *loc. cit.*

expressed in gold dollars. As a consequence, the value is to be computed from the value of gold in relation to the dollar value which obtains under the present practice.[30] Considered in the light of this interpretation the ten thousand dollars permitted by the faculty becomes, in today's dollar, approximately sixteen thousand nine hundred and thirty-one dollars.[31] Although no direct response on the question has been given by the Holy See, responses on related matters indicate that the mind of the Holy See is in agreement with the principle stated above.[32] In view of the author's opinions and the responses of the Sacred Congregation, the computation of the sum named in the faculty in the equivalent value of gold dollars today is admissible in the use of the faculty, and does not constitute an extension of the terms, as is forbidden in canon 67. As a consequence, Ordinaries in the United States [33] are permitted, in virtue of this faculty, to alienate property up to the sum of sixteen thousand nine hundred thirty-one dollars and ninety cents, ($16,931.90) provided that the other provisions are fulfilled.[34]

---

[30] Heston, *The Alienation of Church Property*, p. 111; Doheny, *Practical Problems in Church Finance*, p. 42; "Church Finance and Problems of Alienation"—*The Jurist*, I (1941), 97-107; Ellis, "Triginta Millia Libellarum seu Francorum"-*Periodica*, XXVII (1938), 348-349; Ayrinhac, *Administrative Legislation*, n. 359.

[31] Doheny, (*Practical Problems in Church Finance*, p. 42, fn. 5) gives the actual reduction effected by President Roosevelt, by Presidential Decree, acting under the authority extended him by the National Emergency Act, January 31, 1934, which is from twenty-five and eight-tenths grains of gold, nine-tenths fine, to fifteen and five twenty-firsts grains. Although this decree is not permanent legislation, it is in effect at this writing. Any future change in the gold value of the dollar will affect the sum as contemplated by the faculty.

[32] S. C. Rel., Epist., 13 nov. 1936 (Private: communicated through the office of the Apostolic Delegate); cf. Bouscaren, *The Canon Law Digest*, II, canon 534, and Doheny, *Practical Problems in Church Finance*, p. 93; *S. C. de Prop. Fide*, 10 iul. 1920—Bouscaren, *op. cit.*, II, canon 1532; S. C. resol. 23 ian. 1923—*AAS*, XV, (1923), 513.

[33] The Canadian dollar is considered on a par with the dollar of the United States, cf. Ellis, "Triginta Millia Libellarum seu Francorum"—*Periodica*, XXVII (1938), 352-353.

[34] The interpretation of the term fifteen thousand *pesos*, which is the sum named for South America and other countries in which this faculty is issued, depends upon the specific country in which the faculty is to be used. Some countries use other units of exchange, e. g., Brazil uses the *cruzeiro;* Honduras, the *lempira;* and there is great variation among the others. The Sacred Congregation of the Council did not indicate the *peso* of any particular country. Until such a declaration is obtained, it seems that a safe norm of action is to consider, in South America and the other countries in which the faculty is issued, the fifteen thousand *pesos* as fifteen thousand

There are two provisions which seem to be required for the valid use of the faculty, since the text states that the Ordinary is permitted to alienate ecclesiastical property to the value of ten thousand dollars insofar as (*quatenus*) these provisions are present. The term *quatenus* implies in effect that the Ordinary possesses the faculty only when the provisions are fulfilled, and is therefore to be considered as a term equivalent to the *si* or *dummodo* of canon 39.

First, the transaction must be necessary (*necessitas adsit*), that is to say, a real necessity must be present. Such a necessity, or what may constitute a real necessity, is a variable factor and will depend upon the case and circumstances in question. A transaction to prevent financial loss to the Church would be a transaction implying a real necessity; it seems that transactions to improve or stabilize the position of the Church also contain sufficient necessity in themselves. Other reasons which may be considered as sufficient are to be judged by the Ordinary in the light of the particular case being considered.

Secondly, there must be insufficient time for recourse to the Holy See. In deciding whether or not there is sufficient time, the Ordinary must consider the urgency of the case and the length of time required for recourse to the Holy See.[35] The urgency of the case and the question of sufficient time for communication with the Holy See are closely related and interdependent matters, which are to be considered on their own merits in each single case.

An admonition is contained in the text of the faculty which required that the Holy See should immediately be notified of the transaction upon its completion (*statim ac effecta fuerit*). The notification is to be made upon the completion of the transaction; there is no requirement for the sending of notification that the negotiations have been begun. The length of the delay permitted in the use of the word *statim* by the Sacred Congregation is not determined by the Sacred Congregation. However, in view of the

units of the national currency in relation to their value in gold as determined by the government of that country. Ellis, ("Triginta Millia Libellarum seu Francorum"—*Periodica*, XXVII, 1938, 352-353) lists the value of the currencies of the various countries in which these faculties may be issued.

[35] The time for a response from the Holy See to a submitted application is computed as being from 40 to 50 days; cf. Article 2, Chapter VII of this work.

nature of the faculty and of the acts of alienation, it seems that any delay beyond a week is an abuse of the faculty. The word *statim* is used similarily in canon 204, § 2, in regard to the obligation of an inferior official to inform his superior of actions taken in a matter already referred to the superior. In both the canon and the faculty any reason for delay in reporting the acts are difficult to imagine, unless mere procrastination were a reason of itself. The inconvenience of the Ordinary does not seem a cause which could exist beyond the maximum period of a week. Notification is to be sent to the Sacred Congregation of the Council, the source of this faculty.

CHAPTER IX

FACULTIES FROM THE SACRED CONGREGATION OF RELIGIOUS

Introduction

Faculties issued by the Sacred Congregation of Religious are granted to the Ordinaries mentioned in canon 198, § 1, [1] and may be used in favor of any persons, either as a member of the religious institute or as seeking admission to the religious institute, [2] provided that the favor sought receives express mention in the text of the faculties. Jurisdiction concerning the subject matter of these faculties pertains to the Sacred Congregation of Religious by reason of the legislation of canon 251. Use of the faculties by an Ordinary requires that the Ordinary have that type of jurisdiction which is called non-judicial or voluntary in relation to the petitioner. [3] Thus, according to canon 201, § 3, an Ordinary may use the delegated power of these faculties for the benefits of his subjects, even though they or their subjects, or both, be outside the proper territory of the Ordinary. Use of the faculties for non-subjects renders invalid the acts of an Ordinary performed in virtue of these faculties, [4] unless the text of the respective faculty allows its use in favor of non-subjects.

What Ordinary is to be petitioned in any particular case is determined by the fact of whether or not the necessary bond of jurisdiction exists between the petitioner and the particular Ordinary. A multiplicity of Ordinaries in a given single case is possible. [5] In any particular case the jurisdiction of the Ordinary in regard to religious is governed by the rules of canon 500. [6] Numerous variations and

[1] Cf. Article 2, Chapter V.
[2] Cf. canon 538.
[3] Cf. canon 201, § 3.
[4] Cf. canon 201, § 1.
[5] Costello, *Domicile and Quasi-domicile*, The Catholic University of America Canon Law Studies, n. 60, (Washington, D. C.: The Catholic University of America, 1930), pp. 151-154.
[6] Canon 500, § 1: Subduntur quoque religiosi Ordinario loci, iis exceptis

exceptions occur in the law and are considered in the discussion of the individual faculties treated in this chapter, inasmuch as the rules and exceptions to the rules affect the matter concerned in the faculties and the relation of the subjects who may benefit from the faculties to various Ordinaries.

Article I

Dispensation from Illegitimacy.

> "Dispensandi, ad petitionem Superiorum, super illegitimitate natalium ad ingrediendum in Religionem, quatenus a Constitutionibus Instituti requiratur, dummodo ne agatur de prole sacrilego commercio orta, et dispensati ad munia maiora ne eligantur iuxta praescriptum canon 504."

Illegitimacy as such is not defined in the Code. It is a negative term which points to the status of those who do not possess the qualifications which in attendance at birth are necessary to endow them with a legitimate status. Legitimate children are those who are either conceived or born of a valid or of a putative marriage, unless the parents were, either in view of a solemn religious profession or of the reception of the sacrament of sacred orders, prohibited from the use of their previously contracted marriage at the time when the children were conceived.[7] Children are made legitimate by the subsequent marriage of their parents, provided that the parents were free to contract marriage at the time of conception, during the course of the gestation, or at the time of the children's birth,[8] by the radical sanation of the marriage of the parents,[9] or

qui a Sede Apostolica exemptionis privilegium consecuti sunt, salva semper potestate quam ius etiam in eos locorum Ordinariis concedit.

§ 2: Moniales quae sub iurisdictione Superiorum regularium ex praescripto constitutionum sunt, Ordinario loci subduntur tantum in casibus iure expressis.

§ 3: Nulla virorum religio sine speciali apostolico indulto potest sibi subditas habere religiosis Congregations mulierum aut earum religiosarum curam et directionem retinere sibi specialiter commendatam. Cf. Schaefer, *Compendium de Religiosis ad Normam Codicis Iuris Canonici*, (3, ed., Romae: S.A.L.E.R., 1940), n. 96, p. 91. (Hereafter cited *De Religiosis.*) Creusen-Garasche-Ellis, *Religious Men and Women in the Code*, (4. ed., Milwaukee: The Bruce Publishing Co., 1940), n. 53, p. 39; Capello, *Summa Iuris Canonici*, II, n. 575, p. 137.

[7] Cf. canon 1114.

[8] Cf. canon 1116.

[9] Cf. canon 1138, § 1.

by papal rescript or dispensation.[10] Solemn religious profession has the effect of removing the irregularity of illegitimacy in regard to the reception of sacred orders.[11]

Illegitimates, insofar as they are the subjects in whose favor this faculty may be used, are those who have not the requisites of legitimacy or legitimation reviewed above. Those made legitimate by the subsequent marriage of their parents according to canon 1116 are considered, as far as the canonical effects are concerned, equal to those legitimately born, unless the contrary is expressly stated. Hence, unless the constitutions of a society stated otherwise, persons legitimated by the subsequent marriage of their parents would not stand in need of dispensation by virtue of this faculty.[12]

Illegitimacy is not constituted as an impediment to the valid admission into a religious community by the Code of Canon Law,[13] and as a consequence the faculty is issued for the sake of making possible the granting of a dispensation from the impediment when constituted as such by the constitutions of the community. The text of the faculty states that dispensations may be granted to persons of illegitimate status upon the request of the superior. This does not mean, however, that such dispensations may be given without a sufficient cause. The principle of canon 84 seems applicable, and a proportionate cause is required for the grant of a dispensation. The constitutions of religious communities are given a canonical binding effect upon religious and their Superiors by canon 593, and therefore a cause proportionate to the gravity of the law seems required for a dispensation from the regulations of the constitutions. Causes which possibly could be admitted are: the small number of religious in the community, the especial qualities of the candidate, or similar reasons.

Since it is the Ordinary who performs the act of dispensing, it is he who must be acquainted with the cause and its urgency.[14] A statement of the reason for which the dispensation is being asked

[10] Cf. canon 1051; McDevitt, *Legitimacy and Legislation*, the Catholic University of America Canon Law Studies, n. 138, (Washington, D. C.: The Catholic University of America Press, 1941), pp. 51-56, 58-60.

[11] Cf. canon 984, 1°.

[12] Cf. canon 1117.

[13] Cf. canon 542, 1° and 2°.

[14] Cf. canon 84, § 1: in cases of doubtful causes, cf. § 2 of canon 84.

and why it is deemed necessary, and also an explanation of the urgency of the cause should be contained in the petition for the dispensation made by the superior.

Those persons who were conceived under the accompaniment of a sin of sacrilege on the part of their parents (*sacrilegi*) are explicitly excluded by the text of the faculty from the group of possible beneficiaries. *Sacrilegi* are those whose parents, one or both, were at the time of the conception of the child prevented from entering matrimony or deprived of its use in view either of solemn religious profession or, on the part of the father, of the possession of sacred orders.[15] A dispensation granted in virtue of this faculty to a person who exists as the offspring of a sin of sacrilege on the part of one or both of his or her parents is granted invalidly.[16]

The faculty permits the granting of a dispensation to illegitimates simply for their admission to a religious community; the legislation of canon 504 remains in effect as far as the dispensed person is concerned. It is stated in the faculty that the dispensation may be given provided that the recipient be not elected to any major office, a condition which pertains to the valid use of the faculty.[17]

Ordinaries may use this faculty in favor of any of those persons who are in need of dispensation, and who are within the jurisdiction of the Ordinary.[18] The text of the faculty speaks of entrance into a religious institute (*ad ingrediendum in Religionem*) and this is interpreted to mean admittance to profession.[19] Accordingly, the Ordinary of the person for whom the dispensation is sought will be determined in accord with the norms of canon 92.[20]

In view of the conditions attached to the faculty, it appears that dispensations granted in virtue of this faculty will be better suited to the purpose of the faculty if they are granted in writing. The conditions, such as the condition which states that the law of canon 504, remains in effect, may be stated in the rescript granting the

[15] Cf. canon 1114.

[16] Cf. canon 203, § 1.

[17] Cf. canon 504.

[18] Cf. canon 92, § 1 and § 2: Costello, *Domicile and Quasi-Domicile*, 151-154; Vermeersch-Creusen, *Epitome*, I, n. 217, p. 184.

[19] Cf. canon 48, 1° and 7°; 49.

[20] Novices may acquire a quasi-domicile in the place where they live during the novitiate. Cf. Vermeersch-Creusen, *Epitome*, I, n. 217, p. 184.

dispensation. The execution of a dispensation is properly to be effected in writing, and a record is to be preserved of the grant which was made.[21]

Article 2

Faculty Permitting the Conferral of the Privilege of Canon 821, § 3, on Churches of Religious not Mentioned in the Canon

> "Permittendi celebrationem trium Missarum de ritu in nocte Nativitatis D. N. I. C. in ecclesiis religiosorum non comprehensis in canon 821, § 3, cum facultate pro adstantibus ad S. Synaxim accedendi, ita tamen ut dictae tres Missae ab uno eodemque sacerdote celebrentur."

Canon 821, § 2, permits the celebration of Mass to begin at midnight on the Feast of the Nativity of Our Lord, provided that the Mass be a parochial or a conventual Mass.[22] Thus, the privilege is restricted to churches in which a parochial Mass[23] or a conventual Mass is to be celebrated.[24] All other churches are excluded. Paragraph 3 of canon 821[25] extends the privilege of the celebration of a midnight Mass on the Feast of the Nativity of Our Lord to religious and pious houses which have an oratory attached to them provided that the proper permission for the reservation of the Blessed Sacrament in the oratory has been granted. The canon excludes the churches (*ecclesiae*) of religious through its use of the term oratory (*oratorium*). This latter term cannot be interrupted as inclusive of churches.[26] Thus, the above-listed faculty makes possible in favor of the churches of religious which are not parochial or in which a conventual mass is not offered, the extension of the privilege which

---

[21] Cf. canons 56; 375, § 1.

[22] Canon 821, § 2: In nocte Nativitatis Domini inchoari media nocte potest sola Missa conventualis vel paroecialis, non autem alia sine apostolico indulto.

[23] Cf. canon 216, § 1 and § 3.

[24] Cf. canon 413, § 2.

[25] Canon 821, § 3: In omnibus tamen religiosis seu piis domibus oratorium habentibus cum facultate sanctissimam Eucharistiam habitualiter asservandi, nocte Nativitatis Domini, unus sacerdos tres rituales Missas vel, servatis servandis, unam tantum quae adstantibus omnibus ad praecepti quoque satisfactionem valeat, celebrare potest et sacram communionem petentibus ministrare.

[26] Cf. canons 1161; 1188, § 1.

is conferred by canon 821, § 3, on certain oratories of religious and pious houses.

The term church (*ecclesia*) as used in the text of the faculty is to be understood in the proper meaning of the term, that is, according to the definition given in canon 1161.[27] It is to be noted, however, that public oratories are included in the matter of the faculty in consequence of the legislation of canon 1191, § 1, according to which public oratories are governed by the law which applies to churches.

The use of the masculine form of the noun *religiosorum* does not limit the use of the faculty to churches of men religious. The term may include religious of both sexes.[28] As a consequence ,the faculty may be used in favor of the church of any religious community, provided that the other conditions are fulfilled. In the case, however, of the churches of women religious and men lay religious, the Masses will necessarily have to be celebrated by a priest, either the chaplain or someone else designated by the proper authority.

The nature of the favor granted in the use of this faculty seems to indicate that the privilege of the celebration of Mass beginning at midnight on the Feast of the Nativity of Our Lord is given to the church rather than to a person. The legislation of canon 821, § 3, is concerned simply with the celebration of the Mass in the oratories of religious, and not with the person who should be permitted to celebrate the Mass. The same may be said of this faculty. Who may make use of the privilege is not determined by the text of the faculty. Any priest who may be permitted to celebrate Mass in the churches concerned could, in view of the permission granted through the use of this faculty, offer the Christmas midnight Mass.[29]

Since the privilege is given to the place rather than to any particular person, an Ordinary is limited in the territorial extension of his jurisdiction when he invokes the use of this faculty. The privilege mentioned in the faculty may be conceded only to those churches which are within the territory of his jurisdiction.[30]

---

[27] Canon 1161: Ecclesiae nomine intelligitur aedes sacra divino cultui dedicata cum potissimum in finem ut omnibus Christifidelibus usui sit ad divinum cultum publice exercendum.

[28] Cf. canon 490.

[29] Cf. canons 802-813.

[30] Cf. canons 334, § 1; 352; 368, § 1; 323, § 1; 294, § 1, and 515, § 1.

The faculty requires that the same priest celebrate the three Masses offered. Three Masses *de ritu* are specified, that is, the three Masses of Christmas as found in the Roman Missal, celebrated according to the rubics of the Missal. The three Masses of the Feast of the Nativity of Our Lord are to be celebrated; 1) beginning after midnight; 2) at dawn; and 3) during the day after the recitation of Tierce, that is, in regard to Conventual Masses which are celebrated as part of the Office of the day.[31]

Thus, according to the rubics of the Missal the three Masses are to be offered separately, that is, at three different times during the Feast of the Nativity, and not all three together at midnight, nor at any other hour during the day. It may be concluded, it seems, that the words of the faculty, *"permittendi celebrationem trium Missarum de ritu"*, . . . do not mean that the priest is obliged to celebrate three Masses at midnight, but rather that he may, by the permission granted, celebrate the three Masses at midnight rather than at the times indicated in the rubics. It may be reasoned then that the priest may celebrate at midnight one or two of the three Masses, and then may celebrate the remaining Mass or Masses sometime during the day.[32] This is the notion conveyed by the text of canon 821, § 3, in regard to the celebration of the Masses of Christmas in oratories of religious and pious houses. The canon permits the celebrant to offer all three of the Masses or only one of them. If but one of the Masses is celebrated at midnight, it should be the Mass designated *in nocte* in the Roman Missal.[33]

In the event that the celebrant belong to a rite other than that of the religious who have charge of the church, the priest should

---

[31] Cf. Missale Romanum, (editio III juxta typicam Vaticanam amplificata I, Benziger Brothers, Inc.,: Neo Eboraci, 1944) :*Rubricae Generales Missae*. Tit., XV, n. 4.

[32] Cf. Canon 821, § 2: Vermeersch-Creusen, *Epitome*, II, n. 97. p. 62: Prummer, *Manuale Iuris Canonici* (4 ed., Friburgi-Brisgoviae: Herder, 1927), q 291.

[33] S. R. C., *Ordinis Carthusianorum*, 19 iun. 1875; S. R. C., *Calaguritana et Calceaten*, 13 febr. 1892, ad XXI—*Decreta Authentica Congregationis Sacrorum Rituum ex Actis Euisdem Collecta Eiusque Auctoritate Promulgata sub Auspiciis SS. Domini Nostri Leonis Papae* XIII (5 vols. cum 2 Appendicibus, Romae: Ex Typographia Polyglotta S. C. de Propaganda Fide, 1898-1901; Appendix II, 1927), nn. 3354; 3767, (hereafter cited *S. R. C. Decret. Auth.*); Le Vavasseur-Haegy-Stergy, *Manuel de Liturgie et Ceremonial*, Selon le Rit Romain, (16. ed., 2 vols., Paris: Librairie Lecaffne, J. Gabalda, 1935-1936), II, 262, p. 222. (Hereafter cited *Manuel.*)

celebrate the Masses according to his own rite, but according to the calendar or order of the church.[34]

As in canon 821, § 3, permission to receive Holy Communion is extended to all those who assist at the Masses. No one of the Masses is specified as that at which Holy Communion should be distributed, this matter being left to the convenience of the celebrant. Distribution of Holy Communion is possible, however, at all of the Masses. The legislation of canon 1249 indicates that assistance at midnight Masses celebrated according to the terms of this faculty fulfills the precept of assisting at Mass on the Feast of the Nativity of Our Lord.

Article 3

Dispensation from Advanced Age.

> "Dispensandi super aetatis excessu pro admittendis ad habitum religiosum quatenus a Constitutionibus Instituti requiratur, praevio, in singulis casibus, consensu Superiorissae Generalis, vel Provincialis et respectivi Consilii, dummodo postulantes aetatem 40 annorum ne excesserint et polleant caeteris qualitatibus requisitis."

This faculty is concerned with the impediment of excessive age (*aetatis excessu*) insofar as excessive age is made an impediment to admission by the constitutions of a religious institute for women religious. The faculty uses the words *ad habitum religiosum* to indicate that the faculty may be used for those seeking admission to the novitiate, since it is at the admission to the novitiate that the candidate first receives the religious habit.[35] It is true that an indication of the type of dress which should be worn by postulants prior to their entering the novitiate is made in canon 540, § 2.[36] There seems little doubt, however, that the term *habitum* used in the faculty refers to the *habitus* mentioned in canon 553. The dress recommended for postulants is not designated as a religious habit in the Code of Canon Law.

---

[34] Missale Romanum, *Additiones et Variationes in Rubricis Missalis*, Tit. IV, n. 6.

[35] Canon 553: Novitiatus incipit susceptione habitus, vel alio modo in constitutionibus praescripto.

[36] Canon 540, § 2: Postulantes vestem induant modestam ac diversam a veste novitiorum.

Further support for the conclusion that the admission to the novitiate is the admission spoken of in the faculty is added by the use of the word *postulantes*. The term *postulantes* is used in the text of the faculty as referring to the petitioners for the dispensation, the granting of which is permitted by the faculty. Thus, the Sacred Congregation of Religious implies that those who seek the dispensations are postulants, that is, those who are preparing to enter the novitiate.

The use of the word Superioress (*Superiorissae Generalis*) by the Sacred Congregation of Religious indicates that this faculty is to be used in favor of women religious only. The use of the masculine form of the word could include religious of both sexes; [37] the converse, however, does not seem admissible. The norm of Canon 490, applicable here by way of contrast, limits the term of the Superiors of women religious.

An Ordinary may, then, by virtue of this faculty, dispense his subjects from the impediment of excessive age, when excessive age is made an impediment to admission to religion by the constitutions of an institute. The dispensation should be petitioned from an Ordinary who is competent in the matter, that is, who has the necessary jurisdiction in regard to any single subject. In regard to postulants, the Ordinary with the needed jurisdiction is determined by the rule of canon 94, § 1, and thus there may be several Ordinaries who enjoy competence. Any Ordinary who has jurisdiction over the postulants petitioner, by reason either of domicile or of quasi-domicile, can then dispense the postulant from the impediment for the purpose of entering into religion ,whether the act of entering religion is to be performed within or outside his territory. In cases wherein the condition of obtaining a quasi-domicile are fulfilled by the postulancy, the Ordinary of the place of postulancy has the necessary jurisdiction for the use of this faculty. [38]

The faculty is issued to Ordinaries to allow them to dispense from the impediment of excessive age when, in each case, the consent of the respective Superioress General or Provincial and her Council has been obtained. This consent of the Superiors of the community

[37] Cf. canon 490.

[38] Cf. canon 92, § 2.

appears necessary for the valid use of the faculty.[39] The necessity of the consent of the Superiors follows also from the rule of canon 543, which gives to them the exclusive right of admitting persons to their respective communities.

Two conditions are placed which pertain to the valid use of the faculty.[40] The candidate must not be more than forty years of age, that is to say, she must not have completed her fortieth year. Hence, a dispensation may be given to a candidate up to midnight of the fortieth birthday anniversary; after midnight of the fortieth birthday anniversary the fortieth year is considered completed.[41] In addition to the above mentioned requisite, the candidate must have the other qualities of a prospective novice.[42] A candidate who has been dispensed because of the lack of one or some of the qualities necessary in a candidate, it appears, could not be the recipient of a dispensation from the impediment of excessive age by virtue of this faculty. The condition of possessing the other requisites for admission to the novitiate is a positive one and pertains to the valid use of the faculty.

Provision for the fulfillment of the conditions as stated in the text of the faculty may be contained in the rescript granting the dispensation. This presumes that a written form is used in the grant, which procedure seems the more desirable in view of the nature of the matter concerned. Execution of the dispensation, given in a written form, should be effected in writing and hence recorded.[43]

Article 4

Dispensation from the Canonical Age Required for the Reception of the Priesthood

"Dispensandi, etiam pro religiosis exemptis, super defectu aetatis canonicae ad S. Ordinem presbyteratus, scilicet:

a) super eiusdem defectu usque ad duodecim menses, dummodo ordinandi a suis Superioribus litteras dimissoriales acceperint et ceteras habeant qualitates a sacris

[39] Cf. canon 105, 1°.

[40] Cf. canon 39.

[41] Cf. canon 34, § 3, 3°.

[42] Cf. canons 538; 542, 1° and 2°; and other requirements that may be included in the constitutions of the institute to which the candidate seeks admission.

[43] Cf. Article 1 of this Chapter.

canonibus requisitas ac praesertim curriculum theologicum expleverint ad normam canonis 976, § 2, C. I. C.;
b) super eodem defectu etiam ultra duocecim menses at non ultra sexdecim, dummodo alumni ne gaudeant vel indigeant alia apostolica dispensatione, servatisque ceteris conditionibus, ut sub lit. a)."

The canonical age required in candidates for the reception of the sacred order of the priesthood is twenty-four completed years, as expressed in canon 975.[44] The faculty here listed may be used only in favor of religious who are candidates for the priesthood, but its favor may be extended also to exempt religious. Jurisdiction over the sacrament of Holy Orders, insofar as the reception of orders by candidates other than religious is concerned,[45] pertains to the competency of the Sacred Congregation of the Sacraments. In regard to members of religious societies, competency is exclusively enjoyed by the Sacred Congregation of Religious.[46]

Dispensation from the lack of canonical age when granted by virtue of this faculty may be given for the reception of the priesthood only; the diaconate and subdiaconate are not included. Neither does the faculty confer the power of dispensing from the requirement that the candidate must have completed his prescribed course in theology; rather, the completion of the course is made a condition, under pain of invalidity, for the use of the faculty.[47]

1. The Faculty of a)

The canonical age from which a candidate for the priesthood may be dispensed in the use of this faculty is stated in canon 975 as twenty-four completed years (*vicesimum quartum completum*). Hence without a dispensation a candidate may licitly receive ordination to the priesthood, all other conditions being fulfilled, any time following midnight of his twenty-fourth birthday anniversary, since

[44] Canon 975: Subdiaconatus ne conferatur ante annum vicesimum primum completum; diaconatus ante vicesimum secundum completum; presbyteratus ante vicesimum quartum completum.

[45] In regard to Oriental Catholics, Cf. Chapter V, Article 2, of this work.

[46] Cf. canon 251, § 1; Coetus Peculiaris S. R. E. Cardinalium, resp. 24 mar. 1919-*AAS*, XI (1919), 251; Bouscaren, *The Canon Law Digest*, I. Canon 251.

[47] Cf. canons 39; 976, § 2.

his age, computed according to canon 34, § 3, 3°, is twenty-four completed years at that time. This faculty permits dispensation from any discrepancy up to twelve months, considered according to the calendar.[48] The mention of two conditions necessary for the valid use of the faculty follows the word *dummodo* in the text.[49] The first of these is that the candidate who belongs to an exempt clerical institute receive dismissorial letters from his superior.[50] Secondly, the candidate must have all other requirements that are stated in the Code of Canon Law.[51]

The text of the faculty reads that the candidate must have these canonical requisites *habeant qualitates a sacris canonibus requisitas.* This seems to indicate that a candidate who lacks any of the canonical requisites is excluded from benefitting through the use of this faculty, even though he may have received a dispensation relaxing the law in his particular case. A dispensation is the relaxation of the law in a particular case; it is not to be understood as supplying a defect.[52] It could be argued that the canonical requisites have been reduced in the case of a candidate who has received a dispensation because of a lack of one or more of the requisites determined in the Code of Canon Law. But such reasoning could make a dispensation equivalent to removal of the law. The dispensation is rather a relaxation of it.[53]

A candidate whose ordination is impeded by the presence of an irregularity or an impediment, but who possesses the positive requirements stated in canon 974, does not appear to be excluded from benefitting through the application of this faculty, provided that

---

[48] Cf. canon 34, § 3, 1°: even though "twelve months" *(duodecim menses)* is used in the text of the faculty rather than the word "year", it appears that the rule of canon 32, § 2, does not apply, since there is an implicit indication of the *terminus a quo* required by canon 34, § 3. Therefore, the computation of twelve months as 360 days is not required, and the term is to be considered as twelve calendar months, or one year, transpiring between the twenty-third and twenty-fourth birthday anniversaries of the candidate.

[49] Cf. canon 39, regarding the force of this word as used in rescripts.

[50] Cf. canons 993, 5°; 995, § 1; 964, 2°, 3° and 4°.

[51] Cf. canon 974; S. C. de Rel., instr., 1 dec. 1931—*AAS*, XXIV, (1932), 74; Bouscaren, *The Canon Law Digest*, I, canon 973; Gallagher, *The Examination of the Qualities of the Ordinand,* The Catholic Uniersity of America Canon Law Studies, n. 195, (Washington, D. C.: The Catholic University of America Press, 1944), pp. 99-112.

[52] Cf. canon 80.

[53] Van Hove, *De Privilegiis, De Dispensationibus*, n. 322, p. 304.

proper action is taken by way of dispensing from the irregularity or the impediment. The irregularities and impediments are stated in such a way by the Code of Canon Law as to point to negative rather than to positive requirements in the candidate, that is, they must simply be absent. For example, the Code does not state that a candidate must have been a partner in but one marriage; it simply states that he must not have been a partner in more than one marriage. This distinction between the positive and the negative requirements in the candidate is borne out by the text of paragraph b) of the faculty, the discussion of which will follow.

Especially emphasized in the faculty is the requisite of the completion of the prescribed course in theology.[54] Canon 976 states that the priesthood is not to be conferred until after the middle of the fourth year of the theological course (*post medietatem eiusdem quarti anni*). The fulfillment of this condition pertains to the valid use of the faculty.[55] The computation of the middle of that scholastic term depends upon both the progress of the course and the passage of time.[56] Hence the middle of the fourth year is computed from the point of view of studies completed and time transpired. Three and one-half years must have elapsed from the day upon which the course in theology was begun.[57] For example, a person who commenced the course in theology on September 15, 1947, could not be ordained, without special consideration, before three and one-half years later, that is, March 16, 1951.[58]

If the candidate's twenty-third birthday anniversary occurred on March 15th, 1951, he could be dispensed, provided all other conditions were fulfilled, from the lack of canonical age any time after midnight of the 15th of March, 1951, that is on March 16th. During the elapsed time of three and one-half years the candidate must have completed at least three and one-half years of the four year theology course.[59] The completion of the three and one-half

[54] Cf. canons 976, § 2; 1365, § 2.
[55] Cf. canon 39.
[56] Cf. canon 1365, § 2.
[57] It is not permitted to understand that the term "year" as used in canon 976, § 2, as meaning the academic year, exclusive of vacation periods, that is, as nine months spent in following the course in theology—S. C. Consist., 24 mar. 1911—*Fontes*, n. 2081.
[58] Cf. canon 34, § 3, 3°.
[59] The matter to be covered during the course is under the jurisdiction of

years in the theological study may certainly be considered as accomplished after the lectures of the second semester of the fourth year have begun. It seems that it is also tenable that the middle of the year has been passed when the examinations of the first semester, half term, have been completed. Use of the faculty during the period of the mid-term examinations, or before the mid-term examinations have been given, even though the lectures of the first semester have been completed, does not seem permissible in view of the wording of canon 976, § 2. The canon uses the words "after the mid-term" (*post medietatem eiusdem quarti anni*). This stage is not reached until the student has been found to have completed the first semester of work to the satisfaction of his professors, which fact is determined with at least the aid of mid-term examinations.

The conditions for the use of the faculty of paragraph a) may then be stated thus: the candidate must have completed, to the satisfaction of his professors, who in turn are responsible to the candidate's superiors, three and one-half of the academic years of theological study; and three and one-half years of time computed according to the calendar must have transpired since the candidate's entrance into the theological course. If these two conditions are fulfilled, and if all other requirements on the part of the law and of the faculty are satisfactorily complied with, then the faculty may be used both licitly and validly.

The Faculty of b)

Paragraph b) of the faculty, under the same conditions as required by paragraph a), permits the granting of a dispensation from the lack of canonical age up to and including a discrepancy of sixteen months. Thus, a candidate must have dismissorial letters from his superior, must have spent three and one-half calendar years in the study of theology, and must have completed three one one-half years of the specified course in theological study. In regard to the possession of the canonical requisites the faculty states that in addition to the requirements of paragraph a) the candiate must neither have, nor need, any apostolic dispensation in addition to the one granted in virtue of this faculty. In this requirement the faculty

---

the Sacred Congregation of Seminaries and Universities, the competency of which is set forth in canon 256, § 1.

differs from that contained in paragraph a). The phrase *alia apostolica dispensatione* is all-inclusive; it points to all other dispensations that the candidate may either have received or stand in need of receiving.

The computation of the sixteen months' period follows the same rules as indicated in the faculty of paragraph a) for the computation of the twelve months' period.[60] This is more easily demonstrated by the use of an example. Sixteen months prior to the candidate's twenty-fourth birthday anniversary is the possible date of the dispensation. Thus a candidate who has as his birthday anniversary February 29th could be dispensed, all other conditions being fulfilled, from the lack of canonical age by the use of this faculty, any time following October 29th, that is, on October 30th of the year following his twenty-second birthday anniversary. He must be at least twenty-two years and eight months old.

The faculties contained in both paragraphs a) and b) may be used in favor of all candidates seeking ordination to the priesthood who are religious according to the norms of Canon Law.[61] In each particular case, however, the dispensation must be granted by the Ordinary having the necessary jurisdiction over the petitioner. The privilege of exemption, as enjoyed by some religious, is duly taken into account in the terms of the faculty, *etiam pro religiosis exemptis,* . . . Thus, the Ordinary of the place is the Ordinary who should be petitioned for dispensations which are granted in virtue of this faculty.[62]

In view of the conditions attached to the use of the faculty, e. g., the completion of the course in theology, and the prescription of canon 1010, § 1,[63] concerning the records to be preserved in regard to the ordination of candidates, it seems that the dispensations granted in virtue of this faculty should be issued in the written form.

[60] Cf. canon 34, § 3, 3°.

[61] Canon 488, § 1: In canonibus qui sequuntur, veniunt nomine: 7° Religiosorum, qui vota nuncuparunt in aliqua religione . . . .

[62] Canon 500, § 1: Subduntur quoque religiosi Ordinario loci, iis exceptis qui a Sede Apostolica exemptionis privilegium consecuti sunt, salva semper potestate quen ius etiam in eos locorum Ordinariis concedit.

[63] Canon 1010, § 1: Expleta ordinatione, nomina singulorum ordinatorum ac ministri ordinantis, locus et dies ordinationis notentur in peculiari libro in Curia loci ordinationis diligenter custodiendo, et omnia singularum ordinationum documenta accurate serventur.

The execution of the dispensations should be effected in writing, that is, a notation of their execution should be preserved according to the norm of canon 56.

Article 5
Dispensation from the Want of Dowry

"Dispensandi super dotis defectu cum monialibus et sororibus in toto vel in parte, dummodo status oeconomicus Instituti detrimentum ne patiatur et postulantes talibus sint praeditae qualitatibus, ut eas magnae utilitati Instituto fore certa spes habeatur."

All prospective nuns or sisters who are obliged to furnish a dowry on entering religious institute and have not been exempted from the obligation may be the recipients of dispensations granted in virtue of this faculty. Women entering religion may be required either by the constitutions of the community or by the Code of Canon Law to present to the institute a dowry.[64]

The *moniales* spoken of in the above mentioned canon are defined in canon 488, 7°.[65] Canon 547 states that the dowry is due from nuns at the time of their entrance into the postulancy. The *sorores* spoken of in the faculty are women religious of simple vows, as defined in canon 488, 7°.[66] In respect to congregations of sisters, the prescriptions of the constitutions of their respective institutes are to be followed in regard to the obligation of presenting a dowry.[67]

The jurisdiction necessary on the part of an Ordinary in relation to the person for whom the dispensation is petitioned is determined by the prescription of canon 94, § 1. In the consideration there may

---

[64] Canon 547: In monasteriis monialium postulans afferat dotem in constitutionibus statutam aut legitima consuetudine determinatam.

[65] Canon 488, 7°: . . . *monialium,* religionis votorum sollemnium aut, nisi ex rei natura vel ex contextu sermonis aliud constet, religiosae quarum vota ex instituto sunt sollemnia, sed pro aliquibus locis ex Apostolicae Sedis praescripto sunt simplicia.

Most of the nuns in the United States are permitted simple vows by Apostolic Indult.

[66] Canon 488, 7°: . . . : *sororum,* religiosae votorum simplicium, ...

[67] In the case of institutes of diocesan approval, the Ordinary can dispense from the obligation of the dowry without the powers conceded in this faculty. Cf. canon 548, § 4.

be more than one Ordinary possessing the necessary jurisdiction, as is described in Article 1 of this Chapter. Postulants from whom the dowry is required in Orders of nuns do not enjoy the privilege of exemption enjoyed by the institute.[68]

The dowry of women religious is defined as a certain capital entrusted to the institute by a new member so that the revenue of the dowry may serve for her support. It may consist either of a sum of money or of a quantity of other goods.[69] The presence of these together with the fact that the candidate is unable to provide the dowry in some given case lend the occasion for calling the faculty into use. Primarily the reception of the candidate without a dowry must not be detrimental to the financial and economic status of the institute. This condition answers to the purpose of the law which requires a dowry in support of the candidate during her life in religion.

The second condition is that the candidate be of such a type that her particular qualifications give certain promise of her future great service (*magnae utilitati*) to the institute. Verification of this condition depends upon the needs of the institute considered in the light of the work the institute is engaged in, and on an examination of the qualities of the candidate.

The obligation of determining the existence of the above mentioned condition rests with the Ordinary who issues the dispensation, since it is his obligation, as a delegate, to avoid actions which exceed the terms of this delegation.[70] The rights of an Ordinary with respect to the temporal administration of the goods of institutes of women religious of pontifical approval are somewhat restricted.[71] However, in view of the conditions placed in the faculty, and of the gravity of those conditions as set therein, it

---

[68] Cf. canon 615; Creusen-Garasche-Ellis, *Religious Men and Women in the Code*, n. 310, p. 235.

[69] Kealy, *Dowry of Women Religious*, The Catholic University of America Canon Law Studies, n. 134, (Washington, D. C.: The Catholic University of America Press, 1941), pp. 60-70; Schaefer, *De Religiosis*, n. 228, p. 500; Creusen-Garasche-Ellis, *Religious Men and Women in the Code*, n. 184, p. 143.

[70] Cf. canon 203, § 1.

[71] Cf. Farrell, *The Rights and Duties of the Local Ordinary Regarding Congregations of Women Religious of Pontifical Approval*, The Catholic University of America Canon Law Studies, n. 128, (Washington, D. C.: The Catholic University of America Press, 1941), 138.

seems that the Ordinary has the duty, and consequently the right, to require of the Superioress the information necessary to determine whether or not the conditions are being violated.[72]

Dispensations granted in virtue of this faculty, as is apparent from the text of the faculty and the conditions mentioned therein, are more appropriately granted in writing. Mention of the conditions and of their effect on the validity of the dispensation may be made in the rescript which grants the dispensation. When the dispensation is granted, its execution should be effected in writing, and the proper notation of the dispensation recorded in the curia.[73]

Article 6
The Approval of the Fourth and Fifth Term for Confessors of Religious

> "Confirmandi confessarium ad quartum et quintum triennium, dummodo maioris partis religiosarum, convocatis etiam iis, quae in allis negotiis ius non habent ferendi suffragium, consensus capitulariter ac per secreta suffragia praestandus prius accedat, proviso pro dissentientibus, si quae sint ac velint."

This faculty extends to the fourth and fifth terms of the same ordinary confessor of women religious[74] the permissibility of extension provided for in canon 526 in regard to the second and third terms.[75] The canon and the faculty differ in that the faculty does not include, as does the canon, as a reason for its use the scarcity of priests. However, since the granting of a dispensation from the common law of the Church requires a just and proportionate cause, it seems that the condition of the scarcity of suitable priests, or an

---

[72] Vigilance on the part of the Ordinary in regard to the administration of the temporal goods in congregations of women religious of pontifical approval is required by canon 535; cf. Farrell, *loc. cit.*

[73] Cf. canons 56; 375, § 1.

[74] Cf. canon 520, § 1.

[75] Canon 526: Religiosarum confessarius ordinarius suum munus ne exerceat ultra triennium; Ordinarius tamen eum ad secundum, imo etiam ad tertium triennium confirmare potest, si vel ob sacerdotum ad hoc officium idoneorum penurium aliter providere nequeat, vel maior religiosarum pars, earum quoque quae in aliis negotiis ius non habent ferendi suffragium, in eiusdem confessarii confirmationem, per secreta suffragis, convenerit; dissentientibus tamen, si velint, aliter providendum est.

equivalent proportionately grave cause, must also be attendant upon the use of the faculty, it is difficult to concede that the will of the majority of the religious community, expressed by secret vote, is a sufficient reason for the use of the faculty.[76]

The faculty is concerned with the extension of the number of terms of office or the ordinary confessor, it cannot be interpreted as permitting the dispensation from the requirements of the Code of Canon Law in regard to the ordinary confessors of religious. For example ,the provisions of canon 524, § 1, in regard to the qualities of priests designated as confessors of religious must be complied with; a dispensation from these provisions cannot be granted in virtue of this faculty.[77]

The faculty requires the favorable majority of the community, which majority is to be obtained in secret vote of all the persons concerned, even those who do not ordinarily have the right of voting. This requirement pertains to the valid use of the faculty.[78] The majority is to be obtained by a secret vote (*secreta suffragia*) of the members of the community meeting together (*convocatis*) prior to the reappointment of the confessor.

The faculty is clear in its statement of what is meant by the majority required and the manner in which it is to be obtained. The majority must be computed according to the number of religious in the community. Thus, in a community of twenty persons, including those who do not ordinarily have a vote in the affairs of the community, a majority is eleven. An absolute majority is all that is required.[79]

The faculty does not state that all must meet together; it states rather that all must be called. Thus, if some were unable to meet with the group because of sickness or for some other legitimate reason, their absence would not affect the vote taken, provided that an absolute majority of the number of religious in the community concurred in the voting. The construction, *convocatis etiam iis, quae in aliis negotiis ius non habent ferendi suffragium,* is inserted in way of explanation of the preceding terms, *maioris partis religiosarum,* and in that manner is included within the condition. Hence,

[76] Cf. canon 84, § 1.
[77] Cf. canons 203, § 1; 67.
[78] Cf. canon 39.
[79] Cf. canon 101, § 1, 1°.

the fact that not all the members of the community were present when the vote was taken does not result in the invalid use of the faculty.

However, the requisites subsequently stated, namely, that the vote be taken in a meeting (*capitulariter*), and that the vote be taken secretly, pertain to the valid use of the faculty, since these, considered in the structure of the text, are included in the condition expressed by the *dummodo* clause, that a major part of all those living in the community be in agreement. Thus, these requirements are governed by the *dummodo* of the text, and according to canon 39 pertain to the valid use of the faculty.

The faculty further insists that provision must be made for those who dissent in the voting, if there are dissenters, and if these wish that such provision be made. This part of the faculty repeats the prescript of canon 526 in this regard, but compliance with the preceptive norm is not a factor postulated for the valid use of the faculty.[80]

Use of the faculty is restricted to the appointment of confessors for women religious (*religiosarum*).[81] It may be used by those Ordinaries who receive it and who have the duty according to canon 525 of appointing confessors to communities of women religious.

Article 7

Permission to Celebrate Mass on Holy Thursday in the Houses of Religious

"Permittendi celebrationem SS. Missae Sacrificii Feria V in Coena Domini, facta licentia personis habitualiter in communitate commorantibus sese reficiendi S. Synaxi, etiam ad adimplendum praeceptum paschale."

The text of this faculty restricts its use to the permitting of the celebration of Holy Mass on Holy Thursday; hence it cannot be extended to include the other liturgical functions of Holy Week.[82] The celebration of Mass on Holy Thursday is part of the liturgical

[80] Cf. canon 39: the ablative absolute, *proviso pro dissentientibus*, is independent of the *dummodo clause*. Cf. Van Hove, *De Rescriptis*, n. 137, p. 123.

[81] Cf. canon 67.

[82] Cf. canon 67.

functions of Holy Week, and the celebration of these functions is reserved to cathedrals, parochial or quasi-parochial and conventual churches.[83] Celebration of Holy Mass alone on Holy Thursday is not allowed except by reason of permission such as the permission extended in the use of this faculty.[84]

The permission which can be made available through the use of the faculty may be extended to religious only; the jurisdiction of the Sacred Congregation of Religious is limited, and as a consequence so are the faculties issued by that Congregation.[85] Although the text of the faculty does not state to whom the permission is to be issued ,yet, inasmuch as the restrictions placed on the functions of Holy Week relate to places rather than to persons, it follows that this permission is granted to the Religious house rather than to the priest acting as celebrant. This is to say that the granted permission may be enjoyed by any priest who is permitted to offer Mass. The use of the faculty, in view of the jurisdiction of the Sacred Congregation of Religious, has respect to the place where the Mass may be celebrated. This place is interpreted to be the oratory or the non-conventual church of a religious house. The application of the faculty does not imply a dispensation from the prescript of canon 822, § 1.[86]

Permission to celebrate Mass on Holy Thursday, when granted by virtue of this faculty, includes the permission for those who live habitually in the community to receive Holy Communion, even for the purpose of fulfilling the Paschal precept.[87] The clause *facta licentia* appears in effect to be a restriction placed upon the Ordinary by which he is prevented from exercising his power of not permitting the distribution of Holy Communion, as conceded to the Ordinary in canon 869.[88] Thus, the extension of the privilege of

---

[83] S. R. C., Gortitien, 4 sept. 1875; S. R. C., *Vicariatus Apostolici Victoriae Nyanzensis*, 19 apr. 1890—S. R .C. *Decret. Auth.* nn. 3366; 3724. Cf. Augustine, *Liturgical Law*, 26; Fortescue-O'Connell, *The Ceremonies of the Roman Rite Described* (5. ed., London: Burns, Oates, and Washborne, Ltd., 1934), p. 302.

[84] Cf. Augustine, *Liturgical Law*, p. 27.

[85] Cf. canon 251.

[86] Canon 822, § 1: Missa celebranda est super altare consecratum et in ecclesia vel oratorio consecrato aut benedicto ad normam iuris, salvo praescripto canon 1196.

[87] Cf. canon 859, § 1, § 2 and § 3.

[88] Canon 869: Sacra communio distribui potest ubicunque Missam cele-

celebrating Holy Mass on Holy Thursday does not, in virtue of this faculty, permit the Ordinary to exercise the power which under other circumstances is conceded to him in canon 869.

Nothing is said in the faculty concerning the hour of the celebration of the Mass or of the distribution of Holy Communion. Canon 867, § 4, states that Holy Communion should be distributed during those hours when Mass may be celebrated, unless a reasonable cause exists for distribution at another hour.[89] The rubrics of the Mass for Holy Thursday, however, indicate that the distribution of Holy Communion is to take place following the reception of Holy Communion by the celebrant.[90] Hence, while the distribution of Holy Communion may ordinarily be effected at other times than in connection with the celebration of the Mass, it seems that the prescription of the rubics in relation to the Mass as offered on Holy Thursday must be observed; the faculty contains no dispensation from those rules.

The text of the faculty reads *permittendi,* rather than *dispensandi,* as is found in the other faculties from this Congregation. The use of this term indicates that permission is given to act contrary to the general rule rather than that a relaxation is granted of the general rule in a particular case. Thus a privilege is granted rather than a dispensation. For this reason the cause as demanded in canon 84, § 1, does not seem necessary in the use of this faculty. Further, the privilege may be granted for an indefinite period, even perpetually. Loss of the faculty by the grantor, or the expiration of the faculty, does not terminate the concession, unless a provision in that regard had been made.[91]

The powers of this faculty may be used by an Ordinary (or his delegates) who has received the Quinquennial Faculties and has houses of religious within his jurisdiction. Jurisdiction over the territory rather than over the persons is required, since the faculty

---

brare licet, etiam in oratorio privato, nisi loci Ordinarius, iustis de causis, in casibus particularibus id prohibuerit.

[89] Canon 867, § 4: Sacra communio iis tantum horis distribuantur, quibus Missae sacrificium offerri potest, nisi aliud rationabilis causa suadeat.

[90] Missale Romanum, *Feria V. in Voena Domini.*

[91] Canon 73: Resoluto iure concedentis, privilegia non extinguuntur, nisi data fuerint cum clausula: *ad beneplacitum nostrum,* vel alia aequipollenti. Cf. Chapter V, Article 4, of this work.

concerns the place of celebration of Mass, rather than the person who may celebrate.

It is desirable that the granting of the privilege deriving from the use of this faculty be effected in writing in consideration of the rule of canon 79, especially if the privilege is extended for a number of years.[92] The burden of proof lies on the community, and a written concession greatly facilitates such proof.

Article 8

The Granting of Permission to Nuns to Go Into the Church for the Purpose of Decorating It

"Permittendi monialibus descensum in ecclesiam, ut ipsae eam maiori sollertia mundare et decorare possint, exeuntibus prius ab ecclesia extraneis omnibus, non exceptis ipsis confessario et monasterio inservientibus et extra claustra degentibus; portae illius claudantur et claves Superiorissae tradantur, moniales vero semper binae sint et porta, per quam aditus interior ad ecclesiam patet, duplici clavi claudatur, quarum una a Superiorissa, altera a sanctimoniali ab Ordinario deputanda custodiatur et non aperiatur nisi in casibus enunciatis et cum praescriptis cautelis."

This faculty may be used by Ordinaries having the proper jurisdiction according to canon 500, § 2 and § 3, in favor of those nuns who are bound by law or the papal cloister.[93] Nuns who by virtue of an apostolic indult have only simple vows in the United States, as considered in canon 488, 7°, are not bound by the law of the cloister and hence, do not stand in need of the favor granted through the application of this faculty.[94] The faculty may be used in favor

[92] Canon 79: Quamvis privilegia, oretenus a Sacta Sede obtenta, ipsi petenti in foro conscientiae suffragentur, nemo tamen potest cuiusvis privilegii usum adversus quemquam in foro externo vindicare, nisi privilegium ipsum sibi concessum esse legitime evincat. The principle applies also to privileges granted by an Ordinary.

[93] Canon 597, § 1: In domibus regularium sive virorum sive mulierum canonice constitutis, etiam non formatis, servetur clausura papalis; S. C. Rel., instr., 6 feb. 1924—*AAS*, XVI (1924), 96; Schaaf, *The Cloister*, The Catholic University of America Canon Law Studies, n. 13, (Washhington, D. C.: The Catholic University of America, 1921), p. 135.

[94] Com. Interp., 1 mart. 1921—*AAS*, XIII (1921), 177; Coronata, *Interpretio Authentica*, p. 149.

of nuns only; novices and postulants are not included within the terms.[95] The latter are not, however, bound by the law of the cloister in the same manner as nuns.[96]

The permission extended through the use of the faculty allows nuns to go into the Church for the purpose of cleaning and decorating. The church (*ecclesia*) named in the faculty, so it appears, is the church connected with the monastery, the *templum publicum* mentioned in canon 597, § 2, as being outside the cloister. This conclusion seems proper in view of the effect of the permission, which in view of the conditions contained in the text of the faculty, implies, so to speak, an extension of the cloister to include the church. Thus, nuns going into the church are not in strict parlance, going outside the cloister, but are going into a place designated by virtue of this faculty as being contained within the limits of the cloister. If the faculty were read to mean "a church" rather than "the church", then the permission, instead of being referred to a *descensus in ecclesiam,* as in fact it is, would more properly have to be referred to an *egressus e claustris,* which *egressus* would be necessary if the nuns were permitted to go to a church other than the one connected with the monastery.[97] Hence any permission which, as granted by virtue of this faculty, would allow the nuns to go to a church other than the public church connected with the monastery would appear to involve a violation of the rule of canon 67, and result in an invalid use of the faculty.[98]

The sacristy of the church attached to the monastery is explicitly

---

95 Cf. canon 49.

96 Schaaf, *The Cloister,* p. 135; Schaefer, *De Religiosis,* n. 214, p. 452; n. 250, 2, p. 545.

97 A similar faculty, mentioned in the Instruction of the Sacred Congregation of Religious on the cloister of nuns of solemn vows, is spoken of in connection with the exterior church *(ecclesia exterior)*. The signification of the term seems the same as the term *ecclesia* used in this faculty, viz., the church connected with the monastery. Cf. *AAS,* XVI (1924), 96; Schaefer, *De Religiosis,* p. 728.

98 Nuns going out of the limits of the cloister in consequence of an invalidly granted permission of this nature, seem to be violating the rule of canon 601, § 1, and to incur the penalty of canon 2342, 3°, that is, in the words of the canon, Plectuntur ipso facto excommunicatione Sede Apostolicae simpliciter reservata . . . ; 3° Moniales e clausure illegitime exeuntes contra praescriptum canon 601. Cf. Schaefer, *De Religiosis,* n. 355, p. 724; Barry, *Violation of the Cloister,* The Catholic University of America Canon Law Studies, n. 148, (Washington, D. C.: The Catholic University of America Press, 1942), pp. 213-217.

excluded from the enclosure by canon 597, § 2.[99] Accordingly, it could appear that the term *ecclesia* as used in the text of the faculty, does not include the sacristy of the church. However, in view of the definition of the word church as contained in canon 1161, [100] it may be said that the sacristy, by its nature, is at least indirectly contained in the definition as being set aside from profane uses for use in divine worship, and may certainly be considered as part of the church. The announced purpose of the faculty, cleaning and decorating the church, implies that permission is extended to the sacristy as well as the public portion of the church. It seems therefore necessary to conclude that the permission granted by virtue of this faculty includes the permission for the nuns to go into the sacristy as well as into the main body of the church. The broad interpretation given to the term of these faculties supports this conclusion.

Various conditions are attached to the use of the faculty. The verification of these conditions extends in effect the rule of the cloister temporarily in include the confines of the church. All persons not belonging to the community (*extraneis*) must leave the church before the nuns are allowed to enter it. The term is all-inclusive and, in the words of the faculty, includes the confessor of the nuns and those who are in the service of the monastery but live outside the cloister.[101] In effect, the only persons allowed to remain in the church during the period of occupancy by the nuns are those who are professed nuns and thus are bound by the law of the enclosure.

The outer doors of the church must be locked and the key given to the Superioress. The inner doors of the church, that is, those

[99] Canon 597, § 2: Lege clausurae paplis afficitur tota domus quam communitas regularis inhabitat, cum hortis et viridariis accessui religiosorum reservatis; excluso, praeter publicum templum cum continente sacrario, ...

[100] Canon 1161: Ecclesiae nomine intelligitur aedes sacra divino cultui dedicata eum potissimum in finem et omnibus Christifidelibus usui sit ad divinum cultum publice exercendum.

[101] Extern religious, attached to a monastery but professed with simple vows, are permitted in communities of solemn vows, in order that they may transact the business of the community in the outside world. Such religious are not bound by the law of the cloister, and by the text of this faculty are to be excluded from the church during its occupancy by the nuns. Cf. Coronata, *Interpretatio Authentica*, p. 150; Barry, *Violation of the Cloister*, p. 222.

separating the main body of the church from the vestibule, must also be closed and secured with a double lock and the keys given, one to the Superioress and the other to a nun designated by the Ordinary. These doors are not to be opened except in those cases provided for in the law, and then according to the cautions contained in the law.[102]

In addition to the above mentioned prescriptions, the nuns are to be always two together in the use of this permission. This seems to indicate that the permission cannot be used for one nun singly, but that there must be at least two. In case there are more than two assigned to the task of decorating and cleaning the church through the use of this permission, does the clause *semper binae sint* mean that they must work in pairs, and if so, how close must they remain together? The use of the term *binae* does not necessarily mean that the nuns must work in pairs; if this were the intention of the Sacred Congregation, then the word *par* should have been used. The presence of two nuns in the church fulfills the requirement based on the term *binae,* and therefore any number greater than two also fulfills the requirement.[103]

In view of the severity of the laws concerning the enclosure and the penalty for the violation of it,[104] it seems advisable that this permission, together with a clear statement of the conditions as set forth in the text of the faculty, be extended to communiies in writing.

Article 9

The Granting of Permission to Nuns to Leave the Cloister for Surgical Treatment

> "Permittendi monialibus egressum e claustris urgente casu operationis chirurgicae subeundae, quamvis non secumferat periculum mortis imminentis aut gravissimi mali, per tempus stricte necessarium, praescriptis debitis cautelis."

This faculty, as the faculty treated in Article 8 of this Chapter,

---

[102] The exceptions contained in the law are found in canons 600 and 601. The church during its occupancy by the nuns, according to the conditions of the faculty, is to be considered as part of the cloister.

[103] Cf. canon 49.

[104] Cf. canon 2342, 3°.

may be used by Ordinaries who have the necessary jurisdiction in favor of nuns who are subject to the law of the cloister.[105]

What has been said in Article 8 of this Chapter in regard to those nuns who by apostolic indult have simple vows in the United States, to novices, and to postulants may also be said to obtain in relation to the use of this faculty. Those religious who take temporary vows, as indicated in canon 574, § 1, prior to their taking solemn perpetual vows are bound by the law of the cloister, and hence may be the recipients of favors granted in virtue of this faculty.[106]

Under the terms of the faculty permission may be given to nuns (*moniales*) to leave the cloister for the purpose of any surgical operation, even though there be no danger of death or of very great harm in the absence of such an operation. The term surgical operation does not admit extension to include any and every type of medical treatment.[107]

The need for surgical treatment, however, constitutes a sufficient cause for the granting of the permission, as required by canon 84, § 1, for a dispensation from a law of the Church. The determination of the need for surgical treatment is, by its nature, outside the office of the Ordinary, and is to be learned from the advice and recommendations of those treating the ill nun. The permission may be granted only for such time as is necessary for the treatment, and all proper precautions must be taken.[108] The necessary time cannot be fixed, since it is relative to the individual case and will amount to the minimum prescribed by the surgeon.

The permission granted in the use of this faculty, it seems, should be granted in writing. This seems the proper procedure in view of the strictness of the laws governing the cloister, and the severity of the penalty inflicted upon those who violate it.[109]

---

[105] Cf. canon 597, § 1.

[106] Cf. Barry, *Violation of the Cloister*, p. 208.

[107] Cf. canons 49; 67; the phrase *alius gravissimi mali* is not included in the terms of the faculty.

[108] The rules governing nuns who, with permission, leave the cloister for any period of time are contained usually in the constitutions of the institute, and it is these precautions to which the faculty refers.

[109] Cf. canons 601, § 1; 2342, 3°.

CHAPTER X

FACULTIES FROM THE SACRED CONGREGATION OF RITES

ARTICLE I

THE DEPUTATION OF PRIESTS FOR THE CONSECRATION OF ALTARS

> "Deputandi sacerdotes, si fieri potest, in aliqua ecclesiastica dignitate constitutos, ad altaria fixa et portatilia consecranda, servato ritu et forma Pontificalis Romani; et quoad altaria portatilia etiam adhibita sola rituali formula approbata."

Both fixed and portable altars are named in the faculty as those which a priest may be deputed to consecrate. The altars are simply those which have never been consecrated. Previously consecrated altars which have lost their consecration are indeed subject to re-consecration, but they are treated in the Article following.

The fixed or immovable altar, according to canon 1197, § 1, 1°, is one which has the entire table (*mensa*) together with the supports consecrated as a unit.[1] A portable or movable altar is what is commonly called an altar stone, usually small in comparison with the *mensa* of the immovable altar, and is consecrated as separate from the supports of the altar.[2] Without an apostolic indult, such as this faculty, which permits the relaxation of the prescript of canon 1147, § 1,[3] a priest cannot consecrate either fixed or movable altars.

The faculty uses the term *deputandi.* Hence the power conferred by the faculty is that of naming another to act in the place of the grantor and in his name. This notion implies that the grantor

[1] Cf. canon 1197, § 1, 1°: Bliley, *Altars According to the Code of Canon Law,* The Catholic University of America Canon Law Studies, n. 38, (Washington, D. C.: The Catholic University of America, 1927), p. 51.

[2] Cf. canon 1197, § 1, 2°; Bliley, *op. cit.*, p. 97.

[3] Canon 1147, § 1: Consecratones nemo qui charactere eipscopali careat, valide peregere potest, nisi vel iure vel apostolico indulto id ei permittatur.

possess the necessary power for the act to be performed. Thus the use of the faculty is restricted to Ordinaries possessing the episcopal character, save for the exceptions enacted in canon 294. § 2; 323, § 2.[4] It is to be noted that mention of the consecration of immovable altars is omitted in canon 294, § 2, and hence the consecrating of immovable altars is not extended as a privilege possessed also by vicars and prefects apostolic. Accordingly, these officials cannot, in virtue of this faculty, deputize priests for the consecration of immovable altars. Canon 323, § 2, however, explicitly extends the privilege to abbots and prelates *nullius*. Accordingly, these can in virtue of this faculty depute a priest for the consecration of an immovable altar, provided that all other conditions are fulfilled. Unless a vicar general possess the episcopal character he does not enjoy this faculty.

An Ordinary may in virtue of this faculty depute any priest who is not rendered incapable of receiving favors.[5] In the act of consecrating an altar the deputed priest is bound, as is the Ordinary, by the law concerning the consecration of altars, which law is treated below. If possible, it should be priests who possess some ecclesiastical dignity who are deputed with the power of consecrating altars. Dignities and those who hold them are treated in the Code of Canon Law, canons 391-242, which deal with Cathedral and Collegiate Chapters and their members. The dignitaries are distinguished from the canons and the other members of the chapter by reason of their offices, which offices contain some powers of jurisdiction not common to the chapter.[6] In the United States, Cathedral chapters are replaced by boards of diocesan

---

[4] Cf. canon 1199, § 2; canon 294, § 2: Etiam ii (Vicarii et Praefecti Apostolici) qui charactere episcopali carent, possunt, intra sui territorii fines ac perdurante munere, omnes benedictiones Episcopis reservatas, una pontificali excepta, impertiri, calices, patenas et altaria portatilia cum sacris oleis ab Episcopo benedictis consecrare, indulgentias quiquaginta dierum concedere, confirmationem, primam tonsuram et ordines minores conferre ad normam can. 782, § 3, 957, § 2.

Canon 323, § 2: Si charactere episcopali (Abbas vel Praelatus *nullius*) non sit ornatus et benedictionem, si eam recipere debet, receperit, praeter alia munera quae in can. 294, § 2, describuntur, potest quoque ecclesias et altaria immobilia consecrare.

[5] Cf. canon 36.

[6] Cf. canon 393, § 1: Woywod, *A Practical Commentary on the Code of Canon Law*, I, p. 140; Vermeersch-Creusen, *Epitome*, I, n. 497, p. 367.

consultors,[7] who participate in the rule of the diocese or territory; they do not, however, participate in the liturgical honors accorded the dignitaries and canons of the duly constituted chapters. Thus, the interpretation of the phrase "in some ecclesiastical dignity" is not controlled by the rules governing chapters. However, the principle implied in the word "dignity" (*dignitas*) does obtain, and it is this notion, namely, that priests of some added dignity, either by reason of their ecclesiastical office or because of some liturgical honor conferred upon them should, when it is possible, in the use of this faculty, be deputed for the consecration of altars. This group of priests, *in aliqua ecclesiastica dignitate constituti,* is composed of: 1) the diocesan consultors; 2) those who have been named members of the Pontifical household;[8] and 3) the diocesan officials, such as the synodal and pro-synodal judges, the *officialiis,* the synodal and pro-synodal examiners, etc.[9]

Priests deputized according to this faculty are to use the rite and form as given in the *Pontificale Romanum.*[10] They are bound to observe also the same rules which the bishop must observe in regard to the consecration of fixed and portable altars. In the consecration of a fixed altar which does not accompany the consecration of a church, the formula of the Roman Pontifical proper to the consecration of the altar alone must be used.[11] The deputed priest may not, according to the terms of this faculty, be appointed also for the consecration of a church along with the consecration of an altar.[12] Neither may he be appointed for the consecration of an altar in conjunction with the consecration of a church; the consecration of the church and the consecration of the altar constitute a single

[7] Cf. Beste, *Introductio in Codicem*, p. 278.

[8] Cf. canon 328: Fortescue-O'Connell, *The Ceremonies of the Roman Rite Described*, p. 38.

[9] The possessors of the scholastic degrees of doctor or licentiate are considered as being among the group of those possessing dignities. Cf. canon 1378.

[10] Pontificale Romanum (Ratisbonae, Editio typica, Romae, 1934), Lib. II, Tit., *De altaris consecratione quae fit sine ecclesiae dedicatione;* Tit., *De altaris portatilis consecratione;* Bliley, *Altars According to the Code of Canon Law*, pp. 75-78; Le Vavasseur-Haegy-Stercky, *Manuel*, I, n. 43, p. 45.

[11] Pontificale Romanum, Lib. II, Tit., *De altaris consecratione quae fit sine ecclesiae dedicatione.*

[12] Cf. canon 67.

function, which is to be performed by one and the same bishop.[13]

Although the consecration of a fixed altar can be effected on any and every day, yet it seems more befitting and decorous that it be undertaken on Sunday or a feast day of precept.[14] Every fixed altar should be consecrated with a title, just as churches are consecrated with titles, and it is prescribed that the main altar of the church should have as its primary title the same title as the church. The requirement of a title does not pertain to the valid consecration of an altar.[15]

In regard to the indulgence of one year which the consecrating bishop may grant on the occasion of the consecration of an altar, the Sacred Congregation of Rites replied to a submitted doubt that a priest deputy may not grant the indulgence, but that he may announce the indulgence as having been granted by the bishop who deputized him.[16]

The consecration of a fixed altar pertains to the Ordinary of the place, and even though that Ordinary lacks the necessary episcopal character, his permission must be obtained.[17] This permission can be considered as having been granted along with the act of deputation in the event that the latter is meant to serve a particular instance. Even in those cases in which the deputation is made for an indefinite number of cases, it seems that the permission of the grantor is implicitly contained in it.

The consecration of a portable altar is not regulated by all the rules which govern the consecration of an immovable altar. Any bishop may consecrate a portable altar in any territory; the permission of the local Ordinary is not required.[18] In the performance of the acts of consecration the deputized priests are to use the form according to the Roman Pontifical. However, in the case of port-

---

[13] Cf. Augustine, *Liturgical Law*, p. 433.

[14] Cf. canon 1199, § 3.

[15] Cf. canon 1201, § 1, § 2 and § 4.

[16] S. R. C. 26 oct. 1931: Coronata, *Interpretatio Authentica*, p. 267; Bouscaren, *The Canon Law Digest*, I, canon 1166; *Apollinaris* (Romae, 1928-), IX, (1936), 186. Cf. also canon 913, 1°. The prescription of canon 1166, § 1 and § 2, apply only to the consecration of a church, as is apparent from the wording of the canon.

[17] Cf. canon 1199, § 2; 1155, § 1 and § 2; canon 1157: Non obstante quolibet privilegio, nemo potest locum sacrum consecrare vel benedicere sine Ordinarii consensu.

[18] Cf. canon 1199, § 2: Le Vavasseur-Haegy-Stercky, *Manuel*, n. 43, p. 45.

able altars the act of deputation leaves room for the optional use of the shorter formula.[19] Portable altars may be consecrated on any day.[20] Titles should also be attached to portable altars.[21]

Written records of the fact of consecration, together with the pertinent facts concerning the consecration, such as the title of the altar, the date of the consecration, the name of the consecrator, the fact of his deputation, the name of the deputing bishop, etc., should be preserved. In regard to fixed altars canon 1158 is quite clear concerning the record to be preserved.[21] With regard to the consecration of portable altars the obligation of recording the fact of consecration, together with all the pertinent information, seems to be equally necessary, in view of the later possible need of establishing the fact of consecration in the external forum. It should also be mentioned in the record whether the altar was consecrated as a portable or as a fixed altar. This becomes important in the matter of determining the possible loss of consecration should occasion arise to question such a loss. Portable and fixed altars lose their consecration differently.[22]

A written deputation is not necessary for the deputy's act of valid consecration; however, in view of the nature of the acts permitted through the application of the faculty, it seems advisable that the bishop should effect the deputation in writing. This advisability relates to the deputation for the consecration of either fixed or portable altars. The records of consecration should contain notice of the fact that the consecration was performed by a deputed priest; proof of this deputation is more easily established with an official document of deputation.[23] When the deputation is granted, the execution of it should be recorded in writing, also apart from the rules indicated above.[24]

---

[19] Pontificale Romanum, Lib. II, Tit., *De altaris portatilis consecratione;* Bliley: *Altars According to the Code of Canon Law*, p. 104.

[20] Cf. canon 1201, § 1 and § 3.

[21] Canon 1158: De peracta consecratione vel benedictione redigatur documentum cuius alterum exemplar in Curia episcopali, alterum in ecclesiae archivo servetur.

[22] Cf. Bliley, *Altars According to the Code of Canon Law*, p. 107; further treatment is given this question in the Article which follows.

[23] Cf. canon 200, § 2; 1814.

[24] Cf. canon 56.

Article 2

The Deputation of Priests for the Re-consecration of Altars

> "Deputandi sacerdotes, si fieri potest, in aliqua ecclesiastica dignitate constitutos, ad altaria fixa et portatilia exsecrata consecranda, adhibita breviori formula B pro casibus can. 1200, § 2, Cod. I. C.; dum in casu can. 1200, § 1, iam indulta fuit per ipsum canonem facultas et adhibenda est formula A."

What has been said in the preceding Article concerning the Ordinaries who enjoy the use of the faculty, the priests whom an Ordinary may depute, and the significance of their possessing some ecclesiastical dignity, may also be held to obtain in the use of this faculty.

This faculty is concerned with both immovable and movable altars which have lost their consecration in a manner described in paragraph 2 of canon 1200, that is, 1) by a fracture which is regarded as serious either by reason of the magnitude of the break itself or in regard to the portion of the altar affected, and 2) by a removal of the relics, and a removal or breaking of the cover of the sepulcher, except in those cases in which the removal of the cover is undertaken by the proper authority.[25] Altars within a church do not lose their consecration by reason of the church's loss of consecration.[26] The re-consecration of immovable altars which have lost their consecration in consequence of a separation of the table (*mensa*) from the support (*stipite*) may be commissioned to a priest by the bishop in virtue of the permission extended in paragraph 1 of canon 1200. Thus, the faculty is concerned merely with the mention of this concession.

The faculty prescribed the use of the shorter form, formula *B,* which is found in the appendix of the Roman Ritual, where it is

---

[25] Canon 1200, § 2: Tum altare immobile tum petro sacra amittunt consecrationem:

1°, Si frangantur enormiter sive ratione quantitatis fractionis sive ratione loci unctionis;

2°, Si amoveantur reliquiae aut frangatur vel amoveatur sepulcri operculum, excepto casu quo ipse Episcopus vel eius delegatus operculum amoveat ad illud firmandum vel reparandum vel subrogandum, aut ad visitandas reliquias.

[26] Cf. canon 1200, § 4.

indicated by the Roman numeral II, [27] the rubrics are contained in the Ritual together with the formula.

No special time is indicated for the re-consecration of altars which have lost their consecration. However, in view of the nature of the act, it seems that the days recommended for the consecration of altars may also be applicable for the re-consecration of altars. In regard to the titles of the re-consecrated altars, any change in the title of an immovable altar is forbidden by canon 1201, § 3, which also states that the Ordinary may change the title in the case of portable altars. [28] The deputy of an Ordinary could not, unless mention had been made of the concession of such power in the act of deputation, presume the use of the right to change the title of a portable altar.

The rubrics of formula *A* (I) prescribe that a written record of the re-consecration of an altar, under the same title, should be made. [29] Although the rubric is not repeated in formula *B* (II), its precept is to be observed in the case of immovable altars re-consecrated with the use of formula *B*. This follows from the rule of canon 1158, regarding immovable altars. The similar nature of the re-consecration of portable altars and the later possible need of establishing the fact of re-consecration, as in the original consecration, makes it almost imperative that such a record be preserved in regard to portable altars also. If a deputation of this faculty is made, canon 56 directs that the execution of the delegation be made in writing.

Article 3

Deputation of Priests for the Consecration of Chalices and Patens

> "Deputandi sacerdotes, si fieri potest, in aliqua ecclesiastica dignitate, ad consecrandos calices et patenas; servato ritu forma Pontificalis Romani."

---

[27] *Rituale Romanum Pauli V Pontificis Maximi jussu editum aliorumque Pontificum cura recognitum atque auctoritate Pii Papae XI* (Neo Eboraci: Benziger Brothers, 1945), Appendix, *De consecratione altarium exsecratorum*, I, II; (hereafter cited *Rituale Romanum*. (The formula *A* mentioned in canon 1200, § 1, is indicated in the Ritual by the Roman numeral I.)

[28] Canon 1201, § 3: De Ordinarii licentia mutari quidem potest altaris mobilis, non autem altaris immobilis titulus.

[29] Cf. Rituale Romanum, Appendix, Tit., *De Consecratione altarium exsecratorum*, I.

What has been said in Article 1 of this Chapter in regard to the Ordinaries who enjoy that faculty, of the priests whom an Ordinary may depute and of the significance of their possessing some ecclesiastical dignity, may also be considered as pertaining to the use of this faculty.

The chalices and patens with which the faculty is concerned must fulfill the requirements, as stated in the Roman Missal, in regard to their material and construction.[30] There is no distinction made in the text of the faculty between chalices and patens which have never been consecrated and those which have lost their consecration through damage or profane use, or by being offered for public sale.[31] Thus, vessels which have lost their consecration and have since been repaired may also be consecrated (re-consecrated) in virtue of the concession derived from the use and application of this faculty.[32] The formulas and rubrics, except those which are proper to a bishop, are to be followed and used by a priest in consecrating chalices and patens in consequence of the grant received in virtue of this faculty.[33]

The reasoning applied with reference to the recording of the consecration of altars seems adaptable here, and hence it appears advisable that the fact of the concession be effected in writing,[34] and that a record be preserved of the fact of consecration, together with all pertinent information.[35] This is especially true of sacred vessels which are the property of an institution since their care will pass from one person to another, and accordingly the fact of consecration should be established in such a manner that questions concerning it may be easily settled.

Article 4
To Permit the Omission of the Passion in Masses of Holy Week, in Cases of Priests Binating

"Quando in Missa Hebdomadae Maioris dictur *Passio,*

---

[30] Missale Romanum, *Ritus servandus in celebratione Missae*, Tit., I, n. 1; Le Vavasseur-Haegy-Stercky, *Manuel*, I, n. 61, p. 63; Augustine, *Liturgical Law*, p. 45.

[31] Cf. canon 1305, § 1, 1° and 2°: Chalices and patens do not lose their consecration through the process of replating; cf. canon 1305, § 2.

[32] Cf. canon 67.

[33] Pontificale Romanum, Tit., *De patenae et calicis consecratione*.

[34] Cf. canon 200, § 2.

[35] Cf. canon 56.

pro sacerdotibus qui, praehabita facultate, binas Missas rite celebrant, legendi in una Missa tantum, ex *Passione* postremam partem (*Altera autem die, etc.,*) praemissis: *Munda cor meum, etc.,—Sequentia sancti evangelii secundum* (Matthaeum.)

The *Passion,* the reading of which the faculty concerns, is that account of Our Lord's suffering and crucifixion as recorded by the Evangelists, Matthew, Mark, Luke, and John. It is contained in the Masses of Palm Sunday, of the Tuesday and the Wednesday of Holy Week, and of Good Friday. As a consequence, the foregoing faculty is useful only in regard to the reading of the *Passion* on Palm Sunday, since this is the only one of the days which permits the use of a bination faculty which is issued by the Ordinary.[36]

In the event that by reason of an Apostolic indult, a priest enjoyed the privilege of bination for the remaining days on which the *Passion* is read at Mass, the Ordinary could, by the use of this faculty, dispense the priest from the obligation of reading the *Passion* in one of the Masses on any day that the reading of the *Passion* is required.[37] The priest who has received a dispensation in virtue of this faculty may omit the reading of the *Passion* in either one of the two Masses he celebrates.

The part of the *Passion* which must be said as the gospel of the Mass is clearly indicated in the Missal. It begins with the words,

---

[36] Canon 806, § 2: Hanc tamen facultatem [bis in die offerendi Eucharisticum Sacrificium] impetiri nequit Ordinarius, nisi cùm, prudenti ipsius iudicio, propter penuriam sacerdotum die festo di praecepto notabilis fidelium pars Missae adstare non possit; non est autem in eius potestate plures quam duas Missas eidem sacerdoti permittere. Cf. Augustine, *Liturgical Law,* p. 356, 6, note 41.

[37] In those cases in which priests have an indult which permits them to offer three Masses if the need arises, which indult has been granted for current use in some of the dioceses, the question arises whether the Ordinary may dispense such priests from the reading of the *Passion* in the third Mass in addition to the second. The faculty does not contemplate trination; it mentions only bination *(binas Missas).* It seems therefore that the use of this faculty in favor of a priest saying three Masses in order to allow the omission of the *Passion* in two of them would constitute an extension of the terms of the faculty, which is forbidden by canon 67. Such a dispensation seems to involve an invalid use of the faculty. Cf. canon 203, § 1.

on Palm Sunday, *Altera autem die* . . . This portion is to be read as the gospel of the Mass.

There is no requirement that this dispensation be given in writing. It seems that the application of this faculty can be invoked for priests in such a manner that they enjoy a habitual permission. Since, however, the conceded permission is of the nature of a dispensation from the rubrics, rather than of the nature of a privilege (the permission is dependent upon another indult which prohibits the permission from extending beyond the duration of that indult), any extension of the permission beyond the duration of the Quinquennial Faculties does not seem permissible.[28]

Article 5

To Permit the Blessing of Marriages Outside Mass

> "Benedicendi nuptias extra Missam, vel recitandi preces super coniuges iuxta formulas approbatas, cum potestate subdelegandi."

The blessing of marriages and the prayers referred to in the faculty are found in the Appendix of the Roman Ritual under the title *De Matrimonio* Numbers I and II. They are somewhat different from the solemn nuptial blessing found in the Roman Missal with the nuptial Mass.[29] The rubrics of the marriage blessing imply that when the nuptial Mass is not celebrated the blessing is to be administered at the time of the marriage by the same priest who officiates at the marriage. The faculty does not indicate the availability of any departure from this requirement of the rubrics.

The blessing of a marriage as contained in the Appendix of the Roman Ritual is not the solemn nuptial blessing which canon 1108, § 2 treats of with reference to the solemnization of marriage, and which is by law disbarred from use during the forbidden seasons. Therefore, it is not subject to the restriction which canon 1108, § 2, invokes. Marriage may be contracted any time during the year. It seems that it is to all such marriages that the blessing of marriage

[28] Cf. Article 4, Chapter V, of this work .

[29] Cf. Rituale Romanum, Appendix, *De Matrimonia*, I, II; Number II of the blessing is indicated in the case of the remarriage of a widow who received the nuptial blessing previously; Missale Romanum, *Missae Votivae*, II, *Missa pro Sponso et Sponsa.*

as given outside of Mass becomes applicable. It seems also that the main purpose of the faculty is to provide for the blessing of marriage in those cases in which liturgical law rules out the bestowal of the customary nuptial blessing. It appears then, that the use of the faculty is not limited by the restrictions which are set in canon 1108, § 2.[40] The faculty also permits the Ordinary the power of subdelegation, *cum potestate subdelegandi.*

Article 6
To Permit the Blessing and Investing of the Five Scapulars Under One Formula

"Benedicendi et imponendi quinque scapularia sub unica formula, cum potestate subdelegandi."

The Five Scapulars spoken of in the faculty are the scapulars of:

1) the Most Holy Trinity, the white, blue, and red scapular of the Trinitarians;

2) of the Passion of Our Lord, the red scapular of the Vincentian priests;

3) of the Immaculate Conception, the blue scapular of the Theatine Order of Nuns;

4) of the Seven Sorrows of the Blessed Virgin, the black scapular of the Servite priests; and

5) of Our Lady of Mount Carmel, the brown scapular of the Carmelite priests.[41] The above named five scapulars may be

[40] De Smet (*De Sponsalibus et Matrimonio*, n. 199, p. 168) concluded that the prohibition of solemnities as enacted in canon 1108, § 2, includes not only the solemn nuptial blessing but also any functions over and above the simple celebration of marriage. Commentary on this aspect of the canon is not within the scope of this work; however, it is worthy of mention that the rule of canon 67 does not permit the extension of the terms of the faculty to include anything other than a blessing of the marriage, and therefore it may not be interpreted as permission for any added celebration or solemnity on the occasion of the marriage.

[41] Cf. Fanfani, *De Indulgentiis ad Norman Codicis Iuris Canonici*, (2 ed., Taurini-Romae: Marietti, 1926), definition of scapular, n. 119, p. 126. Sullian, *The Externals of the Catholic Church*, (New York: Kennedy, 1917), pp. 191 ff.

received and worn in one, and as such the one scapular is called the Five Scapulars (*quinque scapularis.*)

Inscription in the association or confraternity of the various scapulars is required by the Code of Canon Law for the participation of the member in the spiritual benefits of the association.[42] The reception of candidates is to be conducted according to the norms of the constitutions of the individual associations, and priests using this faculty are bound to follow the rules for admitting and inscribing new members according as such rules are expressed in the constitutions of the various associations represented by the Five Scapulars.[43]

The formula, expressed in the faculty by means of the phrase *sub unica formula,* is given in the Roman Ritual, Appendix II, *Benedictiones Faciendae a Sacerdotibus Apostolicum Indultum Habentibus,* no. 14, *Formula Brevior Benedicendi et Imponendi Quinque Scapularia.* The faculty permits the use of this form; it does not however dispense from the other rules to be followed in the enrollment of new members. Such an interpretation would imply an extension of the terms of the faculty beyond their scope.[44]

There is no requirement that the faculty be given in writing, and there seems to be no need of a written grant. However, a priest enrolling new members in the scapular by virtue of this faculty will need to make mention of his delegation, and the source from which he received it, and this procedure could be facilitated with a written copy of the delegation.[45] Subdelegation of the faculty is permitted.

Article 7

To Permit the Blessing and Investing of the Five Scapulars on Special Occasions Without Recourse to the Competent Ordinary or Congregation

"Benedicendi et imponendi quinque scapularia sub unica formula absque recursu ad Ordinarios seu Congregationes

---

[42] Cf. canons 692; 694, § 2.

[43] Cf. canon 694; Schaefer, *De Religiosis,* n. 623 ff., pp. 1061 ff.

[44] Cf. canon 67.

[45] S. C. decr. 16 dec. 1910 (*AAS,* III [1917)], 22) states that a scapular medal may be worn by those invested with the Five Scapulars, provided that the person first be invested with the cloth scapular, and that the medal which is worn be blessed by a priest having the faculty to blessing and investing with the cloth scapular.

religiosas competentes, et sine onere inscriptionis in casibus magni concursus, tempore Exercitiorum et Missionum spiritualium, cum potestate suddelegandi."

This faculty repeats the concession of the faculty treated in Article 6 of this Chapter with the added dispensation from the requirements of recourse to either the competent Ordinaries or religious congregations and from the prescribed inscription of the new members. Canon 690, paragraph 1, states that all associations, even those erected by the Holy See, are subject to the jurisdiction of the local Ordinary. Such associations may be further subject to the Congregation with which the association is connected, as in the case of the Scapular of the Most Holy Trinity, which is under the jurisdiction of the Trinitarians. The extent of the association's subjection, and the requirements of recourse to either the Ordinary or the Congregation on the occasion of the reception of new members, will vary with the statutes or constitutions of the particular association.[46]

A priest who shares in this faculty of investing a person with the Five Scapulars is free to dispense with the recourse otherwise required, and is freed of the obligation of enrolling the new members in the manner required by canon 694, § 1. This freedom is granted only during the times of spiritual missions and of special devotions when there are gathered together great numbers (*in casibus magni concursus*) of the faithful who are to be enrolled. The great number or large gathering of the faithful is of course, a factor that is to be considered relatively. What may constitute a considerable gathering on one community may have to be regarded as a small group in another. In this regard the authorized priest is the judge of this matter but he is bound and indeed under the pain of acting invalidly, by the prescript of canon 203, § 1.[47]

The spiritual missions (*Missionum spiritualium*) mentioned in the faculty are those required to be held at least every ten years according to the Code of Canon Law.[48] The faculty may be used,

---

[46] Cf. Schaefer, *De Religiosis*, n. 621, p. 1057.

[47] Canon 203, § 1: Delegatus qui sive circa res sive circa personas mandati sui fines excedit nihil agit.

[48] Cf. canon 1349, § 1.

however, at any time such a mission is held, without respect to the intervening years. The spiritual exercises (*Exercitiorum spiritualium*) contemplated in the faculty are what are known as spiritual retreats, such as are required of persons in certain states in life by various canons in the Code.[49] They are considered to be the days set aside (the number of days varies) for a pattern of spiritual exercises which may be conducted for the laity as well as for religious and clerics.[50]

Retreats for the laity are not excepted from the terms of the faculty. It seems therefore that the faculty can be used on the occasion of such spiritual retreats. With reference to the so-called one-day retreats for the laity, it seems that use of the faculty during a retreat of this type would involve a misuse and therefore would not be permitted. One day "retreats" are rather days of recollection, a distinction which is made by Pope Pius XI in his encyclical letter on the priesthood.[51] This faculty may be subdelegated.

Article 8

Faculty Permitting the Blessing of the Holy Oils With Fewer Than the Required Number of Priests

'Benedicendi sacra olea cum eo presbyterorum et sacrorum ministrorum numero, quo pro loci rerumque adiunctis reperiri poterit, Feria V *in Coena Domini* (pro Episcopo celebrante)."

The ceremonies of Holy Thursday are regulated by the rubrics of the Roman Pontifical which prescribes the number of ministers required for the function of blessing the oils used in the administration of some of the sacraments.[52] According to the rubrics, twelve priests, seven deacons, and seven subdeacons are required for the ceremony.[53] With the use of this faculty the sacred function of blessing the oils may be carried out with fewer than the required

[49] Cf. canons 126; 1001; 541; 571, etc.

[50] Cf. Pius XI, const., "*Summorum Pontificum*", 25 iul, 1922—*AAS*, XIV (1922) 18; ep. 3 dec. 1922—*AAS*, XIV (1922), 627; litt. 20 dec. 1929—*AAS*, XXI, (1929), 689.

[51] *AAS*, XXVIII (1936, 5 ff.

[52] Cf. canon 734, § 1.

[53] Pontificale Romanum, tit, *De officio in feria V. in Coenae Domini;* S. R. C., *Decret. Auth.*, n. 1660.

number of ministers, the number being regulated in the faculty with the terms, *quo pro loci rerumque adiunctis reperiri poterit,* that is, with the number available according to the place and circumstances. This provision cannot be interpreted to mean that the consecration of the oils may take place without any assistant priests; two is indicated as the minimum in a response of the Holy office.[54]

In considering the number of priests available, the bishop is not limited to the priest members of the cathedral staff. The Sacred Congregation of Rites has issued responses indicating that secular priests, subjects of the Bishop, are to be summoned from parishes other than the cathedral.[55] In a case of necessity even regulars from within the territory of the bishop are to be called.[56] Unreasonable distances which would have to be travelled by the priests, the needs of the parishes in which they are stationed, or similar causes which would render their assistance difficult, seem to release the bishop from summoning them, and therefore appear to warrant his use of this faculty.

The faculty is in effect a dispensation from the legislation of the rubrics, and needs a proportionate cause for its use.[57] The cause is expressed in the faculty as inherent in the local circumstances with reference to the number of priests available. If a sufficient number of ministers is available, the faculty cannot be used; however, it seems that if peculiar and unforseen circumstances such as extremely inclement weather or hindering accidents should arise, a bishop could use this faculty even though under ordinary circumstances a sufficient number of priests would be available to him.

The added phrase, *pro Episcopo celebrante,* indicates that this privilege is extended by the Sacred Congregation of Rites for use by the celebrating bishop. Thus, if another bishop, in a case of necessity, were asked to perform the function of the blessing of the

---

[54] S. C. S. Off., Resp., 4 aug. 1859—*Collect,* (1893) n. 485.

[55] Cf. S. R. C., 18 mart. 1679—Gardellini, *Decret. Auth.,* n. 2878.

[56] S. R. C., 11 nov. 1641; Gardellini, *Decret. Auth.,* n. 1354; the term *regulares* may be held to include any priest religious.

[57] Cf. canon 84, § 1.

oils,[58] he could make use of this faculty, if all other provisions are fulfilled.

The same may be said of the vicar general. If the vicar general possesses the episcopal character, and is performing the blessing of the oils on Holy Thursday, he can make use of this faculty, provided all other provisions are fulfilled.

Article 9

Faculty to Permit the Use of the Incensations in the *Missa Cantata*

"Permittendi thurificationem in Missa cantata absque sacris ministris, in Festis tamen duplicibus primae secundae classis, Dominicis et quando Missa cum cantu celebratur coram Ssmo Eucharistiae Sacramento solemniter exposito."

The use of the incensations as indicated in the rubrics of the Roman Missal are limited to Solemn Masses, that is, to sung Masses in which, besides the celebrant, there are also officiating a deacon and a subdeacon. Though the *Missa cantata* is not mentioned in the rubrics, responses of the Sacred Congregation of Rites have excluded the use of incense in such Masses.[59] No exception is made in the rubrics if the *Missa cantata* is celebrated before the Blessed Sacrament exposed.

The faculty extends to the Ordinary the power of permitting the use of the incensations, as they are indicated in the rubrics of the Roman Missal, in the *Missa cantata* on double feasts of both first and second class,[60] on all Sundays, and at those times when a *Missa cantata* is sung before the Blessed Sacrament solemnly exposed.[61] In the faculty no limitation is placed in regard to those

[58] Cf. S. R. C., 8 iun. 1658—Gardellini, *Decret. Auth.*, n. 1896.

[59] S. R. C., *De vacathecas*, 18 mart. 1874, ad I; S. R. C. *Ordinis Minorum Capuccinorum S. Francisci*, 7 dec. 1888, ad III—S. R. C. *Decret. Auth.*, nn. 3328; 3697.

[60] Cf. Breviarium Romanum, *Duae Tabellae ex Rubricis Generalibus Breviarii iuxta Constitutionionem "Divino Afflatu" Reformatis Excerptae* (Turonibus: Mame, 1940); the quality of the feast is always indicated in the Ordo of the place.

[61] Cf. canon 1274, § 1: The incensation of sacred relics, images or statues, in Mass, either solemn or cantata, is forbidden—S. R. C., *Decret. Auth.*, n. 2340.

places in which a priest celebrating a *Missa cantata* may use the privilege of performing the incensations. Hence, the permission may, within the jurisdiction of the granting Ordinary, be bestowed for use in any place where according to the canons Mass may be celebrated.[62]

Although strictly only one server or minister is required at the celebration of a read Mass (*missa lecta*),[63] and consequently only one is required in the celebration of the *Missa cantata,*[64] other servers such as are made necessary by the added duties may be permitted.[65]

The privilege of extending the power by way of further subdelegation is not contained in this faculty; consequently a pastor enjoying this privilege as granted by the Ordinary may not extend it to either the assistants or the visiting priests celebrating Mass in the parish.[66] The Ordinary may, however, give this privilege to all priests of his jurisdiction.

Article 10

To Permit the Use of the *Memoriale Rituum*

> "Permittendi usum *Memorialis Rituum* Benedicti PP. XIII in Ecclesiis seu Oratoriis publicis et semipublicis (non-parochialibus vel quasi-parochialibus) in functionibus Tridui Maioris Hebdomadae et in Benedictione Cinerum, Candelarum et Palmarum; dummodo tamen certo constet decori ac reverentiae sacrorum Mysteriorum satis esse consultum."

The liturgical functions of the days named in the faculty, Candlemas Day, Ash Wednesday, Palm Sunday, and Thursday, Friday, and Saturday of Holy Week, are, according to the rubrics,

---

[62] Cf. canons 822, 823.

[63] Cf. canon 813, § 1.

[64] The rubrics contemplate only the so-called low Mass (read Mass) celebrated without music and sacred ministers, and the Solemn Mass sung according to the rubrics and celebrated with the accompanying ministers of the deacons and subdeacons. The *Missa cantata* is celebrated according to the rubrics of the *Missa lecta,* with such changes as are made necessary in the parts of the Mass which are sung.

[65] Augustine, *Liturgical Law,* pp. 263 ff., lists the servers and their duties in the *Missa cantata.*

[66] Cf. canon 199, § 5.

presumed to be solemn. As a consequence their performance is limited to those churches in which the necessary ministers and furnishings are available.[67]

This faculty permits the Ordinary to extend to churches and oratories, either public or semi-public, which are not parochial or quasi-parochial, the privilege of using the *Memoriale Ritum*[68] in carrying out the functions of the days mentioned above with fewer than the required solemnities.[69]

The privilege is extended to churches and oratories, either public or semi-public, which are neither parochial nor quasi-parochial, rather than to a person. The privilege is to the place in which these functions may be celebrated. Hence, the grant of the privilege pertains to the Ordinary of the place.[70] In order that the privilege may be given validly, certainty is required on the part of the Ordinary that sufficient care has been taken to observe the reverence and propriety due the celebration of these Sacred Mysteries.[71] Clerics are to be employed in assistance at the ceremonies insofar as this is possible.[72]

The permission granted in the use of this faculty may be extended either orally or in writing. It seems, however, that a written grant, containing in the text of the grant reference to the precautions to be followed in the observance of due reverence and care in the use of the *Memoriale Ritum,* would facilitate the grant and use of the privilege.

---

[67] Cf. canon 818: The rubrics of these sacred functions are found in the Roman Missal together with the proper of the Mass on the respective days.

[68] The *Memoriale Rituum* was first issued for use in the smaller parochial churches of Rome, by Benedict XIII, in 1724. The latest edition was ordered by Benedict XV in 1920. There are many English translations available; among the more recent is a translation by the Most Reverend Bartholomew Eustace, first issued in 1935, and reprinted for the third time in 1944, by Joseph F. Wagner, Inc., New York City.

[69] Use of the *Memoriale Rituum* was extended to all parochial or quasi-parochial churches of the Roman rite by Pius VII, in 1821; Cf. S. R. C. *Resolutionis Dubiorum,* 31 iul, 1821, ad 1; S. R. C., Mechlinien., 23 ian. 1876; S. R. C., *Comen.,* 9 dec. 1899, ad 1—S. R. C. *Decret. Auth.,* nn. 2616; 3390; 4049. Cf. also Le Vavasseur-Haegy-Strecky, *Manuel,* I, n. 25, p. 27.

[70] Cf. Chapter V, Article 2, c, of this work.

[71] Cf. canon 39.

[72] Le Vavasseur-Haegy-Stercky, *Manuel,* II, n. 458, pp. 410 ff.

Article II

The Blessing of Objects of Piety, Otherwise Reserved

"Benedicendi obiecta pietatis signo crucis, servatis ritibus ab Ecclesia praescriptis. Occasione tamen visitationis pastoralis, quando multi petunt et plura ac varia exhibent eiusmodi obiecta benedicenda, saepe etiam cum diversis formulis, hisce in casibus permittitur unica formula brevior, dum fit signum crucis super obiecta, nempe: 'Benedicat haec omnia Deus, Pater, et Filius et Spiritus Sanctus, Amen'."

The objects of piety (*obiecta pietatis*) with which this faculty is concerned are those objects whose prime use is to inspire devotion, the benediction of which is reserved to persons having an Apostolic Indult permitting them to confer the blessings, or to members of Religious Orders and Congregations. The blessings in these cases are listed in the Roman Ritual, together with the rubrics governing their administration.[73]

The subdelegation of this privilege is not permitted. In the case of the delegation of the power of orders such a subdelegation is forbidden unless explicit mention is made, in the text of the indult, of the permission to subdelegate.[74] The legislation of canon 1147, § 2, is applicable in the instance of this faculty.[75] Hence its use is enjoyed by all those who receive the faculties according to the rules of canon 66, § 2 and 198, § 1. No territorial restriction is contained in the faculty, so that it seems permissible for the Ordinary to use the powers conceded in the same manner as the privileges of the common law in regard to blessings,[76] that is, any place, even outside the territory of the Ordinary.

In regard to the persons in whose favor the Ordinary may confer

---

[73] Rituale Romanum, Appendix, *Benedictiones Reservatae*, II, *Benedictiones faciendae a sacerdotibus apostolicum indultum habentibus*.

[74] Cf. canon 210.

[75] Canon 1147, § 2: Benedictiones autem impertire potest quilibet presbyter exceptis iis quae Romano Pontifici aut Episcopis aliisve reserventur.

This legislation pertains to the licit conferral of the reserved benedictions as stated in paragraph 3: Benedictio reservata quae a presbytero detur sine necessaria licentia, illicita, est, sed valida, nisi in reservatione Sedes Apostolica aliud expresserit.

[76] Cf. canon 349, § 1, 1°.

the blessings, the prescription of canon 1149 is to be followed, which permits the granting of blessings to all who ask them even catechumens and non-Catholics, with the exception, however, of those Catholics who have been declared incapable of receiving such sacramentals by the law of the Church.[77]

In the use of the faculty the Ordinary is bound to follow the rites of the Church as they are given in the Roman Ritual. Some deviation from the prescribed formulas is permitted on the occasion of the pastoral visitation.[78]

In the words of the faculty the bishop may, during the pastoral visitation when many and various articles are offered for blessing, bless all of them with the simple sign of the cross and one formula, *"Benedicat haec omnia Deus, Pater, et Filius et Spiritus Sanctus. Amen"*. Although the task of performing the pastoral visitation may be accomplished through another, the use of this faculty may not be etxended to the delegate. The delegated visitor may use the faculty only if he has received it from the Holy See, e. g., the vicar general.[79]

Article 12

Permission to Celebrate a Requiem Mass Once Weekly

"Celebrandi Missam de Requie lectam semel in hebdomada ab Ordinario in proprio oratorio; dummodo ne occurrat Festum ritus duplicis primae aut secundae classis, Dominica aut Festum de praecepto etiam suppresso, necnon Octava privilegiata, Feria Quadragesimae, Quatuor Temporum, II Rogationum, Vigilia aut Feria in qua anti-

[77] Cf. canons, 2260; 2275, 2°.

[78] For the interpretation of the words, *servatis ritibus ab Ecclesia praescriptis*, cf. Com. Interp., resp., 12 mart. 1929, ad I—*AAS*, XXI (1929), 170; Bouscaren, *The Canon Law Digest*, canon 349, pp. 209-210. It was answered that these words were not to be understood in the sense that bishops in sacred blessings are forbidden to use a mere sign of the cross when no special formula is prescribed in the liturgical books.

[79] Cf. canons 66, § 2; 368, § 2. Cf. also S. Poenit., resp. 18 iul. 1919, and 10 nov. 1926—*AAS, XI* (1919), 332 and *AAS*, XVIII (1926), 500. The Sacred Penitentiary replied that a bishop could not, either habitually or by way of an individual concession, communicate to his priests the faculties which canon 349, § 1, 1°, accords to bishops, and that the same faculties likewise do not belong to the bishop's vicar general.

cipanda vel primo reponenda est Missa Dominicae: servatis de cetero Rubricis."

The use of this faculty concerns the celebration of a Requiem Mass on those days when its celebration is not permitted by the current liturgical calendar, with the exceptions listed in the text of the faculty. On the days when a Votive Mass is permitted, or on the days when a Requiem Mass may be celebrated for a particular deceased person,[50] there is no need for the privilege of this faculty. The Mass that may be said in virtue of this faculty is the one found in the Missal in the section titled *Missae Defunctorum,* listed as the *Missa Quotidiana Defunctorum.* The low Mass (Missa Lecta) is explicitly mentioned in the faculty, and consequently the faculty cannot be used as a privilege to celebrate either a *Missa Cantata* or a *Missa Solemnis.*

The Mass may be celebrated once each week, but only in the oratory of the Ordinary, and by the Ordinary (ab Ordinario). Thus any other who celebrates Mass in the private oratory of the Ordinary could not use this privilege. The vicar general, by virtue of his office, has the privilege of this faculty; his use of it, however, depends upon his celebration of Mass in his own private oratory (proprio oratorio).

Certain days are excepted by the text of the faculty. They are the double feasts of both the second and first class, the Sundays and Feasts of precept, even though suppressed, the privileged octaves, the ferial days of Lent, the Ember days, the Feria II of the Rogation days, and the vigils or ferial days on which a Sunday Mass is to be anticipated or to which it is to be transferred. An indication of which days of the year will be excluded as a result of the foregoing list is found in the Ordo of the diocese.[51]

The final phrase of the text of the faculty, *servatis de cetero Rubricis* refers to the rubrics of the Requiem Mass, which in some points differ from the general rubrics to be observed in the celebration of Mass, e. g., a special Requiem Mass is indicated for daily

---

[50] Missale Romanum, *Rubricae Generales Missae,* Tit. IV, De Missis votivis S. Mariae et aliis, tit. V *De Missis Defunctorum.*

[51] Cf. Breviarium Romanum, *Kalendarium,* and *Duae Tabellae ex Rubricis Generalibus Breviarii iuxta Constitutionem "Divino Afflatu" reformatis excerptae.*

celebration. They are listed both together and with the proper of the Mass as contained in the Roman Missal and under Title III, *De Missis Defunctorum,* of the section of the Missal, *Additiones et Variationes in Rubricis Missalis ad normam bullae "Divino Amatu et Subsequentium S. R. C. decretorum.*

CHAPTER XI

FACULTIES FROM THE SACRED PENITENTIARY

Introduction

The general norms governing the use of the faculties from the Sacred Penitentiary are contained in an added instruction concluding the text.

> "1. Ordinarius recensitis facultatibus, tum absolvendi a censuris tum dispensandi, pro foro conscientiae, etiam extra sacramentalem confessionem cum suis subditis, et extra dioecesim quoque, quatenus vel ipse vel subditus vel uterque extra dioecesim fuerint, necnon cum non sudditis intra limites proprii territorii, ex speciali Sedis Apostolicae auctoritate ipsi concessa, uti valebit; easque intra fines dioecesis tantum Canonico Poenitentiario necnon Vicariis Foraneis, pro foro pariter conscientiae et in actu sacramentalis confessionis dumtaxat, etiam habitualiter, si ipsi placuit, aliis vero confessariis cum ad ipsum Ordinarium in casibus particularibus poenitentium recursum habuerint, pro exposito casu impertiri poterit, nisi ob peculiares causas aliquibus confessariis specialiter deputandis per tempus, arbitrio suo statuendum, illas communicare iudicabit.
>
> "2. Ordinarius facultatem praefatas Indulgentias concedendi nemini delegare potest, sed per se ipse tantum exercere debet."

The faculties from the Sacred Penitentiary lend themselves to division into two classifications. One group is concerned with the absolution of censures and penalties, and the dispensation from impediments or irregularities. This group comprises the first nine articles of the text. The second group, consisting of one article, article ten, is concerned with the concession of indulgences.

The faculties concerning absolution or dispensation are granted for use in the internal forum (*foro conscientiae*) both sacramental and extra-sacramental, according to the instruction of the Sacred Penitentiary and the jurisdiction of that Tribunal.[1] That is to say, these faculties from the Sacred Penitentiary are to be used for the granting of absolutions and dispensations in the internal forum, either sacramentally or extra-sacramentally; use of the faculties for absolution or dispensation in the external forum is an invalid use of the power.[2]

The faculties are not restricted to occult cases for their use, as are the powers conceded the Ordinary in canon 2237, § 2. Thus, the faculties may be used for absolving a censure or dispensing a vindictive penalty inflicted in consequence of the perpetration of a public delict. The restriction concerns the absolution or the dispensation, which must remain in the internal forum; it does not relate to the nature of the cause of the punishment or irregularity, that is, the delict.

The result of the restriction placed upon the absolutions granted by virtue of these faculties is expressed in canon 2251.[3] Thus, a penitent who receives absolution from a censure by virtue of these faculties may conduct himself as having been absolved in the external forum.

The faculties of absolving and dispensing are to be used by Ordinaries, which term includes vicars general, in favor of their subjects: 1) within the territory of the Ordinary, 2) when either the subject or the Ordinary or both are outside the territory; in favor of non-subjects, but only within the proper territory of the Ordinary. The faculties are not to be used outside the territory of the Ordinary when employed by his delegate, as is explicitly stated in the instructions of the Sacred Penitentiary.

The matter with which these faculties pertaining to absolution and dispensation is concerned is that which, under the common law and ordinary circumstances, is beyond the power of the Ordinary.

---

[1] Cf. canon 258, § 1.

[2] Cf. canon 203, § 1.

[3] Cf. canon 2251: Si absolutio censurae detur in foro externo, utrumque forum afficit; si in interno, absolutus, rèmoto scandalo, potest uti talem se habere etiam in actibus fori externi; sed, nisi concessio absolutionis probetur aut saltem legitime praesumatur in foro externo, censura potest a Superioribus fori externi, quibus reus parere debet, urgeri, donec absolutio in eodem foro habita fuerit.

The powers conceded to the Ordinary or confessors by the Code of Canon Law or by special indult are not considered in this discussion.[4] Thus, those penalties which are enacted in the Code of Canon Law, but are reserved to the Holy See, are the proper objects of the powers conceded in these faculties. It must be remembered, however, that the faculties permit the granting of absolutions and dispensations in the internal forum only. Those reservations which are affected by the faculties remain in effect insofar as the external forum is concerned.[5]

Subdelegation of the faculties for use in the forum of conscience, either sacramentally or extra-sacramentally, may be made by the Ordinary, if he pleases, to the canon penitentiary,[6] and to the vicars forane.[7]

These above mentioned officers may be subdelegated for a period of five years, or for a shorter period according to the mind of the Ordinary and the duration of his faculties. The Ordinary can also subdelegate the faculties, for use in single cases, to other confessors who have recourse to him in particular cases. In some instances the Ordinary is also permitted in view of specific circumstances to subdelegate the powers of the faculties to other confessors for fixed periods of time. The length of the period of time is to be fixed according to the judgment of the Ordinary. Subdelegates of the Ordinary may use the faculties only within the proper territory of the Ordinary.

The forms to be used in the granting of the favors of these faculties are not specified. In the granting of sacramental absolution the form of absolution contained in the Roman Ritual for the sacrament of penance is proper. In the extra-sacramental absolution, the use of the form of the Ritual proper to extra-sacramental absolution is urged, although it is not necessary for the validity of the absolution.[8]

Subdelegation of those faculties which permit the concession of

---

[4] Cf. canons 2237, § 2; 2254; 2290; also Moriarty, *The Extraordinary Absolution from Censures,* The Catholic University of America Canon Law Studies, n. 113, (Washington, D. C.: The Catholic University of America, 1938.)

[5] Cf. canon 2251.

[6] Cf. canon 398, § 1 and § 2; 401, § 1 and § 2.

[7] Cf. canons 445; 217.

[8] Rituale Romanum, Tit., III, cap. 2; cap. 3.

indulgences is prohibited. They are to be used by the Ordinary only. It seems that in this instance the term Ordinary does not include the vicar general, unless he be at the same time a bishop. This conclusion appears permissible from a reply of the Sacred Penitentiary in regard to the faculties extended the bishops in canon 349, § 1, 1°. The response states that these powers cannot be communicated to his priests by a bishop, and that they do not belong to the vicar general.[9] The same interpretation seems applicable in the case of these faculties.

Article 1

Absolution From Reserved Censures and Penalties Incident to Heresy

"Absolvendi quoscumque poenitentes (exceptis haereticis haeresim inter fideles e proposito disseminantibus) a quibusvis censuris et poenis ecclesiasticis ob haereses tam nemine audiente quam coram aliis externatas incursis, postquam tamen poenitens magistros ex professo haereticalis doctrinae, si quos noverit, ac personas ecclesiasticas et religiosas, si quas hac in re complices habuerit, prout de iure, denunciaverit; et quatenus ob iustas causas huiusmodi denunciatio ante absolutionem pergi nequeat, facta ab eo seria promissione denunciationem ipsam peragendi cum primum et quo meliori modo fieri poterit, et postquam in singulis casibus haereses coram absolvente secreto abiuraverit; iniuncta pro modo excessuum gravi poenitentia salutari cum frequentia sacramentorum; et obligatione se retractandi apud personas eorum quibus haereses manifestavit, atque illata scandala reparandi."

Those in whose favor this faculty may be used are all those who, provided they are within the jurisdiction of the Ordinary, have, because of heresy,[10] incurred the penalties of canon 2314, § 1, 1°,

[9] S. Poenit., resp. 10 nov. 1926—*AAS*, XVIII (1926), 500. Cf. footnote at end of Article 11 in the previous Chapter of this work. Cf. also Bouscaren, *The Canon Law Digest*, I, canon 349, p. 209.

[10] Cf. canon 1325, § 2: Post receptum baptismum si quis, nomen retinens christianum, pertinaciter aliquam ex veritatibus fide divina et catholica credendis denegat aut de ea dubitat, haereticus; . . . : MacKenzie, *The Delict of Heresy in Its Commission, Penalization, Absolution*, The Catholic University of America Canon Law Studies, n. 77, (Washington, D. C.:

and who cannot be absolved from the censure because of its reservation according to paragraph 2 of the same canon.[11] The faculty may be used in favor of apostates and schismatics only when they have incurred the censure by reason of heresy, not when the censure is inflicted because of apostasy or schism.[12]

Thus, those who are subject to the laws of the Church,[13] whether they be lay persons, clerics or religious, may be the beneficiaries of the use of this faculty. The sole exception is contained in the words, *exceptis haereticis haeresim inter fideles e proposito disseminantibus,* that is, heretics who make it their business to disseminate heretical teachings among the faithful. Such people cannot be absolved by virtue of this faculty. The exception is couched in such unmistakable terms that it is evident that absolution granted to such persons, in defiance of the exception, is invalid. The reservation of the censure remains in force.

In the words of the faculty the delict of heresy, because of which the penalties are incurred, may be committed in the presence of others or in their absence *tam nemine audiente quam coram aliis externatas incursis.* Absolution granted by virtue of this faculty is confined, however, to the internal forum, as has been explained in the introduction to this Chapter. Should the delict be brought to the external forum of the Ordinary, absolution may be given by means of the power conceded to the Ordinary in canon 2314, § 2,

---

The Catholic University of America 1932), p. 19. Sole, *De Delictis et Poenis,* Romae: Pustet, 1920), n. 314 ff., pp. 222 ff; Vermeersch-Creusen, *Epitome,* II, n. 660, p. 459.

[11] Canon 2314, § 1: Omnes a christiana fide apostatae et singuli haeretici aut schismatici:

1°, Incurrunt ipso facto excommunicationem;

§ 2: Absolutio ab excommunicatione de qua in § 1, in foro conscientiae impertienda, est speciali modo Sedi Apostolicae reservata. Si tamen delictum apostasiae, haeresis vel schismatis ad forum externum Ordinarii loci quovis modo deductum fuerit, etiam per voluntariam confessionem (i. e., non per sacramentalem confessionem) idem Ordinarius, non vero Vicarius Generalis sine mandato speciali, resipiscentem praevia abiuratione iuridice peracta aliisque servatis de iure servandis, sua auctoritate ordinaria in foro exteriore absolvere potest; ita vero absolutus, potest deinde a peccato absolvi a quolibet confessario in foro conscientiae . Abiuratio vero habetur iuridice peracta cum fit coram ipso Ordinario loci vel eius delegato et saltem duobus testibus. Cf. Goodwine, *The Reception of Converts,* The Catholic University of America Canon Law Studies, n. 198, (Washington, D. C.: The Catholic University of America Press, 1944.) pp. 155-163.

[12] Cf. canon 67.

[13] Cf. canons 87; 1325, § 2.

even if the delict is known though voluntary confession. Sacramental confession, by its very nature, is not included in the term of voluntary confession as it is used in the just mentioned canon.

Absolution when imparted by virtue of this faculty is to be given only after certain provisions are fulfilled. The penitent must report according to the process outlined in canon 1936, those who are teaching the heretical doctrine, if he knows who they are, and any religious or ecclesiastical persons who may have been his accomplices in the heresy. The penitent, under the terms of the faculty itself, is excused from the denunciation of the above mentioned persons only when he does not know the teachers of the heretical doctrine. The terminology of the faculty in regard to this provision is held to affect the licit use of the faculty only, and not, it seems, the valid use of the powers of the faculty.[14]

The denunciation may be made either orally or in writing, and to those who may receive the denunciation according to canon 1936 must be added the confessor who is making use of this faculty.[15] In the event that the penitent, because of a just reason, is prevented from making the denunciation, the grantor of the absolution must exact from the penitent a serious promise to the effect the denunciation as early as possible and in the best manner that the penitent is able. What may constitute a just reason for postponing the denunciation will vary with the circumstances of each individual case. The reason must, however, be of sufficient gravity to be proportionate to the rule requiring that the denunciation be made prior to the grant of the absolution.[16]

Insufficient time at the moment of the petition for absolution, lack of a suitable place, or some similar reason, seems to offer a sufficient cause for postponing the denunciation. The Ordinary may authorize another to receive the denunciation from the penitent. But a subdelegate of the Ordinary could not again subdelegate to another the power to receive the denunciation of a penitent, unless

[14] Cf. Van Hove, *Re Rescriptis*, n. 137, p. 123; Provisions introduced in the text of rescripts by the use of the word *postquam* are not held to be conditions pertaining to the valid use of the favors contained in the rescript.

[15] Cf. canon 200, § 1.

[16] Cf. canons 84; 2252; 2254.

he be among those empowered by canon 1936 to receive such denunciation.[17]

From the nature of the crime of heresy it seems that it is only after either the denunciation or a promise such as described above has been received by the confessor that the absolution from the censure should be given. This does not pertain, however, to the valid use of the faculty, as is demonstrated above. The denunciation may be required by the confessor within any reasonable time designated by him. Thus, the absolution from the censure or penalty could be given with the proviso that the proper denunciation be made within two weeks, or one month, dependent upon the circumstances of each case as known to the grantor of the absolution.[18]

The faculty also requires that the penitent make an abjuration of the heresy secretly before the grantor of the absolution.[19] The nature or neresy itself demands an abjuration of the heresy before absolution can be given from the sin; abjuration is a necessary adjunct to contrition.[20]

A penance proportionate to the gravity of the committed offense is to be imposed by the grantor of the absolution. What may constitute a grave penance in a particular case depends upon the person and circumstances of the case. Authors list, as included among grave penances, five decades of the Rosary, assistance at Mass on a day other than one of obligation, and fasting or abstaining from the use of meat for one day.[21] In addition the penitent is to be urged to receive the sacraments frequently, and reminded of the obligation of making reparation for the harm done by his or her defection; that is, to make a retraction of the heresy before those in whose presence the heresy was manifested, and to repair the scandal.

---

[17] Cf. canon 199, § 5.

[18] Cf. canon 2239, § 1.

[19] In the external forum a formal abjuration is required, made before the Ordinary or his delegate and at least two witnesses. Cf. canon 2314, § 2.

[20] Vermeersch, *Theologia Moralis,* III, n. 567, p. 485. Cf. canon 2250, § 2.

[21] Vermeersch, *Theologia Moralis,* III, n. 546, 3, p. 464; Sabetti-Barrett, *Compendium Theologiae Moralis* (27 a. ed., New York: Pustet, 1919), n. 768, p. 729.

Article 2

To Absolve From Censures and Penalties Incurred Through the Use or Defense of Prohibited Books

> "Absolvendi a censuris et poenis ecclesiasticis eos qui libros apostatarum, haeriticorum aut schismaticorum, apostasiam, haeresim aut schisma propugnantes, aliosve per Apostolicas Litteras nominatim prohibitos defenderint aut scienter sine debita licentia legerint vel retinuerint; iniuncta congrua poenitentia salutari ac firma obligatione supradictos libros, quantum fieri poterit, ante absolutionem, destruendi vel Ordinario aut confessario tradendi."

The prohibited books which are named in the faculty are those which are prohibited according to the law of canon 1399, 2°, 3°, 4°, 6°, and 7°, and those which are explicitly condemned by Apostolic letters.[22] The prohibitions of canon 1399 apply also to magazines, periodicals, and pamphlets according to canon 1384, § 2. It seems that this faculty may be used also for the absolution of censures and penalties incurred by reason of the use or defense of such magazines or periodicals. Absolutions from the penalties incurred by the publication or printing or selling of such books is not included in this faculty, and, hence any extension of the powers of the faculty to include such cases is not permitted.[23]

The faculty mentions as the delicts punished by the censures contemplated by this faculty the defense and the deliberate reading and retaining of such prohibited literary works. The penalty for these acts is enacted in canon 2318, § 1, and there designated as an excommunication reserved in a special manner to the Holy See.[24] The penalty is separate and distinct from that which is established for heresy, apostasy, or schism according to canon 2314. That penalty is treated in Article 1 of this Chapter.

The powers of the faculty may be used by an Ordinary in favor of his subjects, either within or outside his proper territory, as is set forth in the instructions of the Sacred Penitentiary. Vicars general

[22] Cf. Chapter VI, Article 1, which treats the faculty to extend permission to read and retain such prohibited books.

[23] Cf. canon 67.

[24] Cf. canon 2318, § 1.

are considered Ordinaries in regard to this act of absolution. Subdelegates are limited to the use of the faculty within the territorial limits of the subdelegating Ordinary's jurisdiction. As in the case of the other faculties for absolving and dispensing, this faculty is also confined to use in and for the forum of conscience, either sacramental or extra-sacramental.[25]

Persons using the faculty are instructed to assign a suitable penance for performance by the penitent and to place upon the penitent the obligation either of delivering the books to the confessor or the Ordinary, or of destroying them. When this is possible, it should be required of the penitent before the absolution is given. As it is stated in this faculty, the requirement does not appear to be necessary for the valid use of the power of absolving.[26]

Article 3

To Absolve From Censure Incurred Through the Impeding of Ecclesiastical Jurisdiction

> "Absolvendi a censuris eos qui impediverint directe vel indirecte exercitum iurisdictionis ecclesiasticae sive interni sive externi fori, ad hoc recurrentes ad quamlibet laicalem potestatem."

This faculty is concerned with the penalty inflicted upon those who, by having recourse to any lay authority whatsoever, impede the exercise of the jurisdiction of the Church in either the internal or the external forum, either directly or indirectly. The text of the faculty uses the same wording as canon 2334.[27]

The penalty is that of an excommunication incurred ipso facto, that is, without the formality of sentence, and reserved in a special

[25] In regard to those who incur this penalty, cf. Chelodi, *Ius Canonicum de Delicitis et Poenis et de Iudiciis Criminalibus* (5 ed., recognita et aucta a Pio Cirotti, Trento: Ardesi, 1943), n. 60, 2, p. 70; Sole, *De Delictis et Poenis*, n. 328, 5°, p. 233.

[26] Cf. canon 39.

[27] Canon 2334: Excommunicatione latae sententiae speciali modo Sedi Apostolicae reservata plectuuntur:

2° Qui impediunt direct vel indirecte exercitium iurisdictionis ecclesiasticae sive interni sive externi fori, ad hoc recurrentes ad quamlibet laicalum potestatem. For the question of who incurs the penalty and how cannon 2334 is to be interpreted, cf. Sole, *De Delicitis et Poenis*, n. 360, p. 265, Vermeersch-Creusen, *Epitome*, III, n. 534, p. 325.

manner to the Holy See. As in the previous faculties discussed, the Ordinary is limited to absolving from the censure in the internal forum, either sacramentally or extra-sacramentally; a subdelegate of the Ordinary may use the faculty only for absolutions given sacramentally.[28]

No penance other than that imposed for the sin involved is prescribed or suggested by the text of the faculty, nor is there in the text of the faculty any mention of conditions which must be fulfilled in the use of the faculty. The grantor of the absolution should, however, impose an appropriate penance according to the law of canon 2248, § 2.

Article 4

To Absolve From Censures and Penalties Incurred Because of Duelling

> "Absolvendi a censuris et a poenis ecclesiasticis circa duellum statutis, in casibus dumtaxat ad forum externum non deductis; iniuncta gravi poenitentia salutari et aliis iniunctis, quae fuerint de iure iniugenda."

The ecclesiastical punishments inflicted upon those who are guilty of duelling, whether fighting, challenging, accepting a challenge, or being a wilful party to a duel even in the sole capacity of a witness, are mainly two, viz.,: excommunication, incurred *ipso facto* and simply reserved to the Holy See, and infamy of law, also incurred *ipso facto*.[29] The penalty of infamy of law, however, is incurred only by the duellists themselves and their seconds. The privation of christian burial spoken of in canon 1240, § 1, 4°, is by its nature a penalty. It is not, however, reserved to the Holy See. The cessation of the privation is delineated in the same canon.[30]

Clerics guilty of the crime of duelling become irregular. Dispensation from the irregularity, in occult cases, is within the jurisdiction of the Ordinary, or of any confessor, if the case is urgent.[31]

---

[28] Cf. Introduction to this Chapter.

[29] Cf. canon 2351, § 1 and § 2; Sole, *De Delictis et Poenis*, n. 392, p. 320; Vermeersch-Creusen, *Epitome*, III, 553, p. 340.

[30] Cf. canon 1240, § 1, 4° and § 2.

[31] Cf. canons 985, 5°; 990, § 1 and § 2.

The powers conceded in this faculty, as in all the faculties deriving from the Sacred Penitentiary, are confined to use in the internal forum, the forum of conscience, either within or outside the sacrament of penance. The powers of this faculty may be used, however, only in those cases which have not been brought into the external forum (*ad forum externum non deductis*).[32]

The meaning of this phrase seems to be that the faculties can be used only in those cases which have not yet been brought before the Church for public action. The external forum (*forum externum*) when spoken of with regard to the exercise of jurisdiction within the Church, concerns public action with public juridical effects.[33] Thus, an Ordinary, or his subdelegate, may use this faculty in those cases which, even though they are public, have not yet been brought into the external forum of the Church. In this the faculty is limited to a greater degree than the faculties which have been discussed previously.[34]

A passage parallel to the exception contained in the faculty is found in canon 2237, § 1, 1°.[35] In this instance the Ordinary may not use the powers of remitting penalties enacted by the common law in those public cases which have been brought into the contentious forum (*ad forum contentiosum deductis*), that is, when the cases have been brought before the proper tribunal of the Church for action in a public manner. This stage in procedural development of the case is held to have been reached when the

[32] The pre-Code faculties read, *ad forum Ordinarii non deductis.* Cf. Putzer, *Commentarium,* n. 251, p. 433. In occult cases the Ordinary does not need the power conceded in this faculty; cf. canon 2237, § 2; Coronata, *Institutiones Iures Canonici,* IV, 137.

[33] Cf. canon 196; Capello, *Summa Iuris Canonici,* I, n. 255; p. 308; Bouscaren-Ellis, *Canon Law,* (Milwaukee: The Bruce Publishing Company, 1946), p. 133; Vermeersch-Creusen, *Epitome,* I, n. 313, p. 258.

[34] The extra-sacramental confession of the penitent as mentioned in canon 2314, § 2, does not appear to be considered as a means of bringing the delicit into the external forum, since it is not explicitly mentioned. Its mention in canon 2314, § 2, is in the manner of an exception in a particular case.

[35] Canon 2237, § 1: In casibus publicis potest Ordinarius poenas latae sententiae iure communi statutas remittere, exceptis:

1°, Casibus ad forum contentiosum deductis;

2°, Censuris Sedi Apostolicae reservatis;

3°, Poenis inhabilitatis ad beneficia, officia dignitates munera in Ecclesia, vocem activam et passivam eorumve privationis, suspensionis perpetuae, infamiae iuris, privationis iuris patronatus et privilegii seu gratiae a Sede Apostolica concessae.

party or parties have been summoned by the tribunal according to law, or have appeared before the court of their own will, for the purpose of litigation.[36]

In view of the similiarity of the terms contained in the faculties, it mav be concluded that the meaning conveyed by the terms of the above mentioned canon applies also to this faculty. That is to say, cases may be held to be introduced into the external forum when the delinquent party has either been legitimately summoned or has appeared of his own volition before the proper tribunal of the Church for the purpose of litigation.[37] Thus *"ad forum externum deductis"* means in application *"ad forum externum publicum deductis"*, that is, the case has become one in which the public authority of the Church manifests an active interest. The preliminary acts of the denunciation, the accusation, the investigation and the rebuke of the delinquent[38] are not considered as being sufficient to constitute the case as being brought before the external forum of the Church.[39]

The precise juridical moment in which the case is brought into the external forum of the Church coincides with that moment when the delinquent party has been either legitimately summoned by the court or has appeared of his own volition for the purpose of litigation. In such cases the Ordinary cannot validly use the powers of this faculty. The moment is determinable from the action taken by the competent Church authority in the case. Once any given case is considered as having been begun, according to canon 1725, § 1, the Ordinary can no longer absolve the censure with which this faculty is concerned.[40] It bears repetition that absolution given in

[36] Canon 1725: Cum citatio legitime peracta fueri aut partes sponte in iudicum venerint: Cf. Augustine, *A Commentary on Canon Law* (8 vols., St. Louis: B. Herder Book Co., Vol. VIII, 3 ed., 1931), 281; Lega,-Bartoccetti, *Commentarius in Iudicia Ecclesiastica iuxta Codicem Iuris Canonici* (3 vols., Romae: Anonima Libraria Cattolica Italiana, 1938-1941), II, 537, 542.

[37] Cf. Vermeersch-Creusen, *Epitome*, III, n. 431, 2; p. 254.

[38] Cf. canons 1934-1935.

[39] Wernz-Vidal, *Ius Canonicum ad Codicis normam exactum*, (7 vols. in 8, Romae: apud Aedes Universitatis Gregorianae, 1923-1938), VIII, n. 214, p. 224.

[40] This conclusion is in keeping with the principle that restrictive conditions are to be interpreted strictly and the favors of the faculties are to be interpreted widely. *Odia restringi et favores convenit ampliari*—R. J. 15, in VI°. Cf. canon 67.

virtue of this faculty can be given only in the internal forum, either sacramentally or extra-sacramentally. The penalty of infamy of law is reserved to the Holy See, [41] further instruction is contained in the text of the faculty. The penitent is to have imposed upon him a grave penance together with all the other demands of the law. [42] The faculty contemplates solely the absolution from the censure incurred by duellists and those held guilty of participation; and obligation resulting from the delict retain their force in regard to the penitent. The two final provisions of the faculty do not, as it appears from the wording of the text, pertain to the valid use of the faculty, and absolutions imparted in virtue of it are validly though illicitly granted if the fulfillment of the two mentioned provisions is slighted, as long, of course, as the other demands are duly complied with. [43]

The terms of the faculty prescribe a grave penance. The gravity of the penance depends upon the particular circumstances of the case in question. Authors list some penances which are considered grave. In reality, it seems that in this matter the judgment of the grantor of the absolution in the light of the circumstances if the individual case is the controlling factor. [44]

Article 5

To Absolve From Censures and Penalties Incurred Because of Membership in Forbidden Societies

"Absolvendi a censuris et poenis ecclesiasticis eos qui nomen dederint sectae massonicae aliisque eiusdem generis associationibus, qua contra Ecclesiam vel legitimas civiles potestates machinantur; ita tamen ut a respectiva secta vel associatione omnino se separent eamque abiurent; denuncient, iuxta can. 2336, § 2, personas ecclesiasticas et religiosas, si quas eidem adscriptas noverint; libros, manuscripta ac signa eamdem respicienta, si qua retineant, in manus absolventis tradant, ad S. Officium quamprimum caute

[41] Cf. canon 2295.

[42] Such as the obligation to make restitution of the damage involved, to repair scandal, etc. Cf. canons 2210, 2354.

[43] Cf. canon 39.

[44] Vermeersch, *Theologia Moralis*, III, n. 546, p. 464; Sabetti-Barrett, *Compendium Theoligiae Moralis*, n. 768, p. 729; cf. canon 2313.

> transmittenda aut saltem, si iustae gravesque causae id postulent, destruenda; iniuncta pro modo culparum gravi poenitentia salutari cum frequentatione sacramentalis confessionis et obligatione illata scandala reparandi."

The Masonic lodge is explicitly named in the faculty; included also are others which are of the same nature. Of these some are forbidden simply under pain of grave sin, while others are forbidden under pain of a censure reserved to the Holy See. The classification of any particular society as being forbidden under pain of censure is the right of the Holy See. If there exists a doubt as to whether a given society is forbidden, or if membership is forbidden under pain of censure, the prescript of canon 15 applies to the effect that no penalty is incurred.[45] Writing of such societies, Ayrinhac (1867-1930) stated: "Such certainly are, besides those nominally condemned, nihilistic, anarchistic and perhaps some socialistic societies. What is to be considered is their end, not the secrecy which they may or may not impose upon their members."[46]

The penalty incurred is an excommunication *ipso facto* reserved in a simple manner to the Holy See.[47] In the case of clerics further punishment is enacted in the prescription of canon 2336, § 1. These penalties are reserved in public cases, according to canon 2237, § 1. They may be absolved, however, in the internal forum, either sacramentally or extra-sacramentally, in virtue of the powers conceded in this faculty.

Several conditions are attached to the use of this faculty. They are introduced collectively with the words *ita tamen ut*, "to the extent that", which, in view of the nature of the crime being considered and the conditions that follow the phrase, may be considered

---

[45] Cf. canon 15: Leges, etiam irritantics et inhabilitantes, in dubio iuris non urgent; in dubio autem facti potest Ordinarius in eis dispensare, dummodo agatur de legibus in quibus Romanus Pontifex dispensare solet.

[46] Ayrinhac-Lydon, *Penal Legislation in the New Code of Canon Law* (Revised edition, New York: Benzinger Brothers, 1944), p. 196. For those who incur the penalties, cf. Ayrinhac-Lydon, *loc. cit.;* Sole, *De Delictis et Poenis*, n. 361, p. 268.

[47] Cf. canon 2335. In occult cases the Ordinary has the power to absolve from the censure in accordance with the norm of canon 2337, § 2.

as expressing the conditions in a manner which pertains to the valid use of the faculty.[48]

First among these conditions is that the penitent must entirely withdraw from the society and abjure the society itself. Passive membership, or so-called nominal membership is, *per se,* not permitted.[49] The abjuration is to be performed before the grantor of the absolution. Since the faculty transmits the powers necessary for its use, the Ordinary or his subdelegate who absolves from the above mentioned penalties necessarily has the power of receiving the abjuration of the penitent.[50]

The penitent must also give the names of, i. e., denounce, any ecclesiastical or religious persons whom he knows as belonging to the society. He is likewise required to submit any books, rituals, or insignia of the society that he might still have in his possession. These are to be submitted to the grantor of the absolution. As in the condition of complete severance of relations with the society, these above mentioned conditions pertain to the valid use of the faculty. In the case of the surrendering of the items described, the absolution may be given on the condition that the surrender be made in the future, within a time set by the grantor of the absolution.[51]

Having received the items named in the faculty, the grantor of the absolution is to transmit them at once to the Holy Office, or, if just and grave cause urge it, he is to destroy them. This is an obligation on the grantor of the absolution, and, as is evident, does not pertain to the valid use of the faculty in behalf of the penitent.

---

[48] The words, *ita tamen ut,* duly considered in the context of the faculty, seem to be included in the rule of canon 39: Conditiones in rescriptis tunc tantum essentiales pro eorundem validatate censentur, cum per particulas *si dummodo,* vel aliam eiusdem significationis exprimuntur.

[49] A response issued by the Holy Office on January 18, 1896, explained that passive membership in some forbidden societies is permitted if: 1) membership had been subscribed in good faith, that is, before the party knew the society was forbidden; 2) no scandal will result from the nominal membership; 3) it is impossible for the party to withdraw without grave loss; and 4) there is no danger of perversion either to the party or his family, and no liklihood of any insistence on a non-Catholic burial. Each case must be referred to the Apostolic Delegate for the permission. This was later changed to include also the Metropolitan, as of June 26, 1913. Cf. Beste, *Introductio in Codicem,* p. 946; Aryinhac-Lydon, *Penal Legislation,* p. 200.

[50] Cf. canon 200, § 1.

[51] Cf. canon 2239, § 1.

There is no doubt that an Ordinary or his subdelegate who acts contrary to this prescription acts wrongfully; nevertheless, the absolution is valid.[62]

Finally, although it does not pertain to the valid use of the faculty, the penitent is to be given a grave and salutary penance,[63] and the obligation of repairing any scandal connected with his having become a member of the society must be duly urged. He is to be reminded, too, of his obligation of availing himself of the reception of the sacrament of confession at frequent intervals.

Article 6

To Absolve From Censures and Penalties Incurred Because of the Violation of a Religious Cloister

> "Absolvendi a censuris et poenis ecclesiasticis eos qui clausurum regularium utriusque sexus sine legitima licentia ingressi fuerint, necnon qui eos introduxerint vel admiserint; dummodo tamen id factum ne fuerit ad finem utcumque graviter criminosum, etiam effectu non secuto, nec ad externum forum deductum; congrua pro modo culpae poenitentia salutari iniuncta."

The use of this faculty, as of the faculty concerning the absolution from the punishment incurred because of participation in duelling, is restricted to those cases involving the violation of the cloister which are not introduced into the external forum, *dummodo . . . nec ad externum forum deductum,* that is to say, in cases which have not been brought before the jurisdiction of the Church in a

---

[62] There is no provision made for the loss sustained by the penitent in the surrender of the books, insignia, etc., as mentioned in the faculty. In some cases, e. g., when jewelled emblems would have to be surrendered, the financial loss could amount to considerable. It seems that a certain amount of loss is justifiable, and that the penitent has no claim against the loss of a reasonable number of books or of plain insignia. However, in the case of richly contrived emblems, it seems that as long as the connection between the society and the emblem is destroyed the provision of the faculty is fulfilled. Consequently, the penitent could recover the intrinsic value of the article, after its efficacy as a symbol has been destroyed. This, it seems, constitutes a sufficient reason for not transmitting the items to the Holy Office. Sale alone of the items does not appear to fulfill the provisions of the faculty expressed in the word *destruenda.*

[63] Cf. Article 1 of this Chapter.

public manner.[54] In virtue of this faculty absolution can be given in the internal forum only; but it may be given either sacramentally or extra-sacramentally.[55]

Those who unlawfully enter the cloister of regulars and those who unlawfully introduce or admit others to it incur the penalties enacted in canon 2342.[56] There are some persons who may lawfully enter the cloister of regulars at all times, and others who may enter lawfully on occasion. The persons are identified in canons 598, § 2; 600, 1°, 2°, 3°, and 4°.[57] In occult cases the Ordinary has the power of absolving and dispensing by virtue of canon 2237, § 2, while in cases involving a doubt of either law or fact, the prescription of canon 15 obtains. Hence the necessity of using the powers contained in this faculty will arise only in those cases in which the penalties enumerated in canon 2342 are certainly incurred, and as is stated above, in which the issue has not been brought into the external forum, that is to say, in those cases which have not been brought before the Church for public action.[58] This condition is imposed under pain of invalidity in the event of the condition's non-fulfillment. Use of the faculty in cases which have been brought before the Church publicly for judgment is beyond its scope.[59]

A further condition is attached to the use of the faculty; it too is essential to the valid use of the faculty. Absolution cannot be

---

[54] Treatment is given the interpretation of the condition, *nec ad forum externum deductum*, in Article 4 of this Chapter.

[55] Subdelegate of the Ordinary can use the faculty only within the territorial jurisdiction of the delegating Ordinary, and then only sacramentally. Cf. Introduction of this Chapter.

[56] Canon 2342: Plectuntur ipso facto excommunicatione Sedi Apostolicae simpliciter reservata:

1° Clausuram monialium violantes, cuiuscunque generis aut conditionis vel sexus sint, in earum monasteria sine legitima licentia ingrediendo, pariterque eos introducentes vel admittentes; quod si clerici sint, praeterea suspendantur per tempus pro gravitate culpae ab Ordinario definiendum;

2° Mulieres violantes regularium virorum clausuram et Superiores aliique, quicunque ii sint, eas cuiuscunque aetatis introducentes vel admittentes; et praeterea religiosi introducentes vel admittentes priventur officio, si quod habeant, et voce activa ac passiva.

[57] For a treatment of these canons as regarding those who incur the penalties for unlawful entrance into the cloister, cf., Creusen-Garesche-Ellis, *Religious Men and Women in the Code*, n. 283, p. 213; Sole, *De Delictis et Poenis*, nn. 373 ff., pp. 287 ff. The faculty does not comprehend the absolution of the censure incurred for unlawful departure.

[58] Cf. for explanation of *nec ad externum forum deductum*, Article 4 of this Chapter.

[59] Cf. canon 39.

granted, in virtue of this faculty, in those cases in which the violation of the cloister was perpetrated for a criminal purpose, even though that purpose remained unachieved.[60] The term *criminosum* in the faculty is to be taken in the sense in which it is used in the Code of Canon Law, that is, as referring to anything gravely sinful and morally imputable.[61] Thus, the determination of the purpose because of which the cloister was violated on the part of the person entering the cloister, or on the part of the one either admitting or introducing that person, is of paramount importance in the use of this faculty. If there be discovered any motive whose fulfillment in the canonical sense stands branded as criminal in nature, then the powers of this faculty cannot be validly used.

The person granting absolution in virtue of this faculty is further advised to impose on the penitent a salutary penance proportionate to the offense committed. This rests as an obligation on the grantor of the favor; it does not pertain to the valid use of the faculty.

Article 7
To Dispense From the Private Vow of Chastity

> "Dispensandi ad petendum debitum coniugale cum transgressore voti castitatis perfectae et perpetuae, privatim post completum XVIII aetatis annum emissi, qui matrimonium cum dicto voto contraxerit, huiusmodi poenitentem monendo, ipsum ad idem votum servandum teneri tam extra licitum matrimonii usum quam si coniugi supervixerit."

The private vow of perpetual and perfect chastity is an impediment in regard to marriage,[62] and as a consequence it does not have an invalidating effect on marriages entered into by a person bound by such a vow if no dispensation has previously been obtained. The vow does, however, render such marriages illicit. It is these cases of illicit marriage that the powers of the faculty con-

---

[60] *Dummodo tamen id (delictum violationis clausurae) factum ne fuerit ad finem utcumque graviter criminosum, etiam effectu non secuto, . . .*
et moraliter imputabilis legis violatio cui addita sit sanctio canonica saltem indeterminata.

[61] Canon 2195, § 1: Nomine delicti, iure ecclesiastico, intelligitur externa

[62] Canon 1058, § 1: Matrimonium impedit votum simplex virginitatis, castitatis perfectae, non nubendi, suscipiendi ordines sacros et amplectendi statum religiosum.

template. The vow of perfect and perpetual chastity renders the contracting and the use of marriage gravely sinful, and it is this condition that the faculty seeks to remedy. The simple and private vow of perfect chastity is the only vow with which the faculty is concerned.

In order that this faculty to dispense from the impeding vow may be used, the vow must be private in nature.[63] Thus, the simple public vows of religious are beyond the scope of this faculty. The distinction between a public and a private vow is that the former is accepted in the name of the Church by a legitimate Superior; all other vows are considered private. As is apparent from the text of canon 1308, § 1, a private vow is not necessarily a secret vow.[64]

The vow of perfect and perpetual chastity to render the use of marriage illicit, must have been made after the completion of the person's eighteenth year, that is, after midnight of the person's eighteenth birthday anniversary,[65] as is stated in canon 1309, which canon reserves the dispensation from the vow to the Holy See.[66] The vow must have been made as binding under pain of grave sin, otherwise it is not considered reserved.[67] The term *absolute*, of canon 1309, although not contained in the text of the faculty, is understood as a necessary attribute of vows, simple and private, of perfect and perpetual chastity, which as reserved to the Holy See, may require dispensing in virtue of this faculty.

The dispensation given in the use of this faculty permits the use of the marriage already contracted, the use of which otherwise is constantly impeded by the presence of a vow of chastity, perfect and perpetual, on the part of one or both of the parties. The faculty cannot be used validly with a view to dispensing from the vow for the purpose of contracting marriage.[68] The dispensation can be

---

[63] Canon 1308, § 1: Votum *est publicum, si* nomine Ecclesiae et legitimo Superiore ecclesiastico acceptetur; secus *privatum*.

[64] The so-called "vows of devotion" elicited by novices are considered private, even though they are taken before witnesses; cf. Creusen-Garesche-Ellis, *Religious Men and Women in the Code*, n. 215, p. 165.

[65] Cf. canon 34, § 3, 3°.

[66] Canon 1309: Vota privata Sedi Apostolicae reservata sunt tantumodo votum perfectae ac perpetuae castitatis et votum ingrediendi in religionem votorum sollemnium, qui emissa fuerint absolute et post completum decimum octavum aetatis annum.

[67] Cf. Vermeersch-Creusen, *Epitome*, II, n. 640, p. 445.

[68] Cf. canon 67.

given only in regard to the particular previously contracted marriage in question. The grantor of the dispensation is directed to make known to the person dispensed that the vow retains its force outside the legitimate use of this particular marriage, and that in the event that this particular marriage is dissolved by death, the vow retains its full effect in regard to any and every prospective marriage.

ARTICLE 8

TO DISPENSE FROM THE OCCULT IMPEDIMENT OF CRIME

> "Dispensandi super occulto criminis impedimento, dummodo sit absque ulla machinatione, et agatur de matrimonio iam contracto; monitis putatis coniugibus de necessaria consensus secreta renovatione, ac iniuncta gravi et diuturna poenitentia.
>
> "Item dispensandi super eodem occulto impedimento, dummodo pariter sit absque ulla machinatione, etiam in matrimoniis contrahendis, iniuncta gravi et diuturna poenitentia salutari."

The power conceded in this faculty permits the dispensation from the occult [69] matrimonial impediment of crime (*crimen*) as described in number one of canon 1075 [70] in marriages which have already been invalidly contracted, as is stated in paragraph one of the faculty, and for marriages to be contracted, as is stated in paragraph two.

The impediment of crime, as described in canon 1075, 2° and 3°, [71] is excluded from the limits of this faculty. The phrase, *dummodo sit absque ulla machinatione,* expresses a condition which affects the valid use of the faculty, [72] that is, the faculty cannot be used validly in those cases in which the impediment of crime arose as the result

[69] Cf. canon 2197, 4°.

[70] Canon 1075, Valide contrahere nequent matrimonium:

1°, Qui perdurante eodem legitimo matrimonio, adulterium inter se consummarunt et fidem sibi mutuo dederunt de matrimonio ineundo vel ipsum matrimonium, etiam per civilem tantum actum, attentarunt;

[71] Canon 1075: Valide contrahere nequeunt matrimonium:

2°, Qui, perdurante pariter eodem legitimo matrimonio, adulterium inter se consummarunt eorumque alter coniugicidium patravit;

3°, Qui, mutua opera physica vel morali, etiam sine adulterio, mortem coniugi intulerunt.

[72] Cf. canon 39.

of plotting, conniving, or devising, as expressed in the term *machinatione*. The elements postulated in the impediment of *crimen*, namely; 1) the concurrent existence of a lawful wedlock; 2) adultery with the promise to marry; 3) the murder of the spouse of either of the parties by one of the parties together with adultery and the promise to marry; and 4) the murder of the spouse of either of the parties, even apart from the crime of adultery, brought about by the mutual cooperation of the two who contemplate marriage, are of such a nature that the only element which lends itself to plotting is the murder of the spouse of one of the parties. Thus, the impediment of crime, as described in numbers 2 and 3 of canon 1075, is beyond the scope of the power granted in this faculty.

Hence the power of this faculty as it is expressed in the text can be used validly only when the impediment is occult in marriages which have been invalidly contracted or are to be contracted, and when the impediment was contracted without any plotting of the murder of the spouse of either party, by either or both of the parties to the marriage.

In the text of the faculty further instructions are contained for the one who grants a dispensation in virtue of the power which the faculty confers. In cases in which marriages have already been invalidly contracted, the parties are to be warned that they must renew their matrimonial consent, since the powers of the faculty do not comprehend the sanation of the invalid marriage in which the parties are now living. Although this admonition does not pertain to the valid use of the dispensatory power, it is self-evident that, unless the parties renew their matrimonial consent, they will not be validly married.[73]

A grave penance of long duration is to be imposed upon all those who are granted a dispensation by virtue of this faculty. As has been mentioned earlier,[74] the imposition of what constitutes a grave penance varies with the persons and the circumstances involved. In the imposition of the requisite penance the grantor of the dispensation will necessarily be guided by his own judgment, formulated in the light of the particular attendant circumstances.

---

[73] Cf. canon 1133, § 1, and canon 1135, § 2.
[74] Cf. Article 1 of this Chapter.

Article 9

To Dispense From the Irregularity Incurred Because of Voluntary Homicide or Abortion

"Dispensandi ab irregularitate ex homicidio voluntario aut abortu, de qua in can. 985, 4°, sed ad hoc dumtaxat ut poenitens ordines iam susceptos sine infamiae vel scandali exercere queat; iniuncto eidem poenitenti onere intra mensum, saltem per epistolam, per alium vel per se, reticito nomine, docendi de omnibus casus circumstantiis, et praesertim quoties delictum patraverit, ad S. P. recurrendi et standi eius mandatis sub poena suspensionis a divinis ipso facto incurrendae."

The irregularity with which the faculty is concerned is stated in canon 985, 4°, as arising either from voluntary homicide or from the crime of abortion, if the intended effect is produced.[75] The irregularity falls not only on those who are directly responsible for the delicts, but also on those who cooperate. Only those who are active cooperators, i. e., accomplices, suffer the full penalty. In each case the participation of any person requires interpretation according to the principles of canon 2209, § 2, and § 3.[76] Only those who are clerics and either the perpetrators of, or active accomplices in, the above mentioned crimes incur the irregularity in relation to which the use of this faculty is made potentially available.

The irregularity, as stated in canon 985, 4°, is the only effect of the delicts there mentioned with which the power of this faculty is concerned. Other effects of the crime, such as those which are mentioned in canon 2350, in regard to the crime of abortion, and 2354, § 4, in regard to homicide perpetuated by clerics, are not considered insofar as the power conceded in this faculty is concerned.

In the words of the text the power conceded through the faculty can be used in favor of clerics who have incurred the above mentioned irregularity, in order that they may exercise the orders they have already received. This proviso pertains to the valid use of the

---

[75] Canon 985: Sunt irregulares ex delicto:
4°, Qui voluntarium homidicium perpetrarunt aut fetus humani abortum procuraverunt, effectu secuto, omnesque cooperantes.

[76] Cf. Vermeersch-Creusen, *Epitome*, III, n. 393, p. 230; Wernz-Vidal, *Ius Canonicum*, VII, n. 117, p. 135.

faculty, and any extension of the power of the faculty to cover other cases cannot be made validly.[77]

Further provision is required in the text, namely, that the exercise of the orders already received may be permitted for the sole consideration that the cleric will escape infamy for himself and obviate the danger of scandal for others (*sed ad hoc dumtaxat ut poenitens ordines iam susceptos sine infamiae vel scandali periculo exercere queat*). In the fulfillment of this condition the grantor of the dispensation is bound to exercise his own judgment as to whether or not this danger exists.[78] One should again recall here that the use of this faculty is confined to the granting of dispensations in the internal forum only; they may be given, however, either within or outside of the sacrament of penance.

The grantor of the dispensation is also required to impose upon the penitent the obligation of having recourse to the Sacred Penitentiary at least by means of a letter, either personally or through the agency of another, explaining fully the circumstances of the case and the number of times the delict has been committed. The penitent can use a fictitious name in making recourse, and he must, prior to receiving a reply, agree to accept the ruling of the Sacred Penitentiary in his regard, as implied in the text of the faculty.[79] A period of one month, thirty days,[80] is given the penitent as the time during which he can effect the recourse. It could seem from the parallel of canons 2252 and 2254 that the penalty for neglecting the obligation of making the recourse is the reincidence of the irregularity.[81] However, the irregularity with which this faculty is concerned is not a censure; hence the reincidence of the same or a similar irregularity does not necessarily follow. On that score, the dispensation granted remains unaffected by the failure to make the required recourse. In view, however; of the parallel nature of the recourse as prescribed in the text of the faculty, and as called

[77] Cf. canon 67.

[78] The infamy spoken of in the faculty is infamy of fact as delineated in canon 2293, § 3: Infamie facti contrahitur, quando quis, ob patratum delictum vel ob pravos mores, bonam existimationem apud fideles probos et graves amisit, de quo iudicium spectat ad Ordinarium.

[79] The recourse prescribed in the text of the faculty closely parallels that which is required in canons 2252 and 2254. Cf. Moriarty, *The Extraordinary Absolution from Censures*, pp. 195-218.

[80] Cf. canon 32, § 2.

[81] Cf. Moriarty, *The Extraordinary Absolution from Censures*, p. 215.

for in canons 2252 and 2254, it seems that some equivalent sanction should be attached to the culpable neglect of the obligation of making the recourse. In the printed text of the faculty obtaining during the quinquennium 1944-1949 there is an unsigned marginal note which indicates that the obligation of recourse is to be imposed by the grantor of the dispensation under pain of suspension *a divinis* incurred *ipso facto.* (The note appears, from the script, to have been added by an official of the Sacred Penitentiary.) It does not appear that such a penalty is permitted on the basis of the similar nature of the irregularity and the above mentioned canons.[82]

The failure of the grantor of the dispensation to impose the obligation of making recourse as prescribed in the faculty, or the neglect of the penitent to do so, does not invalidate the dispensation.[83] The gravity of the respective obligations of both the grantor and the penitent is of a moral rather than a legal nature. No mention of this aspect of the faculty's use is made in the text of the faculty.

Article 10
Faculty to Grant Certain Indulgences

"Concedendi, suetis sub conditionibus:

A) Plenariam Indulgentiam, lucrandam a christifidelibus, qui:

a) Missae, in Pontificalibus ab Ordinario celebratae, die ab ipsomet Ordinario semel in anno in singulis dioecesis locis designanda, adstiterint;

b) ecclesiam vel publicum aut semipublicum oratorium, in actu quo ibi Ordinarius pastoralem Visitationem peregerit, devote visitaverint;

c) tempore dioecesanae Synodi, visitaverint ecclesiam, in qua ipsa Synodus habetur;

d) die generalis communionis, semel in anno, in ecclesia cathedrali vel alia ecclesia ab Ordinario indictae, sacris Epulis ibidem reficiantur;

---

[82] Canon 2219, § 3: Non licet poenam de persona ad personam vel casu ad casum producere, quamvis par adsit ratio, imo gravior, salvo tamen praescripto can. 2231. Cf. canon 20.

[83] Cf. canon 39.

e) tempore Missionum, quae de Ordinarii licentia in dioecesi habentur, saltem dimidium sacrarum concionum audierint;

B) Partialem Indulgentiam CC dierum, acquirendam ab iis, qui cuilibet ex concionibus, de quibus supra sub lit. e), devote interfuerint".[54]

The usual conditions referred to in the opening sentence of the faculty are those conditions which are listed in canons 925-936 of the Code of Canon Law. On the part of the faithful they are principally that the person be baptised, free from the penalty of excommunication, in the state of grace at the time when he finishes the prescribed good works, subject to the grantor of the indulgence, and possessed of the intention of gaining the granted indulgence. The performance of the prescribed good works is also necessary, and these must be done within the time stated by the grantor of the indulgence.[55] By special concession of the Holy See, an Ordinary may also grant the above mentioned indulgences to *peregrini* within his territory.

The Ordinary can gain for himself the indulgences with which this faculty is concerned.[56] It is apparent that the concessions of this faculty are granted to the Ordinary over and above any faculties for the granting of indulgences that he may have from another source.

In the use of these faculties the Ordinary may grant a plenary indulgence on the following occasions:

a) on any day during the year, but once only during the year in various designated places of the diocese, the day and place to be

---

[54] This faculty which imparts permission to the Ordinary to concede indulgences on certain occasions cannot be committed to others. The faculty may be used by the vicar general only when his personal status fits him for the use of the faculty, that is, when he possesses the character of the episcopacy. Cf. the Introduction to the present Chapter.

[55] Canon 925, § 1: Ut quis capax sit sibi lucrandi indulgentias, debet esse baptizatus, non excommunicatus, in statu gratiae saltem in fine operum praescriptorum, subditus concedentis.

§ 2: Ut vero subiectum capax eas revera lucretur, debet habere intentionem saltem generalem eas acquirendi et opera iniuncta implere statuto tempore ac debito modo secundum concessionis tenorem.

[56] Lepicier, *Indulgences, Their Origin and Development*, (3. ed., revised, London: Burne, Oates, Washbourne, Ltd., 1928), p. 60.

designated by the Ordinary, to all those who assist at a Pontifical Mass celebrated by the Ordinary;

b) during the regular canonical visitation, to all those who devoutly visit the church or oratory being visited by the Ordinary;[87]

c) during the time of the holding of the diocesan synod, to all the faithful who visit the church in which the synod is being held;

d) once a year, at the time of a General Communion, either at the cathedral church or at some other church of the diocese, designated by the Ordinary, to all those who receive Holy Communion at that time;

e) to all those of the faithful who attend at least half of the instructions of a mission which is being held in the diocese with the permission of the Ordinary.[88]

Paragraph B of the text permits the Ordinary to grant an indulgence of 200 days to all those attending a mission, such as the one mentioned above, for each instruction they attend. This partial indulgence can apparently be granted in addition to the plenary indulgence granted in virtue of paragraph A of this faculty.

It is to be noted that with reference to the concessions listed above, a certain performance of good works is conditional to the grant of each indulgence, either the visit to a church, or the attendance at a mission, or the reception of Holy Communion.[89] The performance

---

[87] This faculty cannot be committed to a person together with the delegation of the task of visitation. It seems, however, that the Ordinary may follow the procedure indicated with respect to the granting of indulgences by a person deputed to consecrate a church or an altar. Cf. Coronata, *Interpretatio Authentica,* p. 267; Chapter X, Article 10, of this work. The bishop is permitted, on the occasion of the consecration of an altar or of a church, to grant the authorized indulgence through the agency of the person deputed to perform the consecration, that is, the employment of the bishop's deputy as an *executor necessarius* to announce the grant of the indulgence is permitted. It appears permissible to make use of the same procedure in the granting of the indulgence at the time of the canonical visitation, since the use of a necessary executor does not violate the prohibition against subdelegation.

[88] Since no further restriction is placed on the use of this portion of the faculty, it is evident that it may be used as often as a mission is held in the diocese with the permission of the Ordinary.

[89] The rule of canon 931, which permits the performance of the prescribed good works within a reasonable time, e. g., confession and communion within the octave following the day for which the indulgence is granted ,or confession within the octave preceding that day, and communion on the day previous to the day for which the indulgence is granted, applies also to the

of the good works postulated in this manner by the faculty pertains to the valid acquisition of the indulgences by the faithful. For example, a person who did not attend any of the instructions of a mission could not gain any of the indulgences attached to that attendance.

The nature of the granting of indulgences requires that their concession be promulgated in some manner. There is no indication of any specific form in the text of the faculties; in this the Ordinary is left free to follow his own desires. Any method which is in the mind of the Ordinary convenient and effective may be used.

indulgences granted in virtue of this faculty, that is, insofar as the nature of the required work does not prevent it, e. g., assistance at a Pontifical Mass celebrated by the bishop as in paragraph A, a) of the faculty.

APPENDIX

Rules Regarding Fees

The following eight rules are appended to the text of the faculties. They regulate the administration of the faculties conceded by the various Sacred Congregations. In the faculties which obtain for the years 1944 - 1949, no change is indicated; the rules contained in the faculties issued in 1939 remain in effect. In most cases the rules are in themselves self-explanatory.

1. No fee is to be exacted for the granted permission to read and retain prohibited books.

2. No fee is to be exacted for concessions given in virtue of the faculties granted by the Sacred Penitentiary; these concessions are to be issued absolutely free of charge.

3. A fair and suitable offering is to be required by the Ordinary of those who are able to make the offering for marriage dispensation and sanations granted in virtue of the faculties issued by the Holy Office and the Sacred Congregation of the Sacraments. The amount of this fee is to be in keeping with the practice obtaining in the curias.[1]

4. With regard to the faculties concerning the alienation of ecclesiastical property (in n. 5 of the faculties issued by the Sacred Congregation of the Council) it is meet that there be made to the Holy See an offering proportionate to the benefits obtained or the usefulness of the alienation, according to the judgment of the Ordinary.

5. For all other indults granted in virtue of these faculties the fee asked should be fifteen lire.[2]

---

[1] Canon 1056: Excepta modica aliqua praestatione ex titulo expensarum cancelariae in dispensationibus pro non pauperibus, locorum Ordinarii eorumve officiales, reprobata quavis contraria consuetudine, nequent, occasione concessae dispensationis, emolumentum ullum exigere, nisi haec facultas a Sancta Sede expresse eis data fuerit; et si exegerint, tenentur ad restitutionem. Cf. also canon 1507.

[2] Stenger, *(The Mortgaging of Church Property,* The Catholic University *of America Canon Law Studies,* n. 169 [Washington, D. C.: The Catholic

6. These fees (*taxae*) may be moderated or dispensed from entirely when the need arises, either because of the poverty of those who seek the indults or in view of other just causes, according to the prudent and conscientious judgment of the Ordinary.

7. At the end of each year the sum total of all fees and offerings collected for indults granted in virtue of these faculties shall be sent to the Holy See, through the Sacred Consistorial Congregation. Tabulation of the fees and offerings shall be made on separate sheets, separated according to the Sacred Congregation to which the matters pertain.

8. The Ordinary may add incident to the issuance of each indult, even a matrimonial indult according to canon 1056, a fee of five lire, ($1.70) which the Ordinary may retain for the purpose of applying it to the necessities of either himself or his diocese, without prejudice to the rule given in n. 6.

University of America Press, 1942], p. 135) gives a simple formula, based upon the revised dollar as presented by the authors, (cf. Doheny, *Practical Problems in Church Finance,* p. 42; also Chapter VIII, Article 5, of this work) for the conversion of lire or francs into a corresponding sum of dollars. The sum in lire or francs multiplied by .338638 establishes the equivalent in United States dollars. Thus, the sum of fifteen lire becomes, in United States coin, five dollars and ten cents ($5.10).

CONCLUSIONS

1. The Institute of Quinquennial Faculties, as described in canon 66 of the Code of Canon Law, cannot be said to be an entirely new institution of the Code. It is rather the developed idea of Apostolic Faculties as evolved in the course of the development and administration of Ecclesiastical Law. pp. 6 - 10.

2. By their nature, Quinquennial Faculties are a necessary institution in the legal system of the Church. pp. 20 - 21; 50.

3. The formulas of the Quinquennial Faculties as they are issued today are not of such a nature that they cannot be altered as circumstances require; it is necessary therefore to consider carefully each new transcript of the faculties as often as they are renewed. pp. 22 - 27.

4. It is beyond the power of the bishop to restrict the use of the faculties which the vicar general shares with him; the vicar general enjoys the faculties by reason of his office. p. 55.

5. In their interpretation, the Quinquennial Faculties are to be considered according to the broad meaning of the text, not, however, extensively or restrictively. p. 64.

6. The Quinquennial Faculties may be used in favor of all those who are not prohibited from receiving favors from the Church. In this regard each particular faculty must be considered separately. p. 62.

7. There are many exceptions to be found within the text of the individual faculties. Each text must be carefully considered. p. 64.

8. The faculties granted by the Holy Office may be used in favor of Oriental Catholics; those granted by the remaining Sacred Congregations may not be used in favor of Oriental Catholics unless first the proper delegation is received by the Ordinary from the Sacred Congregation for the Oriental Church. p. 62.

9. In the use of the faculties it is desirable that the Ordinary follow that style of the Roman Curia. p. 69.

10. In the administration of the favors conceded by the faculties, the Ordinary may employ executors. However, in those faculties which cannot permissibly be subdelegated to others the use of the voluntary executor is not permitted, but the use of a necessary executor seems admissible. p. 67 - 68.

BIBLIOGRAPHY

SOURCES

Acta Apostolicae Sedis, Commentarium Officiale, Romae, 1909—.

Acta et Decreta Sacrorum Conciliorum Recentiorum, Collectio Lacensis, 7 vols., Friburgi Brisgoviae, 1870-1890.

Acta Sanctae Sedis, 41 vols., Romae, 1865-1908.

Bourscaren, T. Lincoln, *The Canon Law Digest,* 2 vols., Milwaukee: The Bruce Publishing Co., Vol. I, 1934; Vol. II, 1943.

Brevarium Romanum, Turonibus: Mame, 1940.

Bullarum Diplomatum et Privilegiorum Sanctorum Romanorum Pontificum Taurinensis Editio, 24 vols., et Appendix, Augustae Taurinorum, Neapoli, 1857-1872.

Canones Apostolorum et Conciliorum Saeculorum IV-VII, 2 vols., ed. H. Th. Bruns, Berolini, 1839.

Canones et Decreta Sacrosancti Oecumenici Concilii Tridentini, Romae, ex Typographia Polyglotta S .C. de Propaganda Fide, 1882.

Codex Iuris Canonici Pii X Pontificis Maximi iussu digestus Benedicti Papae XV auctoritate promulgatus, Romae Typis Polyglottis Vaticanis, 1917, (reimpressio, 1934).

Codicis Iuris Canonici Fontes, cura Emi Petri Card, Gasparri editi, 9 vols. Romae (postea Civitate Vaticana): Typis Polyglottis Vaticanis, 1923-1939, (Vols. VII, VIII et IX ed. cura et studio Emi Iustiniani Card. Seredi).

Collectanea S. Congregationis de Propaganda Fide, 2 vols., Romas; Typographia Polyglotta S. C. de Propaganda Fide, 1893.

Collectanea S. Congregationis de Propaganda Fide, 2 vols., Romae: Typographia Polyglotta S. C. de Propaganda Fide, 1907.

Coronata, Matthaeus Conte a, *Interpretatio Authentica Codicis Iuris Canonici et circa Ipsum Sanctae Sedis Iurisprudentia* 1916-1940, Romae: Marietti, 1940.

Corpus Iuris Canonici, Editio Lipsiensis II, (E. Richter-E. Friedberg), 2 vols., Lipsiae, 1879-1881.

Decreta Authentica Congregationis Sacrorum Ritum ex Actis Eiusdem Collecta eiusque Auctoritate Promulgata sub Auspiciis SS. Domini Nostri Leonis Papae XIII, 5 vols., cum 2 Appendicibus, Romae: ex Typographia Polyglotta S. C. de Propaganda Fide, 1898-1901; Appendix II, 1927.

Decretum Gratiani Emendatum et Notationibus Illustratum una cum Glossis, Romae, 1582.

Decretales D. Gregorii Papae IX, una cum Glossis Restitutae, Romae, 1582.

Gardellini, A., *Decreta Authentica Congregationis Sacrorum Rituum octis eiusdem collecta,* 3. ed., 4 vols., cum appendicibus, Romae, 1856-1887.

Jaffé, Phillippus, *Regesta Pontificum Romanorum, ab condita ecclesia ad annum post Christum natum MCXCVIII,* 2. ed., correctam et auctam auspiciis Guliemi Wattenbach, curaverunt S. Loewenfeld, F. Kaltenbrunner, P. Ewald, 2 vols., Lipsiae, 1885-1888.

Mansi, Joannes Dominicus, *Sacrorum Conciliorum Nova et Amplissima Collectio,* 53 vols., in 60, Paris, Arnhem, Leipzig, 1901-1927.

Memoriale Ritum, Benedict XIII, 1724, Benedict XV, 1920; English translation by Bartholomew, Eustace, 3. printing, New York: Joseph F. Wagner, 1944.

Migne, J. P., *Patrologiae Cursus Completus, Series Latina*, 221 vols., Paris, 1844-1864.

Missale Romanum, editio III juxta typicam Vaticanam amplificata I, Neo Eboraci: Benziger Brothers, Inc., 1944.

Pontificale Romanum Summorum Pontificum iussu editum a Benedicto XIV et Leone XIII Pontificibus Maximis recognitum et castigatum, Ratisbonae, Neo-Eboraci et Cincinnati: Pustet, 1891.

Ritulae Romanum Pauli V Pontificis Maximi iussu editum aliorumque Pontificum cura recognitum atque auctoritate Pii Papae XI, Neo-Eboraci: Benzinger Brothers, 1945.

Schroeder, H., *Canons and Decrees of the Council of Trent*, St. Louis: Herder, 1941.

Syllogr praecipuorum documentorum recentium Summorum Pontificum et S. Congregationis de Propaganda Fide necnon aliorum SS. Congregationum Romanorum ad usum Missionarionum, Typis Polyglottis Vaticanis, 1939.

Thiel, A., *Epistolae Romanorum Pontificum Genuinae a S. Hilario usque ad Pelagium*, Vol. 1, *Epistolae Romanorum Pontificum a S. Hilario usque ad S. Hormisdam*, Brunsbergae, 1868.

INSENT PAGE xi **

Corpus Iuris Civilis, 3 vols., Berolini, 1928-1929. *Institutiones*, quas recognovit P. Krueger, ed. stereotypa 15., 1928; *Digesta* quas recognovit T. Mommensen et retractavit P. Krueger, ed. stereotypa 15., 1928; *Codex Iustinianus*, quem recognovit et retractavit P. Krueger, ed. stereotypa 10., 1929; *Novellae*, quas recognovit R. Schoell, et absolvit G. Kroll, ed. stereotypa 5., 1928.

AUTHORS

Augustine, Charles (Bachofen, Charles Augustine) *Liturgical Law*, St. Louis: Herder, 1931.

————————*A Commentary on Canon Law, 8 vols., St. Louis:* B. Herber Book Co., Vol. VIII, 3 ed., 1931.

Ayrinhac, H. A., *Administrative Legislation in the New Code of Canon Law*, New York: Longmans, Green & Co., 1928.

————————, *Penal Legislation in the New Code of Canon Law*, Revised edition, New York: Benzinger Brothers, 1944.

Baart, Peter A., *Legal Formulary*, 2 ed., New York, 1898.

Barry, Garrett Francis, *Violation of the Cloister*, The Catholic University of America Canon Law Studies, n. 148, Washington D. C.: The Catholic University of America Press, 1942.

Benedictus XIV, *De Synodo Dioecesana*, 2 vols., Prati, 1844.

Beste, Udalricus, *Introductio in Codicem*, editio altera, Collegeville: St. John's Abbey Press, 1944.

Blat, Albertus, *Commentarium Textus Codicis Iuris Canonici*, 5 vols., in 6, Romae: Collegio Angelico, 1919-1927.

Bliley, Nicholas Martin, *Altars According to the Code of Canon Law*, The Catholic University of America Canon Law Studies, n. 38, Washington, D. C.: The Catholic University of America, 1927.

Bouscaren, T. Lincoln-Ellis, Adam C., *Canon Law*, Milwaukee: The Bruce Publishing Co., 1946.

Brys, J., *De Dispensatione in Iure Canonico, praesertim apud Decretistas et Decretalistas usque ad Medium Saeculum Decimum Quartum*, Burgis: Beyaert, 1925.

Cappello, Felix, *Summa Iuris Canonici in usum Scholarum Concinnata*, 3 vols., Romae: Universitas Gregoriana, Vol. I., 3. ed., 1938; Vol II, 3. ed., 1939; Vol. III, 1936.

———, *Summa Iuris Publici Ecclesiastici*, 3. ed. Universitas Gregoriana, Romae, 1932.

———, *Tractatus Canonico-Moralis de Sacramentis*, 3 vols., in 6, Romae: Marietti, 1932-1939.

Chelodi, Ioannes, *Ius Canonicum de Personis*, 3. ed., curavit Pius Ciprotti, Vicenza; Societa Anonima Tipografica, 1942.

———, *Ius Canonicum de Delictis et Poenis et de Iudiciis Criminalibus*, 5 ed., recognita et aucta a Pio Ciprotti, Vicenza: Societa Anonima Tipografica, 1943.

Cicognani, A.-O'Hara, J.-Brennan, F., *Canon Law*, 2. ed., revised, 1935, Westminster, Maryland: The Newman Bookshop, 1946.

Coronata, Mattheus Conte a, *Institutiones Iuris Canonici*, 5 vols., Taurini: Marietti, 1928-1936.

Costello, John Michael, *Domicile and Quasi-Domicile*, The Catholic University of America Canon Law Studies, n. 60, Washington, D. C.: The Catholic University of America, 1930.

Creusen, Joseph-Ellis, Adam-Garesche, Edward, *Religious Men and Women in the Code*, 4. English ed., translated from the 5. French ed., Milwaukee: The Bruce Publishing Co., 1940.

De Smet, Aloysius, *De Sponsalibus et Matrimonio*, 4. ed., (inde a Codice altera) Brugis; Beyaert, 1927.

Doheny, William, *Canonical Procedure in Matrimonial Cases*, Vol. II, *Informal Procedure*, Milwaukee: The Bruce Publishing Co., 1944.

———, *The Impediment of Crime*, The Catholic University of America Canon Law Studies, n. 69, Washington, D. C.: The Catholic University of America, 1931.

Dubé, Arthur Joseph, *The General Principles for the Reckoning of Time in Canon Law*, The Catholic University of America Canon Law Studies, n. 144, Washington, D. C.: The Catholic University of America Press, 1941.

Duskie, John Aloysius, *The Canonical Status of Orientals in the United States*, The Catholic University of America Canon Law Studies, n. 48, Washington, D. C.: The Catholic University of America, 1928.

Fanfani, Ludovicus, I., *De Indulgentiis ad Normam Codicis Iuris Canonici*, 2. ed., Raurnin, Romae: Marietti, 1926.

Farrell, Benjamin Francis, *The Rights and Duties of the Local Ordinary Regarding Congregations of Women Religious of Pontifical Approval*, The Catholic University of America Canon Law Studies, n. 128, Washington, D. C.: The Catholic University of America Press, 1941.

Feije, Henricus, J., *De Impedimentis et Dispensationibus Matrimonialibus*, 3. ed., Lovanii, 1885.

Ferraris, Lucius, *Prompta Bibliotheca, Canonica, Iuridica, Moralis, Theologica necnon Ascetica, Polemica, Rubristica, Historica*, ed. novissima, 9 vols., Romae, 1885-1889.

Fortescue, Adrian-O'Connell, J. B., *The Ceremonies of the Roman Rite Described*, 5. ed., London: Rurns, Oates & Washbourne, Ltd., 1934.

Gallagher, Thomas Raphael, *The Examination of the Qualities of the Ordinand*, The Catholic University of America Canon Law Studies, n. 195, Washington, D. C.: The Catholic University of America Press, 1944.

Gasparri, Petrus, *Tractatus Canonicus de Matrimonio*, ed. nova, 2 vols., Romae: Typis Polyglottis Vaticanis, 1932.

Goodwine, Joseph Gerard, *The Reception of Converts*, The Catholic University of America Canon Law Studies, n. 198, Washington, D. C.: The Catholic University of America Press, 1944.

Harrigan, Robert J., *The Radical Sanation of Invalid Marriages*, The Catholic University of America Canon Law Studies, n. 116, Washington, D. C.: The Catholic University of America, 1938.

Hefele, C., Leclercq, H., *Histoire des Conciles*, 10 vols., in 19, Paris, 1907-1938.

Heneghas, John Joseph, *The Marriages of Unworthy Catholics*, Canons 1065 and 1066, The Catholic University of America Canon Law Studies, n. 188, Washington, D. C.: The Catholic University of America Press, 1944.

Heston, Edward Louis, *The Alienation of Church Property in the United States*, the Catholic University of America Canon Law Studies, n. 132, Washington, D. C.: The Catholic University of America Press, 1941.

Keller, Charles Frederick, *Mass Stipends*, The Catholic University of America Canon Law Studies, n. 27, Washington, D. C.: The Catholic University of America, 1925.

Kealy, Thomas M., *Dowry of Women Religious*, The Catholic University of America Canon Law Studies, n. 134, Washington, D. C.: The Catholic University of America Press, 1941.

Keene, Michael James, *Religious Ordinaries and Canon 198*. The Catholic University of America Canon Law Studies, n. 135, Washington, D. C.: The Catholic University of America Press, 1942.

Lega, Michael, *Commentarius in Iudicia Ecclesiastica iuxta Codicem Iuris Canonici, curante Victorio Bartoccetti*, 3 vols., Romae: Anonima Libraria Carrolica Italiana, 1938-1941.

Le Vavasseur, Leon-Haegy, Joseph, Stercky, Louis,*Manuel de Liturgie et Ceremonial selon le Rit Romain*, 16, ed., 2 vols.,· Paris, Librarie Lecoffre: J. Gabalda, Vol. I, 1935; Vol. II, 1936.

Lepicier, Alexis, *Indulgences, Their Origin and Development*, 3. ed., revised, London: Burns, Oates & Washbourne, Ltd., 1928.

Louis, William Francis, *Diocesan Archives*, The Catholic University of America Canon Law Studies, n. 137, Washington, D. C.: The Catholic University of America Press, 1941.

Lynch, George Edward, *Coadjutors and Auxiliaries of Bishops*, The Catholic University of America Canon Law Studies, n. 238, Washington, D. C.: The Catholic University of America Press, 1947.

MacKenzie, Eric, F., *The Delict of Heresy in Its Commission, Penalization, Absolution*, The Catholic University of America Canon Law Studies, n. 77, Washington, D. C.: The Catholic University of America, 1932.

Many, S., *Praelectiones de Locis Sacris*, Paris, 1904.

Marbach, Joseph Francis, *Marriage Legislation for the Catholics of the Oriental Rites in the United States and Canada*, The Catholic University of America Canon Law Studies, n. 243, Washington, D. C.: The Catholic University of America Press, 1946.

Mergentheim, L., *Die Quinquennalfakultäten pro foro externo. Ihre Entstehung und Einteilung in Deutschen Bistümern*, 2 vols., Stuttgart, 1908.

Miller, Newton Thomas, *Founded Masses According to the Code of Canon Law*, The Catholic University of America Canon Law Studies, n. 34, Washington, D. C.: The Catholic University of America, 1926.

Monin, A., *De Curia Romana*, Lovanii, 1912.

Moriarty, Francis E., *The Extraordinary Absolution from Censures*, The Catholic University of America Canon Law Studies, n. 113, Washington, D. C.: The Catholic University of America, 1938.

Motry, Hubert L., *Diocesan Faculties According to the Code of Canon Law*, The Catholic University of America Canon Law Studies, n. 16, Washington, D. C.: The Catholic University of America, 1922.

McDevitt, Gilbert Hoseph, *Legitimacy and Legitimation*, The Catholic University of America Canon Law Studies, n. 138, Washington, D. C.: The Catholic University of America Press, 1941.

O'Mara, William A., *Canonical Causes for Matrimonial Dispensation*, The Catholic University of America Canon Law Studies, n. 96, Washington, D. C.: The Catholic University of America, 1935.

O'Neill, William H., *Papal Rescripts of Favor*, The Catholic University of America Canon Law Studies, n. 57, Washington, D. C.: The Catholic University of America, 1930.

Payen, G., *De Matrimonio in Missionibus ac Potissimum in Sinis: Tractatus Practicus et Casus*, 2. ed., 3 vols., Zi-Ka-Wei: Typographia T'OU-SE-WE, 1935-1936.

Petrovits, Joseph, J. C., *The New Church Law on Matrimony*, 2d. ed., Philadelphia: Joseph McVey, 1926.

Pirhing, Ernricus, *Jus Canonicum in V Libros Decretalium distributum*, ed., noviss., 5 vols., Dilingae, 1722.

Prummer, D. M., *Manuale Iuris Canonici*, 4. ed., Friburgi Brisgoviae, 1927.

Putzer, Joseph, *Commentarium in Facultates Apostolicas*, 4. ed., New York, 1897.

Reiffenstuel, Anacletus, *Ius Canonicum Universum*, 4 vols., Venetiis, 1735.

Reilly, Edward, M., *The General Norms of Dispensation*, The Catholic University of America Canon Law Studies, n. 119, Washington, D. C.: The Catholic University of America Press, 1939.

Roelker, Edward G., *Principles of Privilege According to the Code of Canon Law*, The Catholic University of America Canon Law Studies, n. 35, Washington, D. C.: The Catholic University of America, 1926.

Ryan, Gerald Aloysius, *Principles of Episcopal Jurisdiction*, The Catholic University of America Canon Law Studies, n. 120, Washington, D. C.: The Catholic University of America Press, 1939.

Sabetti, A.-Barrett, T., *Compendium Theologiae Moralis*, 27a ed., Neo Eboraci: Frederick Pustet Co., Inc ., 1919.

Schaaf, Valentine Theodore, *The Cloister*, The Catholic University of America Canon Law Studies, n. 13, Washhington, D. C.: The Catholic University of America, 1921.

Schaefer, Timotheus, *Compendium de Religiosis ad Normam Codicis Iuris* Canonici, Munster in W.: Ex Officina Libaria Aschendorff, 1940.

Schenk, Francis J., *The Matrimonial Impediments of Mixed Religion and Disparity of Cult*, The Catholic University of America Canon Law Studies, n. 51, Washington, D. C.: The Catholic University of America, 1929.

Schmalzgrueber, Franciscus, *Ius Ecclesiasticum Universum*, 5 vols., in 12, Romae, 1843-1845.

Shea, John G., *History of the Catholic Church in the United States*, 4 vols., New York, 1886-1892.

Slafkosky, Andrew Leonard, *The Canonical Episcopal Visitation of the Diocese*, The Catholic University of America Canon Law Studies, n. 142, Washington, D. C.: The Catholic University of America Press, 1941.

Smith, S. B., *Elements of Ecclesiastical Law*, 5. ed., 3 vols., New York, 1883.

Sole, Jacobus, *De Delictis et Poenis*, Romae: Pustet, 1920.

Sullivan, John F., *The Externals of the Catholic Church*, New York: Kennedy, 1917.

Thomassinus, Ludovicus, *Vetus et Nova Ecclesiae Disciplina Circa Beneficia et Beneficiarios*, 3 vols., Venetiis, 1730.

Van Hove, A., *De Privilegiis, De Dispensationibus*, Commentarium Lovaniense in Codicem Iuris Canonici editum a magistris et doctoribus Universitatis Lovaniensis, Vol. I, Tomus V, Mechliniae—Romae: H. Dessain, 1939.

——————, *De Rescriptis*, Commentarium Lovaniense in Codicem Iuris Canonici editum a magistris et doctoribus Universitatis Lovaniensis, Vol. I, Tomus IV, Mechliniae—Romae: H. Dessain, 1936.

Vermeersch, Arthurus-Creusen, Josephus, *Epitome Iuris Canonici*, 3 vols., Romae: H. Dessain, Vol. I, 6. ed., 1937; Vol. II, 5. ed., 1934; Vol. III, 5. ed., 1936.

Vromant, G., *Facultates Apostolicae quas Sacra Congregatio de Propaganda Fide delegare solet Ordinariis Missionum, Commentaria in Formula Tertiam*, Museum Lessianum—Section Theologique, n. 16, Lovain: Editions du Museum Lessianum, 1926.

Wahl, Francis S., *The Matrimonial Impediments of Consanguinity and Affinity*, The Catholic University of America Canon Law Studies, n. 90, Washington, D. C.: The Catholic University of America, 1934.

Wernz, Francis X., *Ius Decretalium*, 2.. ed., 6 vols., Romae et Prati, 1906-1913.

Wernz, Francis X., Vidal, P., *Ius Canonicum ad Codicis normam exactum*, 7 vols., in 8, Romae: apud Aedes Universitatis Gregorianae, 1923-1938.

Woywood, S., *A Practicle Commentary on the Code of Canon Law*, 9. printing, revised by Callistus Smith, 2 vols., New York: Joseph F. Wagner, 1945.

ARTICLES

Doheny, William J., "Church Finance and Problems of Alienation", *The Jurist*, I, (1941), 97-107.

Ellis, A. C., "Triginta Millia Libellarum seu Francorum", *Periodica* XXVII, (1938), 348-349.

Plöchl, Willibald M., "Quinquennial Faculties extended by the S. Congregation for the Oriental Church to Latin Ordinaries", *The Jurist*, VI (1946), 73-76.

Vermeersch, Arthurus, "Commentaria de Formulis Facultatum Quas S. Congregatio de Propaganda Fide Concedere Solet", *Periodica*, XI (1922), (33)-(143).

PERIODICALS

Apollinaris, Romae, 1928—.

Ecclesiastical Review, (originally *The American Ecclesiastical Review*), Philadelphia, 1889-1943; Baltimore, 1944—.

Il Monitore Ecclesiastico, Romae, 1876—

Jurist, The, Washington, D. C.: The Catholic University of America, 1941—.

Periodica de Religiosis et Missionariis (later, *Periodica de Re Canonica et Morali utili praesertim Religiosis et Missionariis*, Brugis, 1905—.

ABBREVIATIONS

AAS—*Acta Apostolicae Sedis.*

ASS—*Acta Sanctae Sedis.*

Collect. (1893)—*Collectanea S. C. De Propaganda Fide* (1893).

Collect. (1907)—*Collectanea S. C. de Propaganda Fide* (1907).

Fontes—*Codicis Iuris Canonici Fontes,* cura . . . Emi Card. Gasparri editi.

Jaffé—*Regesta Pontificum Romanorum* (edited by Ewald, Kaltenbrunner, Loewenfeld).

Mansi—*Sacrorum Conciliorum Nova et Amplissima Collectio.*

MPL—Migne, *Patrologiae Cursus Completus, Series Latina.*

ALPHABETICAL INDEX

Canon Law Studies*

1. Freriks, Rev. Celestine *A., C.P.P.S., J.C.D.*, Religious Congregations in Their Evternal Relations, 121 pp., 1916.
2. Galliher, Rev. Daniel M., O. P., J.C.D., Canonical Elections, 117 pp., 1917.
3. Borkowski, Rev. Aurelius L. O.F.M., J.C.D., De Confraternitatibus Ecclesiastics, 136 pp., 1918.
4. Castillo, Rev. Cayo, J.C.D., Disertacion Historico-Canonica sobre la Potestad del Cabildo en Sede Vacante o Impedida del Vicario Capitular, 99 pp., 1919 (1918).
5. Kubelbeck, *Rev.* William J., S.T.B., J.C.D., The Sacred Penitentiaria and Its Relation to Faculties of Ordinaries and Priests, 129 pp., 1918.
6. Petrovits, Rev. Joseph J. C., S.T.D., J.C.D., The New Church Law on Matrimony, X-461 pp., 1919.
7. Hickey, Rev. John J., S.T.B., J.C.D., Irregularities and Simple Impediments in the New Code of Canon Law, 100 pp., 1920.
8. Klekotka, Rev. Peter J., S.T.B., J.C.D., Diocesan Consultors, 179 pp., 1920.
9. Wanenmacher, Rev. Francis, J.C.D., The Evidence in Ecclesiastical Procedure Affecting the Marriage Bond, 1920 (Printed 1935).
10. Golden, Rev. Henry Francis, J.C.D., Parochial Benefices in the New Code, IV-119 pp., 1921(Printed 1925).
11. Koudelka, *Rev.* Charles J., J.C.D., Pastors, Their Rights and Duties According to the New Code of Canon Law, 211 pp., 1921.
12. Melo, Rev. Antonius, O.F.M., J.C.D., De Exemptione Regularium, X-188 pp., 1921.
13. Schaaf, Rev. Valentine Theodore, O.F.M., S.T.B., J.C.D., The Cloister, X-180 pp., 1921.
14. Burke, Rev. Thomas Joseph, S.T.D., J.C.D., Competence in Ecclesiastical Tribunals, IV-117 pp., 1922.
15. Leech, Rev. George Leo, J.C.D., A Comparative Study of the Constitution "Apostolicae Sedis" and the "Codex Juris Canonici," 179 pp., 1922.
16. Motry, Rev. Hubert Louis, S.T.D., J.C.D., Diocesan Faculties According to the Code of Canon Law, II-167 pp., 1922.
17. Murphy, Rev. George Lawrence, J.C.D., Delinquencies and Penalties in the Administration and the Reception of the Sacraments, IV-121 pp., 1923.
18. O'Reilly, Rev. John Anthony, S.T.B., J.C.D., Ecclesiastical Sepulture in the New Code of Canon Law, II-129 pp., 1923.
19. Michalicka, Rev. Wenceslas Cyrill, O.S.B., J.C.D., Judicial Procedure in Dismissal of Clerical Exempt Religious, 107 pp., 1923.
20. Dargin, Rev. Edward Vincent, S.T.B., J.C.D., Reserved Cases According to the Code of Canon Law, IV-103 pp., 1924.
21. Godfrey, Rev. John A., S.T.B., J.C.D., The Right of Patronage According to the Code of Canon Law, 153 pp., 19224.
22. Hagedorn, Rev. Francis Edward, J.C.D., General Legislation on Indulgences, II-154 pp., 1924.
23. King, Rev. James Ignatius, J.C.D., The Administration of the Sacraments to Dying Non-Catholics, V-141 pp., 1924.

* From nn. 1-100 inclusive only n. 25 is still obtainable. From n. 101 onward all numbers are available except the following: 101-114, 116, 118, 120, 122, 123 and 162.

24. WINSLOW, REV. FRANCIS JOSEPH, M.M., J.C.D., Vicars and Prefects Apostolic, IV-149 pp., 1924.
25. CORREA, REV. JOSE SERVELION, S.T.L., J.C.D., La Potestad Legislativa de la Iglesia Catolica, IV-127 pp., 1925.
26. DUGAN, REV. HENRY FRANCIS, A.M., J.C.D., The Judiciary Department of the Diocesan Curia, 87 pp., 1925.
27. KELLER, REV. CHARLES FREDERICK, S.T.B., J.C.D., Mass Stipends, 167 pp., 1925.
28. PASCHANG, REV. JOHN LINUS, J.C.D., The Sacramentals According to the Code of Canon Law, 129 pp., 1925.
29. PIONTEK, REV. CYRILLUS, O.F.M., S.T.B., J.C.D., De Indulto Exclaustrationis necnon Saecularizationis, XIII-289 pp., 1925.
30. KEARNEY, REV. RICHARD JOSEPH, S.T.B., J.C.D., Sponsors at Baptism Accordin gto the Code of Canon Law, IV-127 pp., 1925.
31. BARTLETT, REV. CHESTER JOSEPH, A.M., LL.B., J.C.D., The Tenure of Parochial Property in the United States of America, V-108 pp., 1926.
32. KILKER, REV. ADRIAN JEROME, J.C.D., Extreme Unction, V-425 pp., 1926.
33. MCCORMICK, REV. ROBERT EMMETT, J.C.D., Confessors of Religious, VIII-266 pp., 1926.
34. MILLER, REV. NEWTON THOMAS, J.C.D., Founded Masses According to the Code of Canon Law, VII-93 pp., 1926.
35. ROELKER, REV. EDWARD G., S.T.D., J.C.D., Principles of Privilege According to the Code of Canon Law, XI-166 pp., 1926.
36. BAKALARCZYK, REV. RICHARDUS, M.I.C., J.U.D., De Novitiatu, VIII-208 pp., 1927.
37. PIZZUTI, REV. LAWRENCE, O.F.M., J.U.L., De Parochis Religiosis, 1927. (Not Printed.)
38. BLILEY, REV. NICHOLAS MARTIN, O.S.B., J.C.D., Altars According to the Code of Canon Law, XIX-132 pp., 1927.
39. BROWN, MR. BRENDAN FRANCIS, A.B., LL.M., J.U.D., The Canonical Juristic Personality with Special Reference to its Status in the United States of America, V-212 pp., 1927.
40. CAVANAUGH, REV. WILLIAM THOMAS, C.P., J.U.D., The Reservation of the Blessed Sacrament, VIII-101 pp., 1927.
41. DOHENY, REV. WILLIAM J., C.S.C., A.B., J.U.D., Church Property: Modes of Acquisition, X-118 pp., 1927.
42. FELDHAUS, REV. ALOYSIUS H., C.P.P.S., J.C.D., Oratories, IX-141 pp., 1927.
43. KELLY, REV. JAMES PATRICK, A.B., J.C.D., The Jurisdiction of the Simple Confessor, X-208 pp., 1927.
44. NEUBERGER, REV. NICHOLAS J., J.C.D., Canon 6 or the Relation of the Codex Juris Canonici to the Preceding Legislation, V-95 pp., 1927.
45. O'KEEFE, REV. GERALD MICHAEL, J.C.D., Matrimonial Dispensations, Powers of Bishops, Priests, and Confessors, VIII-232 pp., 1927.
46. QUIGLEY, REV. JOSEPH A. M., A.B., J.C.D., Condemned Societies, 139 pp., 1927.
47. ZAPLOTNIK, REV. JOHANNES LEO, J.C.D., De Vicariis Foraneis, X-142 pp., 1927.
48. DUSKIE, REV. JOHN ALOYSIUS, A.B., J.C.D., The Canonical Status of the Orientals in the United States, VIII-196 pp., 1928.
49. HYLAND, REV. FRANCIS EDWARD, J.C.D., Excommunication, Its Nature, Historical Development and Effects, VIII-181 pp., 1928.
50. REINMAN, REV. GERALD JOSEPH, O.M.C., J.C.D., The Third Order Secular of Saint Francis, 201 pp. 1928.
51. SCHENK, REV. FRANCIS J., J.C.D., The Matrimonial Impediments of Mixed Religion and Disparity of Cult, XVI-318 pp., 1929.

52. Coady, Rev. John Joseph, S.T.D., J.U.D., A.M., The Appointment of Pastors, VIII-150 pp., 1929.
53. Kay, Rev. Thomas Henry, J.C.D., Competence in Matrimonial Procedure, VIII-164 pp., 1929.
54. Turner, Rev. Sidney Joseph, C.P., J.U.D., The Vow of Poverty, XLIX-217 pp., 1929.
55. Kearney, Rev. Raymond A., A.B., S.T.D., J.C.D., The Principles of Delegation, VII-149 pp., 1929.
56. Conran, Rev. Edward James, A.B., J.C.D., The Interdict, V-163 pp., 1930.
57. O'Neill, Rev. William H., J.C.D., Papal Rescripts of Favor, VII-218 pp., 1930.
58. Bastnagel, Rev. Clement Vincent, J.U.D., The Appointment of Parochial Adjutants and Assistants, XV-257 pp., 1930.
59. Ferry, Rev. William A., A.B., J.C.D., Stole Fees, V-136 pp., 1930.
60. Costello, Rev. John Michael, A.B., J.C.D., Domicile and Quasi-Domicile, VII-201 pp., 1930.
61. Kremer, Rev. Michael Nicholas, A.B., S.T.B., J.C.D., Church Support in the United States, VI-136 pp., 1930.
62. Angulo, Rev. Luis, C.M., J.C.D., Legislation de la Iglesia sobre la intencion en la application de la Santa Misa, VII-104 pp., 1931.
63. Frey, Rev. Wolfgang Norbert, O.S.B., A.B., J.C.D., The Act of Religious Profession, VIII-174 pp., 1931.
64. Roberts, Rev. James Brendan, A.B., J.C.D., The Banns of Marriage, XIV-140 pp., 1931.
65. Ryder, Rev. Raymond Aloysius, A.B., J.C.D., Simony, IX-151 pp., 1931.
66. Campagna, Rev. Angelo, Ph.D., J.U.D., Il Vicario Generale del Vescovo, VII-2$5 pp., 1931.
67. Cox, Rev. Joseph Godfrey, A.B., J.C.D., The Administration of Seminaries, VI-124 pp., 1931.
68. Gregory, Rev. Donald J., J.U.D., The Pauline Privilege, XV-165 pp., 1931.
69. Donohue, Rev. John F., J.C.D., The Impediment of Crime, VII-110 pp., 1931.
70. Dooley, Rev. Eugene A., O.M.I., J.C.D. Church Law on Sacred Relics, IX-143 pp., 1931.
71. Orth, Rev. Clement Raymond, O.M.C., J.C.D., The Approbation of Religious Institutes, 171 pp., 1931.
72. Pernicone, Rev. Joseph M., A.B., J.C.D., The Ecclesiastical Prohibition of Books, XII-267 pp., 1932.
73. Clinton, Rev. Connell, A.B., J.C.D., The Paschal Precept, IX-108 pp., 1932.
74. Donnelly, Rev. Francis B., A.M. S.T.L., J.C.D., The Diocesan Synod, VIII-125 pp., 1932.
75. Torrente, Rev. Camilo, C.M.F., J.C.D., Las Procesiones Sagradas, V-145 pp., 1932.
76. Murphy, Rev. Edwin J., C.P.P.S., J.C.D., Suspension Ex Informata Conscientia, XI-122 pp., 1932.
77. MacKenzie, Rev. Eric F., A.M., S.T.L., J.C.D., The Delict of Heresy in its Commission, Penalization, Absolution, VII-124 pp., 1932.
78. Lyons, Rev. Avitus E., S.T.B., J.C.D., The Collegiate Tribunal of First Instance, XI-147 pp., 1932.
79. Connolly, Rev. Thomas A., J.C.D., Appeals, XI-195 pp., 1932.
80. Sangmeister, Rev. Joseph V., A.B., J.C.D., Force and Fear as Precluding Matrimonial Consent, V-211 pp., 1932.

81. JAEGER, REV. LEO A., A.B., J.C.D., The Administration of Vacant and Quasi-Vacant Episcopal Sees in the United States, IX-229 pp., 1932.
82. RIMLINGER, REV. HERBERT T., J.C.D., Error Invalidating Matrimonial Consent, VII-79 pp., 1932.
83. BARRETT, REV. JOHN D. M., S.S., J.C.D., A Comparative Study of the Third Plenary Council of Baltimore and the Code, IX-221 pp., 1932.
84. CARBERRY, REV. JOHN J., PH.D., S.T.D., J.C.D., The Juridical Form of Marriage, X-177 pp., 1934.
85. DOLAN, REV. JOHN L., A. B., J.C.D., The Defensor Vinculi, XII-157 pp., 1934.
86. HANNAN, REV. JEROME D., A.M., S.T.D., LL.B., J.C.D., The Canon Law of Wills, IX-517 pp., 1934.
87. LEMIEUX, REV. DELISE A., A.M., J.C.D., The Sentence in Ecclesiastical Procedure, IX-131 pp., 1934.
88. O'ROURKE, REV. JAMES J., A.B., J.C.D., Parish Registers, VII-109 pp., 1934.
89. TIMLIN, REV. BARTHOLOMEW, O.F.M., A.M., J.C.D., Conditional Matrimonial Consent, X-381 pp., 1934.
90. WAHL, REV. FRANCIS X., A.B., J.C.D., The Matrimonial Impediments of Consanguinity and Affinity, VI-125 pp., 1934.
91. WHITE, REV. ROBERT J., A.B., LL.B., S.T.B., J.C.D., Canonical Ante-Nuptial Promises and the Civil Law, VI-152 pp., 1934.
92. HERRERA, REV. ANTONIO PARRA, O.C.D., J.C.D., Legislacion Ecclesiastica sobra el Ayuno y la Abstinencia, XI-191 pp., 1935.
93. KENNEDY, REV. EDWIN J., J.C.D., The Special Matrimonial Process in Cases of Evident Nullity, X-165 pp., 1935.
94. MANNING, REV. JOHN J., A.B., J.C.D., Presumption of Law in Matrimonial Procedure, XI-111 pp., 1935.
95. MOEDER, REV. JOHN M., J.C.D., The Proper Bishop for Ordination and Dimissorial Letters, VII-135 pp., 1935.
96. O'MARA, REV. WILLIAM A., A.B., J.C.D., Canonical Causes for Matrimonial Dispensations, IX-155 pp., 1935.
97. REILLY, REV. PETER, J.C.D., Residence of Pastors, IX-81 pp., 1935.
98. SMITH, REV. MARINER T., O.P., S.T.Lr., J.C.D., The Penal Law for Religious, VII-169 pp., 1935.
99. WHALEN, REV. DONALD W., A.M., J.C.D., The Value of Testimonial Evidence in Matrimonial Procedure, XIII-297 pp., 1935.
100. CLEARY, REV. JOSEPH F., J.C.D., Canonical Limitations on the Alienation of Church Property, VIII-141 pp., 1936.
101. GLYNN, REV. JOHN C., J.C.D., The Promoter of Justice, XX-337 pp., 1936.
102. BRENNAN, REV. JAMES H., S.S., M.A., S.T.B., J.C.D., The Simple Convalidation of Marriage, VI-135 pp., 1937.
103. BRUNINI, REV. JOSEPH BERNARD, J.C.D., The Clerical Obligations of Canons 139 and 142, X-121 pp., 1937.
104. CONNOR, REV. MAURICE, A.B., J.C.D., The Administrative Removal of Pastors, VIII-159 pp., 1937.
105. GUILFOYLE, REV. MERLIN JOSEPH, J.C.D., Custom, XI-144 pp., 1937.
106. HUGHES, REV. JAMES AUSTIN, A.B., A.M., J.C.D., Witnesses in Criminal Trials of Clerics, IX-140 pp., 1937.
107. JANSEN, REV. RAYMOND J., A.B., S.T.L., J.C.D., Canonical Provisions for Catechetical Instruction, VII-153 pp., 1937.
108. KEALY, REV. JOHN JAMES, A.B., J.C.D., The Introductory Libellus in Church Court Procedure, XI-121 pp., 1937.
109. MCMANUS, REV. JAMES EDWARD, C.SS.R., J.C.D., The Administration of Temporal Goods in Religious Institutes, XVI-196 pp., 1937.

110. MORIARTY, REV. EUGENE JAMES, J.C.D., Oaths in Ecclesiastical Courts, X-115 pp., 1937.
111. RAINER, REV. ELIGIUS GEORGE, C.SS.R., J.C.D., Suspension of Clerics, XVII-249 pp., 1937.
112. REILLY, REV. THOMAS F., C.SS.R., J.C.D., Visitation of Religious, VI-195 pp., 1938.
113. MORIARITY, REV. FRANCIS E., C.SS.R., J.C.D., The Extraordinary Absolution from Censures, XV-334 pp., 1938.
114. CONNOLLY, REV. NICHOLAS P., J.C.D., The Canonical Erection of Parishes, X-132 pp., 1938.
115. DONOVAN, REV. JAMES JOSEPH, J.C.D., The Pastor's Obligation in Prenuptial Investigation, XII-322 pp., 1938.
116. HARRIGAN, REV. ROBERT J., M.A., S.T.B., J.C.D., The Radical Sanation of Invalid Marriages, VIII-208 pp., 1938.
117. BOFFA, REV. CONRAD HUMBERT, J.C.D., Canonical Proviisons for Catholic Schools, VII-211 pp., 1939.
118. PARSONS, REV. ANSCAR JOHN, O.M.Cap., J.C.D., Canonical Elections, XII-236 pp., 1939.
119. REILLY, *Rev.* EDWARD MICHAEL, A.B., J.C.D., The General Norms of Dispensation, XII-156 pp., 1939.
120. RYAN, REV. GERALD ALOYSIUS, A.B., J.C.D., Principles of Episcopal Jurisdiction, XII-172 pp., 1939.
121. BURTON, REV. FRANCIS JAMES, C.S.C., A.B., J.C.D., A Commentary on Canon 1125, X-222 pp., 1940.
122. MIASKIEWICZ, REV. FRANCIS SIGISMUND, J.C.D., Supplied Jurisdiction According to Canon 209, XII-340 pp., 1940.
123. RICE, REV. PATRICK WILLIAM, A.B., J.C.D., Proof of Death in Prenuptial Investigation, VIII-156 pp., 1940.
124. ANGLIN, REV. THOMAS FRANCIS, M.S., J.C.D., The Eucharistic Fast, VIII-183 pp., 1941.
125. COLEMAN, REV. JOHN JEROME, J.C.D., The Minister of Confirmation, VI-153 pp., 1941.
126. DOWNS, REV. JOHN EMMANUEL, A.B., J.C.D., The Concept of Clerical Immunity, XI-163 pp., 1941.
127. ESSWEIN, REV. ANTHONY, ALBERT, J.C.D., Extrajudicial Penal Powers of Ecclesiastical Superiors, X-144 pp., 1941.
128. FARRELL, REV. BENJAMIN FRANCIS, M.A., S.T.L., J.C.D., The Rights and Duties of the Local Ordinary Regarding Congregations of Women Religious of Pontifical Approval, V-195 pp., 1941.
129. FEENEY, REV. THOMAS JOHN, A.B., S.T.L., J.C.D., Restitutio in Integrum, VI-169 pp., 1941.
130. FINDLAY, REV. STEPHEN WILLIAM, O.S.B., A.B., J.C.D., Canonical Norms Governing the Deposition and Degradation of Clerics, XVII-279 pp., 1941.
131. GOODWINE, REV. JOHN, A.B., S.T.L., J.C.D., The Right of the Church to Acquire Property, VIII-119 pp., 1941.
132. HESTON, REV. EDWARD LOUIS, *C.S.C.*, PH.D., S.T.D., J.C.D., The Alienation of Church Property in the United States, XII-222 pp., 1941.
133. HOGAN, REV. JAMES JOHN, A.B., S.T.L., J.C.D., Judicial Advocates and Procurators, XIII-200 pp., 1941.
134. KEALY, REV. THOMAS M., A.B., Litt.B., J.C.D., Dowry of Women Religious, IX-152 pp., 1941.
135. KEENE, REV. MICHAEL JAMES, O.S.B., J.C.D., Religious Ordinaries and Canon 198, V-164 pp., 1942.
136. KERIN, REV. CHARLES A., S.S., M.A., S.T.B., J.C.D., The Privation of Christian Burial, XVI-279 pp., 1941.

137. LOUIS, REV. WILLIAM FRANCIS, M.A., J.C.D., Diocesan Archives, X-101 pp., 1941.
138. McDEVITT, REV. GILBERT JOSEPH, A.B., J.C.D., Legitimacy and Legitimation, X-347 pp., 1941.
139. McDONOUGH, REV. THOMAS JOSEPH, A.B., J.C.D., Apostolic Administrators, X-217 pp., 1941.
140. MEIER, REV. CARL ANTHONY, A.B., J.C.D., Penal Administrative Procedure Against Negligent Pastors, XI-240 pp., 1941.
141. SCHMIDT, REV. JOHN ROGG, A.B., J.C.D., The Principles of Authentic Interpretation in Canon 17 of the Code of Canon Law, XII-331 pp., 1941.
142. SLAFKOSKY, REV. ANDREW LEONARD, A.B., J.C.D., The Canonical Episcopal Visitation of the Diocese, X-197 pp., 1941.
143. SWOBODA, REV. INNOCENT ROBERT, O.F.M., J.C.D., Ignorance in Relation to the Imputability of Delicts, IX-271 pp., 1941.
144. DUBE, REV. ARTHUR JOSEPH, A.B., J.C.D., The General Principles for the Reckoning of Time in Canon Law, VIII-299 pp., 1941.
145. McBRIDE, REV. JAMES T., A.B., J.C.D., Incardination and Excardination of Seculars, XX-585 pp., 1941.
146. KROL, REV. JOHN T., J.C.D., The Defendant in Contentious Trials, XII-207 pp., 1942.
147. COMYNS, REV. JOSEPH J., C.SS.R., A.B., J.C.D., Papal and Episcopal Administration of Church Property, XIV-155 pp., 1942.
148. BARRY, REV. GARRETT FRANCIS, O.M.I., J.C.D., Violation of the Cloister, XII-260 pp., 1942.
149. BOLDUC, REV. GATIEN, C.S.V., A.B., S.T.L., J.C.D., Les Etudes dans les Religions Clericales, VIII-155 pp., 1942.
150. BOYLE, REV. DAVID JOHN, M.A., J.C.D., The Juridic Effects of Moral Certitude on Pre-Nuptial Guarantees, XII-188 pp., 1942.
151. CANAVANA REV. WALTER JOSEPH, M.A., Litt.D., J.C.D., The Profession of Faith, XII-143 pp., 1942.
152. DESROCHERS, REV. BRUNO, A.B., PH.L., S.T.B., J.C.D., Le Premier Concile Plenier de Quebec et le Code de Droit Canonique, XIV-186 pp., 1942.
153. DILLON, REV. ROBERT EDWARD, A.B., J.C.D., Common Law Marriage, X-148 pp., 1942.
154. DODWELL, REV. EDWARD JOHN, PH.D., S.T.B., J.C.D., The Time and Place for the Celebration of Marriage, X-156 pp., 1942.
155. DONNELLAN, REV. THOMAS ANDREW, A.B., J.C.D., The Obligation of the Missa pro Populo, VII-131 pp., 1942.
156. ELTZ, REV. LOUIS ANTHONY, A.B., J.C.D., Cooperation in Crime, XII-208 pp., 1942.
157. GASS, REV. SYLVESTER FRANCIS, M.A., J.C.D., Ecclesiastical Pensions, XI-206 pp., 1942.
158. GUINIVEN, REV. JOHN JOSEPH, C.SS.R., J.C.D., The Precept of Hearing Mass, XIV-188 pp., 1942.
159. GULCYNSKI, REV. JOHN THEOPHILUS, J.C.D., The Desecration and Violation of Churches, X-126 pp., 1942.
160. HAMMILL, REV. JOHN LEJ, M.A., J.C.D., The Obligations of the Traveler According to Canon 14, VIII-204 pp., 1942.
161. HAYDT, REV. JOHN JOSEPH, A.B., J.C.D., Reserved Benefices, XI-148 pp., 1942.
162. HUSER, REV. ROGER JOHN, O.F.M., A.B., J.C.D., The Crime of Abortion in Canon Law, XII-187 pp., 1942.
163. KEARNEY, REV. FRANCIS PATRICK, A.B., S.T.L., J.C.D., The Principles of Canon 1127, X-162 pp., 1942.

164. LINAHEN, REV. LEO JAMES, S.T.L., J.C.D., De Absolutione Complicis In Peccato Turpi, 114 pp., 1942.
165. McCLOSKEY, REV. JOSEPH ALOYSIUS, A.B., J.C.D., The Subject of Ecclesiastical Law According to Canon 12, XVII-246 pp., 1942.
166. O'NEILL, REV. FRANCIS JOSEPH, C.SS.R., J.C.D., The Dismissal of Religious in Temporary Vows, XIII-220 pp., 1942.
167. PRINCE, REV. JOHN EDWARD, A.B., S.T.B., J.C.D., The Diocesan Chancellor, X-136 pp., 1942.
168. RIESNER, REV. ALBERT JOSEPH, C.SS.R., J.C.D., Apostates and Fugitives from Religious Institutes, IX-168 pp., 1942.
169. STENGER, REV. JOSEPH BERNARD, J.C.D., The Mortgaging of Church Property, 186 pp., 1942.
170. WALDRON, REV. JOSEPH FRANCIS, A.B., J.C.D., The Minister of Baptism, XII-197 pp., 1942.
171. WILLETT, REV. ROBERT ALBERT, J.C.D., The Probative Value of Documents in Ecclesiastical Trials, X-124 pp., 1942.
172. WOEBER, REV. EDWARD MARTIN, M.A., J.C.D., The Interpellations, XII-161 pp., 1942.
173. BENKO, REV. MATTHEW ALOYSIUS, O.S.B., M.A., J.C.D., The Abbot *Nullius*, XVI-148 pp., 1943.
174. CHRIST, REV. JOSEPH JAMES, M.A., S.T.L., J.C.D., Dispensation from Vindicative Penalties, XIV-285 pp., 1943.
175. CLANCY, REV. PATRICK M. J., O.P., A.B., S.T.Lr., J.C.D., The Local Religious Superior, X-229 pp., 1943.
176. CLARKE, REV. THOMAS JAMES, *J.C.D.*, Parish Societies, XII-147 pp., 1943.
177. CONNOLLY, REV. JOHN PATRICK, S.T.L., J.C.D., Synodal Examiners and Parish Priest Consultors, X-223 pp., 1943.
178. DRUMM, REV. WILLIAM MARTIN, A.B., J.C.D., Hospital Chaplains, XII-175 pp., 1943.
179. FLANAGAN, REV. BERNARD JOSEPH, A.B., S.T.L., J.C.D., The Canonical Erection of Religious Houses, X-147 pp., 1943.
180. KELLEHER, REV. STEPHEN JOSEPH, A.B., S.T.B., J.C.D., Discussions with Non-Catholics: Canonical Legislation, X-93 pp., 1943.
181. LEWIS, REV. GORDIAN, C.P., J.C.D., in Religious Institutes, XII-169 pp., 1943.
182. MARX, REV. ADOLPH, J.C.D., The Declaration of Nullity of Marriages Contracted Outside the Church, X-151 pp., 1943.
183. MATULENAS, REV. RAYMOND ANTHONY, O.S.B., A.B., J.C.D., Communication, a Source of Privilgeses, XII-225 pp., 1943.
184. O'LEARY, REV. CHARLES GERARD, C.SS.R., J.C.D., Religious Dismissed After Perpetual Profession, X-213 pp., 1943.
185. POWER, *Rev.* CORNELIUS MICHAEL, J.C.D., The Blessing of Cemeteries, XII-231 pp., 1943.
186. SHUHLER, REV. RALPH VINCENT, O.S.A., J.C.D., Privileges of Regulars to Absolve and Dispense, XII-195 pp., 1943.
187. ZIOLKOWSKI, REV. THADDEUS STANISLAUS, A.B., J.C.D., The Consecration and Blessing of Churches, XII-151 pp., 1943.
188. HENERHAN, REV. JOHN JOSEPH, S.T.D., J.C.D., The Marriages of Unworthy Catholics: Canons 1065 and 1066, XVI-213 pp., 1944.
189. CARROLL, REV. COLEMAN FRANCIS, M.A., S.T.L., J.C.L., Charitable Institutions.
190. CIESLUK, REV. JOSEPH EDWARD, Ph.B., S.T.L., J.C.D., National Parishes in the United States, VI-178 pp., 1944.
191. COBURN, REV. VINCENT PAUL, A.B., J.C.D., Marriages of Conscience, XII-172 pp., 1944.

192. Connors, Rev. Charles Paul, C.S.Sp., A.B., J.C.D., Extra-Judicial Procurators in the Code of Canon Law, X-94 pp., 1944.
193. Coyle, Rev. Paul Raymond, A.B., J.C.D., Judicial Exceptions, X-142 pp., 1944.
194. Fair, Rev. Bartholomew Francis, A.B., S.T.L., J.C.D., The Impediment of Abduction, XII-122 pp., 1944.
195. Gallagher, Rev. Thomas Raphael, O.P., A.B., S.T.Lr., J.C.D., The Examination of the Qualities of the Ordinand, X-166 pp., 1944.
196. Gannon, Rev. John Mark, S.T.L., J.C.D., The Interstices Required for the Promotion to Orders, XII-100 pp., 1944.
197. Goldsmith, Rev. J. William, B.C.S., S.T.L., J.C.D., The Competence of Crurch and State over Marriage—Disputed Points, X-128 pp., 1944.
198. Goodwine, Rev. Joseph Gerard, A.B., S.T.B., J.C.D., The Reception of Converts, XIV-326 pp., 1944.
199. Kowalski, Rev. Romuald Eugene, O.F.M., A.B., J.C.D., Sustenance of Religious Houses of Regulars, X-174 pp., 1944.
200. McCoy, Rev. Alan Edward, O.F.M., J.C.D., Force and Fear in Relation to Delictual Imputability and Penal Responsibility, XII-160 pp., 1944.
201. McDevitt, Rev. Vincent John, Ph.B., S.T.L., J.C.L., Perjury.
202. Martin, Rev. Thomas Owen, Ph.D., S.T.D., J.C.D., Adverse Possession, Prescription and Limitation of Actions: The Canonical "Praescriptio," XX-208 pp., 1944.
203. Miklosovic, Rev. Paul John, A.B., J.C.L., Attempted Marriages and Their Consequent Juridic Effects.
204. Mundy, Rev. Thomas Maurice, A.B., S.T.L., J.C.D., The Union of Parishes, X—164 pp., 1944.
205. O'Dea, Rev. John Coyle, A.B., J.C.D., The Matrimonial Impediment of Nonage, VIII-126 pp., 1944.
206. Olalia, Rev. Alexander Ayson, S.T.L., J.C.D., A Comporative Study of the Christian Constitution of States and the Constitution of the Philippine Commonwealth, XII—136 pp., 1944.
207. Poisson, Rev. Pierre-Marie, C.S.C., A.B., Ph.L., Th.L. J.C.L., Droits Patrimoniaux des Maisons et des Eglises Religieuses.
208. Stadalnikas, Rev. Casimir Joseph, M.I.C., J.C.D., Reservation of Censures, X-141 pp., 1944.
209. Sullivan, Rev. Eugene Henry, S.T.L., J.C.D., Proof of the Reception of the Sacraments, X—165 pp., 1944.
210. Vaughan, Rev. William Edward, J.C.D., Constitutions for Diocesan Courts, X-210 pp., 1944.
211. Paro, Rev. Gino, S.T.D., J.C.L., The Right of Apostolic Legation.
212. Balzer, Rev. Ralph Francis, C.P., J.C.D., The Computation of Time in a Canonical Novitiate, X—227 pp., 1945.
213. Dougherty, Rev. John Whelan, A.B., S.T.L., J.C.D., De Inquisitione Speciali, XII—195 pp., 1945.
214. Dziob, Rev. Michael Walter, J.C.D., The Sacred Congregation for the Oriental Church, XII—181 pp., 1945.
215. Eidenschink, Rev. John Albert, O.S.B., B.A., J.C.D., The Election of Bishops in the Letters of Pope Gregory the Great, VII—200 pp., 1945.
216. Gill, Rev. Nicholas, C.P., J.C.D., The Spiritual Prefect in Clerical Religious Houses of Study, X—140 pp., 1945.
217. Hynes, Rev. Harry Gerard, S.T.L., J.C.D., The Privileges of Cardinals, XII-183 pp., 1945.
218. McDevitt, Rev. Gerald Vincent, S.T.L., J.C.D., The Renunciation of an Ecclesiastical Office, XIV—179 pp., 1945.

219. MANNING, REV. JOSEPH LEROY, J.C.D., The Free Conferral of Offices, VIII—116 pp., 1945.
220. MEYER, REV. LOUIS G., O.S.B., A.B., S.T.B., J.C.D., Alms-Gathering by Religious, XII—163 pp., 1945.
221. O'DONNELL, REV. CLETUS FRANCIS, M.A. J.C.D., The Marriage of Minors, XII—268 pp., 1945.
222. PRUNSKIS, REV. JOSEPH, J.C.D., Comparative Law, Ecclesiastical and Civil, in Lithuanian Concordat, X—161 pp., 1945.
223. SWEENEY, REV. FRANCIS PATRICK, C.SS.R., J.C.D., The Reduction of Clerics to the Lay State, X—199 pp., 1945.
224. VOGELPOHL, REV. HENRY JOHN, J.C.D., The Simple Impediments to Holy Orders, XVI—190 pp., 1945.
225. BROCKHAUS, REV. THOMAS AQUINAS, O.S.B., A.B., J.C.D., Religious who are Known as *Conversi*, X—127 pp., 1945.
226. GRIESE, REV. N. ORVILLE, S.T.D., J.C.D., The Marriage Contract and the Procreation of Offspring, XVI-224 pp., 1946.
227. BOUDREAUX, REV. WARREN LOUIS, J.C.L., The *"ab acatholicis nati"* of Canon 1099, § 2.
228. BOWE, REV. THOMAS JOSEPH, A.B., J.C.D., Religious Superioresses, VIII-206 pp., 1946.
229. DIEDERICHS, REV. MICHAEL FERDINAND, S.C.J., J.C.D., The Jurisdiction of the Latin Ordinaries over their Oriental Subjects, XIV-153 pp., 1946.
230. DINGMAN, REV. MAURICE JOHN, A.B., S.T.L., J.C.L., The Plaintiff in Contentious Trials.
231. FRISON, REV. BASIL, C.M.F., M.MUS., J.C.D., The Retroactivity of Law, X-221 pp., 1946.
232. GALVIN, REV. WILLIAM ANTHONY, M.A., J.C.D., The Administrative Transfer of Pastors, XII-288 pp., 1946.
233. GORACY, REV. JOSEPH C., J.C.L., The Diriment Matrimonial Impediment of Major Orders.
234. HALE, REV. JOSEPH FRANCIS, M.A., S.T.L., J.C.L., The Pastor of Burial.
235. HENRY, REV. JOSEPH ARTHUR, A.B., J.C.D., The Mass and Holy Communion: Inter-Ritual Law, XII-138 pp., 1946.
236. LINENBERGER, REV. HERBERT, C.PP.S., J.C.L., The False Denunciation of an Innocent Confessor.
237. LOWERY, REV. JAMES MARTIN, A.B., J.C.D., Dispensation from Private Vows, XII-266 pp., 1946.
238. LYNCH, REV. GEORGE EDWARD, A.B., S.T.L., J.C.D., Coadjutors and Auxiliaries of Bishops, X-107 pp., 1947.
239. LYNCH, REV. TIMOTHY, M.S.SS.T., J.C.D., Contracts between Bishops and Religious Congregations, XIV-232 pp., 1946.
240. MCCLUNN, REV. JUSTIN DAVID, A.B., S.T.L., J.C.D., Administrative Recourse, VII-142 pp., 1946.
241. LOHMULLER, REV. MARTIN NICHOLAS, A.B., J.C.D., The Promulgatio nof Law, XII-140 pp., 1947.
242. MCGRATH, REV. JAMES, A.B., J.C.D., The Privilege of the Canon, XII-156 pp., 1946.
243. MARBACH, REV. JOSEPH FRANCIS, A.B., J.C.D., Marriage Legislation for the Catholics of the Oriental Rites in the United States and Canada, XIV-314 pp., 1946.
244. SHIMKUS, REV. BERNARD ALOYIUS, A.B., J.C.L., The Determination and Transfer of Rite.
245. SMITH, REV. VINCENT MICHAEL, A.B., S.T.L., J.C.L., Ignorance Affecting Matrimonial Consent.

246. WACHTRLE, REV. PAUL ANTHONY, A.B., J.C.L., The Baptism of the Children of Non-Catholics.
247. CROTTY, REV. MATTHEW MICHAEL, J.C.L., The Recipient of First Holy Communion.
248. EAGLETON, REV. GEORGE, S.T.B., J.C.L., The Quinquennial Faculties, Formula IV.
249. GIBBONS, REV. MARION LEO, C.M., J.C.L., Domicile of the Wife Unlawfully Separated from Her Husband.
250. KELLY, REV. BERNARD MATTHEW, S.T.L., J.C.D., The Functions Reserved to Pastors, IX-141 pp., 1947.
251. KILCULLEN, REV. THOMAS JOHN, LL.M., J.C.D., The Collegiate Moral Person as Party Litigant, X-150 pp., 1947.
252. LAFONTAINE, REV. GERMAIN JOSEPH, W.F., J.C.L., Relations Canoniques entre le Missionaire et Ses Superieurs.
253. LANE, REV. LORAS THOMAS, J.C.L., Matrimonial Procedure in Ordinary Court of Second Instance.
254. LOVER, REV. JAMES FRANCIS, C.Ss.R., J.C.L., The Master of Novices.
255. MCNICHOLAS, REV. TIMOTHY JOSEPH, J.C.L., The *Septimae Manus* Witness.
256. MAROSITZ, REV. JOSEPH JOHN, M.S.C., J.C.L., Obligations and Privileges of Religious Promoted to the Episcopal or Cardinalitial Dignities.
257. MURPHY, REV. FRANCIS JOSEPH, J.C.L., Legislative Powers of the Provincial Council.
258. O'BRIEN, REV. ROMAEUS WILLIAM, O.Carm., J.C.L., The Provincial Superior in Religious Orders of Men.
259. PFALLER, REV. BENEDICT ANTHONY, O.S.B., J.C.L., *The ipso facto* Effected Dismissal of Religious.
260. POPEK, REV. ALPHONSE SYLVESTER, J.C.L., The Rights and Obligations of Metropolitans.
261. RISTUCCIA, REV. BERNARD JOSEPH, C.M., J.C.L., Quasi-Religious.
262. SONNTAG, REV. NATHANIEL LOUIS, O.F.M.Cap., J.C.L., Censorship of Special Classes of Books.
263. STADLER, REV. JOSEPH NICHOLAS, J.C.L., Frequent Holy Communion.
264. SZAL, REV. IGNATIUS JOSEPH, J.C.L., The Communication of Catholics with Schismatics.
265. WAGNER, REV. URBAN STANLEY, O.F.M.Conv., J.C.D., Parochial Substitute Vicars and Supplying Priests, IX-126 pp., 1947.

BIOGRAPHICAL NOTE

George B. Eagleton was born November 17, 1912, at Decatur, Nebraska. He was received into the Catholic Church on December 24, 1933, in Yerington, Nevada, and in September of the following year, entered St. Joseph's Preparatory Seminary, Mountain View, California, from which he graduated after two years and was admitted to St. Patrick's Seminary, Menlo Park, California. In 1938 he was sent to the North American College, Rome, Italy, to continue his studies at the Pontifical Gregorian University, where he received the degree of Bachelor of Sacred Theology in 1939. In 1940, because of the European War, he was transferred to the School of Sacred Theology, The Catholic University of America, Washington, D. C. He was ordained to the Sacred Priesthood by the Most Reverend Thomas K. Gorman, D.D., D. Sc. Hist., in St. Thomas Aquinas Cathedral, Reno, Nevada, February 1, 1942. In September, 1944, he entered the School of Canon Law at The Catholic University of America, where he received the degree of the Baccalaureate in Canon Law in June, 1945, and of the Licentiate in Canon Law in June, 1946.

www.ingramcontent.com/pod-product-compliance
Lightning Source LLC
LaVergne TN
LVHW050240080826
844660LV00012B/565

* 9 7 8 0 8 1 3 2 2 4 2 6 8 *